Thinking Teams / Thinking Clients

Thinking **Teams** / Thinking **Clients**

KNOWLEDGE-BASED TEAMWORK

Anne Opie

Columbia University Press

New York

COLUMBIA UNIVERSITY PRESS
Publishers Since 1893
New York   Chichester, West Sussex

Library of Congress Cataloging-in-Publication Data

Opie, Anne.
   Thinking teams/thinking clients : knowledge-based teamwork / Anne Opie.
      p. cm.
   Includes bibliographical references and index.
   ISBN 0-231-11684-5 (cloth : alk. paper) — ISBN 0-231-11685-3 (pbk. : alk. paper)
   1. Health care teams.   2. Health care teams—New Zealand.   I. Title.

   R729.5.H4 O65 2000
   362.1'068—dc21   00-043173

Casebound editions of Columbia University Press books are printed
on permanent and durable acid-free paper.
Printed in the United States of America

c 10 9 8 7 6 5 4 3 2 1
p 10 9 8 7 6 5 4 3 2 1

Contents

Acknowledgments

I would like to record my gratitude to the members of the teams and the families and clients who took part in this research. In a project such as this, their agreement and participation are crucial for the study even to get off the ground. I am also much indebted to the three members of the research advisory group—Maureen Bobbett, Robyn Munford, and Ulla Preston—who provided valuable input at critical times.

I was delighted to be able to work again with Brenda Watson, who produced highly professional transcripts of the audiotaped data, a task that required considerable patience and attention to detail, given the difficulties of transcribing group discussions.

I am greatly indebted to John Michel, executive editor at Columbia University Press, for his positive response to this text. I would like, too, to thank the anonymous readers who commented on the manuscript; one in particular made detailed suggestions that assisted in a substantial revision of some sections of the text.

My family, as always, encouraged, supported, rallied around, and provided help at critical moments. My thanks to Rachel and Joss for their assistance with some mundane but necessary collating and editing tasks. I am especially indebted to Brian, who was, as always, available for lengthy discussions at inconvenient moments over the whole life of the project and, in particular, provided an invaluable, knowledgeable, and close critique of drafts of chapters 2 and 9 and the manuscript of the *Sociological Research Online* article (incorporated into this text as chapter 7). My debt to my family for their continued love and support (practical and

emotional) during my working on what was for different reasons a challenging research project is huge. I hope that this text is a worthy outcome
of that support.

I would like to thank two journals for permission to reproduce
already published work. Chapter 7 was first published as "Teams as
Author: Narrative and Knowledge Creation in Case Discussions in
Multidisciplinary Teams" in *Sociological Research Online* (1997) 2 (3),
http://www.socresonline.org.uk/socresonline/2/3/filename. Chapter 8 is a
revised and expanded version of the article " 'Nobody's Asked Me for
My View': Issues of Empowerment in Family Meetings with Multidisciplinary Health Teams," published in *Qualitative Health Research* 8, no. 2
(1998): 188–209.

I would also like to thank the Health Research Council of New
Zealand, which funded this project, and Victoria University of Wellington, which acted as host institution during my three-year contract as a
senior research fellow with the Health Services Research Centre.

Anne Opie
Wellington

Thinking Teams / Thinking Clients

Part One

Thinking Teamwork

Mapping the Terrain Ahead

In 1992, as part of a differently focused study, I observed social workers in action in multidisciplinary health teams in New Zealand. In one of these teams there was a considerable amount of bonhomie, laughter, and joking (occasionally against the patients). In a relatively strict order of speaking, the various health professionals reported back on their work with each patient, and decisions were made about discharge. This team was considered a good one to be on because people got along well and there were lots of jokes, which mitigated the overall stress of the work. There were, nonetheless, occasions when some of the social workers spoke angrily outside of the meetings about how decisions were made and about which members of the team held power, and they outlined strategies by which they frustrated or held up decisions with which they did not agree.

Things did not run so smoothly on another team. No one said much about the work that they, as individual health professionals, were carrying out with patients. The tension in the air could have been cut with a knife. In individual interviews with me all team members spoke angrily and often at considerable length about the professional (and at times personal) shortcomings of a particular associate (as it happened, a social worker), who, in his turn, bitterly castigated them (Opie 1995). The only point of agreement was that this was not a good team.

It was easy to arrive at the conclusion that this second team was dysfunctional. For all the seeming smoothness and good humor of the first team, however, I became skeptical about agreeing too readily with the account or representation of it as a "good team." The criteria used to arrive at these judgments in both instances focused almost exclusively on the issue of members' "dysfunctionality" or "functionality." Concerns about the quality of care and adequacy of care plans that were being developed were strictly a more marginal issue. I became increasingly convinced that it was not sufficient to think about teamwork primarily in relation to members' psychological state (i.e., this person is dysfunctional) and/or the quality of his or her interpersonal interactions during a team meeting. I considered for several reasons that this familiar focus on teamwork was in fact diverting attention from issues of more significance, even though at that point I could not fully define what they were.

Three years later, in 1995, I began a qualitative research project exploring the "effectiveness" of teamwork, involving teams in the research in three health care settings. It is this project that has enabled me to give some substance to my dissatisfaction with the way teamwork has typically been construed. First, a focus on members' interaction does not actively engage with an account of what *work* teams exist to undertake. Put another way, organizations establish teams to carry out certain tasks. Focusing primarily on members' relationships in teams excludes attention to what task the team is meant to discharge and how well it does so. Second, such a focus excludes any attention to the organizational setting in which teams work. It does not provide any discussion of the organization's role in establishing and promoting teamwork, whether it has developed an account of what the work is and how it is to be done, or whether it relies on somewhat vague, general rhetorical statements about the value of teamwork and members' pulling together. Third, given the substantial resources invested in teams by organizations at a time when health care budgets in many countries are being or have been significantly cut back, I was struck by the typical absence of references in the teamwork literature to criteria by which the effectiveness of teamwork could be understood and assessed, and by the difficulties the members of the teams in my research and their managers had in defining what effective teamwork was and what factors contributed to the production of effective teamwork.

The focus of this book is in some important respects different from that of much of the related health care and social work literatures. My objective in the following pages is to outline the book's idiosyncratic features and their significance for thinking about or conceptualizing effective teamwork and to provide an overview of the book as a whole. Substantive discussion of these features is presented in the relevant chapters.

The Contribution to the Field

Based as it is on a detailed analysis of transcripts of team discussions or reviews of clients among members of multidisciplinary health care teams, this book makes major contributions to the understanding and development of teamwork (with a particular emphasis on teams in health care) and to the literature on service delivery in health care and on professional work.

    1. Unlike much of the literature on teamwork in health care, this book emphasizes the importance of the organizational contexts in which teams work. A basic axiom is that teamwork does not occur in an organizational vacuum. Instead, teams exist because they have an organizationally mandated purpose and role. Therefore, the organizations in which the teams exist must develop some reasonably sophisticated account of the work that teams are to do, how that work is to be produced, and how effectiveness can be conceptualized and observed. The ability of any team to then match that account is affected by organizational resourcing, including training, and by the existence of key organizational documentation and procedures that reinforce the organization's account.

    2. I have defined effective teamwork as *knowledge-based* work. In making a distinction between *information* and *knowledge,* I am drawing on Marc Porat's definition of information as "data that has been organized and communicated" and Daniel Bell's definition of knowledge as "a set of organized statements of facts or ideas, presenting a reasonable judgement or an experimental result, which is transmitted to others through some communication medium in systematic form" (cited in Castells 1996:17 n. 27). "Knowledge" therefore takes "information" and works with it to arrive at something more than the previously communicated "facts."

    3. Conceptualizing teamwork as knowledge-based represents a considerable paradigmatic shift in the teamwork literature in health care, where references to such a mode of work are sparse (although somewhat less so in some of the more recent management literature). My foregrounding of the significance of knowledge-based work turns in part on the assumptions (1) that the work of the team is the production of discussions or reviews of clients' situations and how they are to be progressed and (2) that each member of the team is there as a representative of a particular discipline *because* the different perspectives of or knowledge about the client held by those different disciplines are necessary to achieve effective

work with that client. A major task facing a team as it develops care plans is to attend to and work productively with the different accounts or representations of clients held by its members from different disciplines as well as those accounts held by clients and families. I have accordingly defined effective work in the following manner:

An effective team is one that attends to and works with the different knowledges of clients and their situations that are made available to it through discipline-specific accounts and accounts of clients and families (which may also differ from each other). The work of the team requires engagement with such differences (rather than marginalizing or suppressing them) to ensure, as clients' circumstances evolve, the continued elaboration and revision of team goals and care plans. The ongoing development of effective work will focus primarily on evaluations of teams' processes of knowledge production and creation. The organizational discourses inscribing teamwork are also critical to the effectiveness of that work.

4. The concept of "team" also includes the client and the client's family, although these people may quite often not be present at all team meetings where the client's progress is discussed. A knowledge-based team is one that recognizes the importance of the *different* knowledge held by a client and/or family about their situation, and it ensures that this knowledge is included in the team's deliberations rather than being marginalized or overlooked.

5. Analysis of the audio-taped and transcribed reviews produced by the teams participating in the research about their clients has enabled me to produce a map of the features of an effective knowledge-based team discussion. I am not aware of a similar map (or model) in the relevant literature. The dimensions of this map of effective, knowledge-based work, discussed at some length in chapter 6, are the following:

- A focused orientation or introduction to each client that informs and to some extent therefore structures the ensuing discussion;
- The production of knowledge spirals through discussion of the focus and development of work with that client;
- Identification and recording of issues, and members' tasks and goals, in conjunction with an evolving *team* objective;
- A focused closure to the discussion, where the minutes taker ensures that all issues and tasks, and the goals or objectives of both the team and each constituent discipline, identified in the preceding discus-

sion are written into the minutes and are confirmed by the team; and

- A continual engagement throughout the above process with the knowledge and perspectives of clients and families, including their inflection by ethnicity and cultural difference.

Two additional issues pertaining to knowledge-based teamwork need to be noted here. First, not all clients have complex situations, and of those that do, not all have complex situations all the time. Although a discussion of a client who has a relatively straightforward situation or with whom the work is progressing well would be structured by some of the dimensions of this map, it would be unlikely to be informed by all of them. The map of effective teamwork is therefore specifically designed to assist teams when they are reviewing clients whose current situation is complex and/or when the team is uncertain about the appropriate direction(s) of its work.

Second, by and large, the teams involved in the research did not engage in knowledge-based discussions. This was not surprising, given the dominant focus on team dynamics in the training that a very few members had received, most members' lack of any training in teamwork, and, at the research sites, the lack of anything other than the most basic organizational account of teamwork. What this means, however, is that the elements describing the map of effective teamwork have been informed more by what was absent from the team reviews that I taped and observed than by what was present. In this context, the last chapter, "Performing Knowledge Work," is of specific interest because it engages directly with organizational conceptualizing of teamwork, with the effects of that in relation to key organizational procedures and processes, and with the ways in which organizational development and training could be structured to enable the production of knowledge-based teamwork.

6. Much of the literature on teamwork has been substantially undertheorized. In contrast to those undertheorized accounts, this one relies extensively on postmodern theory. Indeed, I would argue strongly that I would not have been able to develop the representation of teamwork presented in this book *without* critical attention to that theoretical perspective. Why such a claim? What are some of the ways that postmodern theory directed my gaze and structured my analysis, thereby enabling me to attend to issues that are absent in other teamwork literature?

First, I do not write of team members—John, Sue, and Jack. By writing instead from a position that foregrounds how individuals are produced within discourse, I am seeking to make clear how each team member's conceptualization of a client's situation is the result of that member's location within discourses, particularly those discourses that structure his or her discipline-based knowledge and bear on his or her professional behaviors. All disciplines, explicitly or implicitly, claim privileged knowledge, yet in all cases that knowledge is partial and can never provide the full account to which it aspires. Further, because some disciplines (and their knowledge base) lack the power and status of others, their accounts are less likely to be sought or more fully worked with. A major task facing an interprofessional team is to work productively with the different knowledges represented by its members in order to achieve well-informed care plans for clients. Defining the task in this fashion draws attention to the necessity to attend to and manage discipline-engendered power issues and to understand such issues as an inevitable outcome of the different degrees of power adhering to the various disciplinary constructions of knowledge. It accordingly foregrounds the management of issues of disciplinary power within a team as a significant team task. Correspondingly, it does not place weight on accounts that emphasize an individual's pathology as the locus of a team's difficulty with power issues.

Second, postmodern theory is also concerned with how disciplinary power is simultaneously inclusive and exclusive. It is therefore attentive to what happens on the margins and to how attending to the small comment, or the easily lost reference, can allow the team to rethink the ways in which they are responding to the issues under discussion.

Third, postmodern theory also draws attention to the production and management of "difference" as a key issue in knowledge-based work. Part of the work of an effective team is to identify and explore, rather than suppress, the different accounts of the client circulating within it and therefore of the different work to be undertaken that is implicit in such accounts.

What the above discussion points to is the close relationship between theory and the development of this account of effective, interprofessional team practices. I recognize that readers who are less familiar with postmodern theory but who wish to follow the theoretical dimensions of the text are likely to find it necessary to read closely the account of the key concepts in chapters 2 and 4. I have, however, discussed throughout the course of the book how a postmodern reading of teamwork requires different questions and issues to be addressed, how it therefore alters not only how teamwork is typically conceptualized but how this different mode requires different types of interactions between organizations, team members, and their clients. Furthermore, I have also addressed how this reading allows for the development of differently shaped and structured interprofessional discussions. The inclusion of lengthy extracts from team reviews as an integral part of the text in part 2 allows me to demonstrate how the above issues closely inform my analysis.

Before outlining the content and focus of the remaining chapters of this book, I want to comment on two further issues. As I have just noted, I have included in the text typically lengthy extracts from the teams' reviews of their clientele in order to demonstrate the data with which I was working and my reading of that data. These extracts, of course, refer to clients whose real names had to be removed. I have identified clients by number (P1, P2, and so on), not by name. I decided against allocating each client a pseudonym for two reasons, both practical and theoretical. The practical reason was that I found it difficult to think quickly of many pseudonyms while I was working over the transcripts, and using numbers was easier. The more substantive theoretical reason for not creating pseudonyms at a later date for those clients referred to in the team discussions was that the focus of the analysis was not on individual clients (Mary, Denis, Dave) and their situations. At the outset of the study, I often felt that if I had a fuller grasp of the "case" I would be better able to develop an analysis of teamwork. I then came to realize that this was substantially the wrong focus. Past histories and voluminous details are not always relevant. More to the point, the teams were working with this client at *this* point in time. What was significantly more important in the context of teamwork was not a client's history but what different knowledges team members produced about the client and his or her history in relation to current issues (which could include some reference to past work). The focus of the research, therefore, is on how teams produce reviews and work with their collective knowledge, generated in the course of team reviews, to advance the care of a client or patient. It is not on what happened to clients. As a consequence of this focus, I have produced only minimal accounts of clients' situations and for reasons of confidentiality I have changed key factors about the clients discussed in this text.

The second point I wish to discuss refers to my use of the word *knowledges* (a word that my computer persistently informs me is unacceptable) rather than *knowledge*. Here again my objective has been to emphasize how knowledge-based teamwork builds on the range of different accounts, informed by differently located, differently focused, disciplinarily structured knowledges about a client available at any one time within a team.

The word *knowledges* is intended to keep to the fore how my reading of effective teamwork relies on teams working productively with those differently focused knowledge domains, the different accounts or representations of clients created by these, and the implications of such differences for the development of work foci and case plans.

The Structure of the Book

A central motif running through this book is that of maps and mapping and, by extension, traveling/exploring. The value of this motif is that it highlights movement, a shift from the familiar, a redrawing of previously stable boundaries, and, inherent in the process, the presence of uncertainty and its simultaneously existing other, possibility. This chapter has begun the mapping process by providing an outline of the terrain to come, thereby demonstrating the work still to be done to develop the connections across less familiar spaces. Chapter 2 explores how teamwork might look when viewed from a postmodern theoretical position, and how so doing requires the shifting of familiar boundaries to take into account rather different territories/modes of conceptualizing. The mapping motif recurs in chapter 4, beginning with the quotation from Curnow's "Landfall in Unknown Seas" and continuing in my writing of the fieldwork and analytical processes as traveling/journeying, of being (uneasily) on the edges of (off) the map. And it builds in indirect references to the recent postmodern anthropological critique of how stock-in-trade tropes and rhetorical devices disguised the unacknowledged operations of power within much previous anthropological writing. So, too, in the section on textual motion/traversal, I engage with Barthes's concept of the text not as that which is caught in one place or able to be reduced to a final definitive reading but as that which is generative, productive of different sites/sights. Finally, the concept and processes of mapping are present in different ways in the chapters in part 2, each one of which is concerned to map/engage with or contribute to the different dimensions of the map of effective teamwork presented in chapter 6.

Let me now provide some more detailed signs of the journey ahead.

My objectives in part 1, "Thinking Teamwork," are to provide an account of the rationale for the study and to discuss in some detail the theoretical, methodological, and contextual dimensions of the study.

Chapter 2, "Shifting Boundaries," begins this work. It falls into four sections. The first, "Thinking Teamwork," sets the scene for conceptualizing teamwork as knowledge-based work, exploring the contribution of this book to the existent literature on teamwork, setting out the assumptions and issues that underpin the analysis, and identifying key methodological issues that have contributed to my focus on the production of effective teamwork. The second section, "Thinking in the Postmodern" attends to the contribution of postmodern theory to this text. The third section, "Discourse, Representation, and 'the Body'" moves into the substantive discussion of key theoretical issues, focusing on issues of discourse, representation, power, the body, and difference. The fourth section, "Reviewing the Literature," discusses the current literature on teamwork and identifies a number of issues embedded in but overlooked by this literature. It reports first on how the concept "effectiveness" has been addressed in the context of quality of interaction in some of the recent literature in relation to team type, collaboration, and members' interdependence. It then moves to focus on three other much more marginalized domains pertaining to effectiveness and quality of interaction: the relationship between clients, families, and teams; the organizational dimension in the production of effective teamwork; and the production of knowledge-based teamwork.

In chapter 3, "The Teams and Their Organizational Locations," I discuss aspects of recent political changes to health organizations and the policy environment in health care in Aotearoa/New Zealand (also drawing parallels between the Aotearoa/New Zealand environment and that of the United States, Australia, and Canada) as context to the production of teamwork by the teams in the research study. A description of the teams (client focus, membership, and so forth) follows, including an account of some specific features of the teams' organizational locations and a discussion of the competing narratives circulating within those teams about their focus and appropriate work. In the final part of the chapter, I analyze members' commentary on three everyday but necessary elements of organizational work that affect the production of effective teamwork: the production and focus of job descriptions, the provision and content of orientation programs, and the training in teamwork provided by the hospitals in which the teams were located.

I begin chapter 4, "Researching the Interprofessional: Theory/Practice/Site," with an account of beginning the research. "Setting Out" reports on a journey, of venturing into unknown terrain. This account of this journey remains unfinished. The text moves into a discussion of "text" and "intertext" (Barthes 1986) and thence to an account of the data collected and methodological issues raised by the research.

Part of the work of a methodology is to map key research processes that contribute to the intellectual/conceptual focus and development of the analysis. This is, I believe, difficult to do (especially if there is a modernist emphasis on transparency and replicability) because while certain techniques can be followed—for example, in coding—no number of lists of what codes the researcher identified in the data can properly explain what is an intellectual process that enabled a series of connections to be made between and across data, literature, and different domains of knowledge and experience. Analysis requires the use of a range of techniques of working with the data *and* also operates on a much more difficult-to-map conceptual level. My recollection of this or that text can suddenly assist in working through an impasse; another researcher may, as a result of different textual references and intellectual and personal experiences, arrive at a somewhat different interpretation of the same data. Rather than relying on conventional sociological texts, I have brought Umberto Eco's (1985) *Reflections on "The Name of the Rose"* into play here because Eco's delightful discussion of textual constraints and freedoms both seems highly apposite and is able to catch neatly the very dimensions of research that are so difficult to verbalize.

Drawing parallels, then, between Eco's account of how he came to write *The Name of the Rose* and the production of an analysis in qualitative research, I discuss aspects of the development of the analysis. I also take what became a key theoretical concept, that of "narrative," to discuss how my use of this word developed over time to produce a more complex and differently focused analysis from what I had initially managed.

Part 2, "Displaying Teamwork," focuses on analyses of the data collected during the fieldwork. I survey the topography of teamwork, working from three data sets, each providing a different mode of apprehending teamwork and engaging with the notion of "effective" teamwork. Each of these sets overlaps the others and works with some of the same issues from different locations.

Chapter 5, "Mapping Effectiveness: Achieving a 'More Subtle Vision,'" draws on the texts of team members. The chapter falls into two sections. The first section, "Thinking Teams/Thinking Effectiveness," highlights the degree to which factors seen as contributing to effective teamwork are structured by location, attending, for example, to the implications of different disciplines' accounts of the structure of an "effective" team discussion. The analysis in the second section, "Difference Patterns and Increasing Subtlety of Vision in Team Practices," is informed by a limited number of texts of interviews with team members, chosen because of the more developed critique of teamwork that they offered. Describing effective work as informed less by reflexivity and more by "diffraction" in order to arrive at a "more subtle vision" (Haraway 1997b:33–34), I attend in this analysis to the tension identified in these members' texts between the concept of the "supportive" team and the role of questioning in the production of effective work. Finally, I suggest that teamwork that is able to acknowledge not only the existence of difference but also its implications and material effects requires a more complex understanding of the role of the team leader than was demonstrated at the research sites by their organizations and the teams.

Chapter 6, " 'We Talk About the Patients and Then We Have Coffee': Making and Shaping Team Discussions," presents my map of an effective knowledge-based team discussion. I draw on Deleuze and Guattari's (1983) theory of lines to discuss the concept of the "shape" of such a discussion, emphasizing its recursive and spiraling form. The remainder of the chapter discusses the key features of the map in the context of transcripts of segments of team reviews and identifies strategies for advancing knowledge-based work. The chapter concludes with a discussion of the need for clear decision-making processes and provides further commentary on the leader's role in the production of effective teamwork.

In chapter 7, "Teams as Author: Narrative and Knowledge Creation in Case Discussions," I develop an analysis of transcripts of team discussions audio-taped over several consecutive weeks about a further two clients. This chapter revisits and extends aspects of the analysis in chapter 6 through locating the analysis in postmodern narrative theory. The analysis is developed from narratives produced during team reviews about two users—one a quadriplegic, the other a psychiatric patient. The chapter focuses first on the identification and explanation of significant differences between the narratives produced by medical and interprofessional teams; second, on the identification of a suppressed dimension (both in the literature on health care teams and in the practice of these teams) with respect to the management of difference in the development of complex interprofessional team narratives; and third, on how teams work with the different professional knowledges represented by their members. The final section of the chapter defines teamwork as primarily a process of knowledge work and knowledge creation, discussing some of the organizational conditions that facilitate such work.

In chapter 8, " 'Nobody's Asked Me for My View': Clients' Empowerment in Interprofessional Teamwork," I discuss the tensions in the concept of empowerment and then, in the context of that discussion, provide a detailed analysis of two team meetings between teams and clients and families. One of these meetings, involving a moderately demented frail elderly woman and her niece, highlights some complex issues with respect to assumptions about the "empowering" nature of such meetings. The second meeting, conducted with a young woman with a degenerative physical condition and members of her family, provides alternative criteria by which the empowering nature of family meetings can be evaluated. Finally, I discuss the wider implications (for teams and for organizations concerned with the development of effective teamwork) for structuring more empowering, rather than less empowering, family meetings and involving families and clients more in the work of the team.

In chapter 9, "Performing Knowledge Work," I review the main strands of my argument about the significance of knowledge-based teamwork as a critical mode of teamwork in organizations concerned with productive use of professional time. In order to highlight the key role of organizations in developing and sustaining knowledge-based teamwork, I return to the organizational representation of teamwork with respect to the mundane organizational factors bearing on the production of teamwork that are discussed in chapter 3: the organizational accounts of teamwork accessed through job descriptions, the orientation of new staff to teamwork, and the types of training made available to team members. The focus of the discussion is how a knowledge-based organization could attend to these factors.

2

Shifting Boundaries

Thinking Teamwork

When human service agencies bring professionals from different disciplines together in teams, their organizational objectives typically emphasize achieving better coordinated and collaborative work to improve the quality of care offered to clients (Perkins and Tryssenaar 1994; Whorley 1996) and, through this process, to contribute to organizational efficiency and effectiveness.[1] Indeed, such teams are mandatory in some countries in some service domains, such as child abuse (Gilgun 1988) and assessment services for older people (Solomon and Mellor 1992). Teamwork rhetoric thus emphasizes the possibilities of a more integrated (if not holistic) professional approach to clients' needs. The work of one professional is frequently contingent on, or affected by, the work of another. Further, Atkinson (1995) has commented pertinently on how in modern medicine the care that clients receive requires input from a range of different disciplines. This care, then, is dispersed across different disciplinary sites. Each of the participating disciplines has its own processes, priorities, and modes of decision making, and each one will produce a different account or representation of the client, the client's needs, and the work that should be effected. As Atkinson has noted, teamwork, by bringing representatives of the various disciplines involved in the client's care together to allow them to address these different and at times competing accounts, is intended to provide that actual and conceptual point of intersection at which the multiple fragmented representations of the client's body are reassembled.

Teamwork thus enables each professional involved in the care of a particular client to gain a more complex understanding of the relationship of his or her work to that of other professionals, thereby contributing to better-coordinated care. Such coordinated, effective, nuanced care, so the rhetoric runs, contributes to organizational efficiency. It should also be more empowering of clients because clients, defined as "team members" and hence consulted by health professionals, are able to insert their concerns and desires directly, or through the advocacy of another, into the complex processes of team decision making.

The teamwork literature in health care abounds with articles that base their conception of the value of teamwork on such an account. This rhetorical construction, however, is immediately thrown into question when, in the same articles, it is placed against the significantly less sanguine accounts of the realities of teamwork in the context of a variety of seemingly endemic problems. Many such articles conclude with discussions of ways in which teams may better achieve some of their intended objectives.

Where does *Thinking Teams/Thinking Clients* fit into what is an already extensively traversed field?

This book is intended to make a significant contribution to the literature on teamwork. In contrast to much of the existing literature, this text goes beyond the rehearsal of consistently identified problems about teamwork and the production of a conclusion constituted by a generalized, short discussion of how these problems may be remedied. Instead it seeks to contribute to current research on the borders of the paradigmatic boundaries policing the concept "teamwork" by addressing dimensions of that research that are largely untheorized and marginalized in the literature, and thereby challenging the current dominant paradigms that define teamwork.[2]

In broad terms, the paradigmatic shift in the accounts or representations of teamwork that are the subject of this book has involved my recasting teamwork as primarily concerned with and derived from knowledge-based work, thereby eschewing the more familiar and dominant focus on interpersonal relations between team members. I argue that teams improve their effectiveness in what are currently changing and leaner organizational environments by addressing how they manage the different (disciplinary) knowledges represented by their various members. The particular, theorized contribution of this book to the field is achieved through the production of a reading or analysis of transcripts of team reviews that is closely informed by postmodern theory. An outcome of this work is that it enables a map to be sketched of the constituting features of effective modes of teamwork.

The following issues and assumptions, discussed at more length throughout the book, underpin the analysis of teamwork that I present.

- Much of the literature on teamwork continues to reflect its historical location within philosophies of personal growth and development and consequently focuses on the management of interpersonal relations within the team as critical to effective work. The question that needs to be asked is whether, in a context of changing organizational imperatives and redefinitions of professional work, this focus now provides (if indeed it ever did provide) an adequate account of teamwork or will enable teams to contribute to desired organizational outcomes.

- My re-siting of teamwork as knowledge-based work is not intended to deny that some attention to the interpersonal dimension of team relations has its place. Discussions require some degree of civility. This dimension is not, however, attended to in any detail in this book because my explicit agenda is to shift the focus of attention from how members interact as individuals to how professionals on a team engage with the differently structured, differently powerful discipline-based knowledges represented by the various team members, and with that differently located knowledge held by clients and families. Further, as this text demonstrates, the production of knowledge-based work imposes its own structure on how discussions progress and how effective teamwork is produced, and this structure is very different from that of a team focusing on its dynamics.

- Teamwork happens within organizations. The organizational objective in establishing teams is to advance organizational interests. The ultimate goal is not team effectiveness per se but the achievement of organizational effectiveness via teamwork (Mankin, Cohen, and Bikson 1995).

- There are few grounds for thinking that a team will be effective (or efficient) simply because an organization puts a group of people together and tells them they are a "team." The production of more effective teamwork is assisted by some organizational clarity about the roles and objectives of teams and the processes by which effective work will be achieved. I argue that organizations wishing to obtain effective work require elaborated and fluid accounts of what quality teamwork might look like and how such work might be structured. I have used the word *fluid* to highlight the importance of teams' not adopting or entrenching highly prescriptive and rigid practices (Barker 1993). In reference to "structure," my emphasis is significantly less on the actual physical structure of teams (an issue discussed at some length by Ovretveit 1993) than on the process of the work of the team as it engages in its discussions and reviews of clients.

• Effective teamwork involves engaging with the different knowledges represented by the members of the team, clients, and families. As are all professionals at the beginning of the twenty-first century, team members are engaged with knowledge work. Knowledge work in an interprofessional team involves the identification and articulation of information relevant to one's disciplinary perspective and is related to the ability to conceptualize. It is constituted by the interrelating of the different knowledge domains and the different modes of practice represented by team members. Clients' well-being is affected by the ways in which team members articulate their own discipline-based knowledge and collectively manage the intersection of knowledges generated by different disciplinary perspectives. Conceptualizing teamwork as knowledge work has organizational and institutional implications for the nature of the training in teamwork provided within specific disciplines.

• Addressing the often overlooked fact that teams are located within organizations highlights the intersection between the production of effective teamwork and organizational responsibilities for resourcing teams and ensuring members' access to professional education and ongoing training. These are both necessary to teams' abilities to critique and refine their own practices, processes that are regarded as necessary in the development of effective and accountable professional work (Fook 1996).

• The development of knowledge-based teamwork and therefore the development of more critical practices involves the team's reviewing and critiquing its different outputs. Such outputs include, for example, the minutes of the team meetings, minutes of meetings with clients and families, the processes and outcomes of clients' reviews, and the team's case plans. Process is also an important dimension for critique. In this text, however, and in contradiction to its more familiar association, the term *process* in knowledge-based work refers to questions about, for example, how a team structures and develops discussions of each client and with what result; how it produces and works with (different) narratives or accounts of clients; how it pools and then works with its collective knowledge base; how it involves clients and families and their differently located knowledge in decision making; whether and how it sets team goals (not just discipline-specific goals) that evolve as a client's situations change; how it allocates time for discussion of each client; whether what members say is audible to their colleagues; and what procedures work to allow the team to operate smoothly. These are very different issues from the issues that need to be addressed when teamwork is conceptualized and practised from a group dynamics perspective, where the focus is likely to be on whether the team has an initiator or an aggressor, whether its communication is open and honest or exhibits hostility and lack of trust between members.

The multiple and overlapping referents in the book's title, *Thinking Teams/Thinking Clients,* directly pertain to this alternative paradigm or mode of representing teamwork. The phrase "thinking teams" directs attention to how, within organizational worlds, teamwork is conceptualized and to the implications of such conceptualization. It also directs attention to how professionals practice such work. The concept of teamwork as a knowledge-based activity emphasizes how teamwork is constituted (in specific times and places and institutional settings) by fluid yet structured "thinking" and engagement with the range of discipline-specific knowledges available within any one team.

"Thinking clients" refers to how teams think about/discuss their clients and the outcomes of such thoughts/discussions, how clients think about their circumstances, and how their thinking is accessed and included in teams' work. "Thinking clients" also directs attention to the narratives or stories through which teams express this client-focused thinking and to the nature or outcome of that thinking. On the one hand, it refers to the (different) descriptions and their embedded representations of clients and families that teams develop in the course of their discussions and the consequences of such descriptions/representations in shaping the work to be undertaken. On the other hand, "thinking clients" refers to the plans generated by team reviews.

A key question driving this research had to do with how to think about effectiveness. This question was all the more necessary because in the literature the criteria describing "effectiveness" are too often implicit or have too narrow a reference, and evaluations of teamwork are often limited by an absence of discussion of the wider environments in which teams operate. In Aotearoa/New Zealand, where this study was carried out, a key element of that external environment as it has impacted service delivery in health care has been the restructuring of primarily public health systems designed to produce better-quality services from reduced public health budgets. Other Western countries, such as the United Kingdom, Canada, and Australia, have had experiences similar to those of Aotearoa/New Zealand.

In light of policies focusing on the production of more effective and efficient modes of service, a primary research objective was to map the key features of effective interprofessional teamwork (that is, teams constituted by representatives of more than one discipline). Three things followed from this objective. First, I define team discussions or reviews of clients as those occasions on which teams meet formally as teams to undertake a significant dimension of teamwork in health care: the production of care plans for and with clients or patients. Second, unlike much of the literature on teams in health care, this study was not conducted from the perspective of a particular discipline. It is not therefore concerned, as some of the literature is, with making a point about the value of, or privileging, a particular discipline in relation to others, or engaging in disciplinary power contests by asserting that particular skills are or should be located within specific disciplines (Abramson and Mizrahi 1986).

Third, a map of teamwork could not be developed only on the basis of observation of team meetings or surveys of and/or interviews with team members, which is the basis for much of the writing in the field. These methodologies alone cannot provide sufficient access to how teams go about carrying out their work, that is, the production of care plans. In order to achieve the kind of rich, textured analysis of actual team practices that is typically missing in the teamwork literature, this study's research design had as a central feature the complete recording and transcription of sequential team discussions or reviews of clients.

As a consequence, this text does not engage in idealized, generalized statements of what teams do. Nor does it rely on how members of one or more disciplines reported that they had discharged their roles, although it does address how they conceptualized various dimensions of teamwork.

The substantive analysis, focused on the development of a map of the structure of an effective team discussion (and the organizational implications of such a map), engages analytically with the complex texts of actual team reviews. A key assumption of this research is that a critical analysis of teamwork requires a methodology providing full access to team practices and interactions, rather than relying only on observations and reports by researchers and team members on the ways in which teams worked or on what members believed they did or said or what they thought they were supposed to do. Unlike most research on teamwork, then, the methodology employed in this study called for audio-taping of team discussions.

Audio-taping discussions, however, cannot in itself guarantee a valuable research outcome. For example, Midgley, Burns, and Garland (1996) audio-taped clinical discussions but provided no access to the transcripts and no analysis of those discussions other than a descriptive account of limited features (attendance, allocation of meeting time, and percentages of time focused on certain tasks, such as information exchange and initiation of interactions). Their generalized statements about the value of "good communication" as assisting in the "effective coordination of community psychiatry" (71) and their commentary on how "increased familiarity with each other as individuals leads to mutual trust and improved cooperation"(71) hardly broke new ground and offered no clarification of how effectiveness might be conceptualized and evaluated. In other words, what is also critical to the production of innovative research is the theoretical framework closely informing the analysis.

There are four tasks to be accomplished in the remainder of this chapter. In the introductory section, "Thinking in the Postmodern" I outline why working within postmodern theory makes a difference to the resultant analysis. In the second section, "Discourse, Representation, and 'the Body,'" I provide an account of those three key theoretical terms and the two additional key concepts to which they give rise ("power" and "difference") that inform the analysis presented in this text. In the third section, "Reviewing the Literature," I discuss issues in the literature on teamwork. In the fourth section, "Thinking Effectiveness," I address how the concept "effectiveness" in teamwork has been discussed in the literature in order to identify a series of issues affecting the quality of processes in teamwork and the ability of members to work more knowledgeably. First, I discuss how in teamwork literature effectiveness is mediated by three processes: the quality of interaction in relation to team type (whether multidisciplinary, interdisciplinary, or transdisciplinary); the achievement of collaboration; and member interdependence. Then I attend to a further three factors affecting the effectiveness of a team's work, factors that are much more marginalized or suppressed in discussions of effectiveness. These are the extent to which clients and families are involved in teams' work; the organizational development of teamwork; and the production of knowledge-based teamwork, including a key dimension of that work, the productive management of difference.

Thinking in the Postmodern

Postmodern theory, drawing extensively on European philosophical traditions and yet representing a rupture from some of those traditions' key assumptions about the nature of humankind, has been in circulation for about the last fifty years. Over that time, but more in the last three decades (and especially since the mid-1980s), when some of the key European texts became more available in English, postmodern theory has come to inform writing and thinking in a range of diverse disciplines and modes of intellectual inquiry in English-speaking countries.

What do postmodern strategies of reading and analysis contribute to the reading of teamwork and the analysis of actual team practices in this text? While I have demonstrated their particular value in relation to the analyses of team reviews and the account of teamwork that I present in subsequent chapters in this book, I wish to highlight three areas of particular significance. First, as a general proposition, I argue that the value of an analysis informed by a postmodern theory of discourse is that it immediately directs attention to the power relations through which representations are produced and circulate, and thus persistently draws attention to how the institutional possession of power results in the perspectives about the weighting of factors or the significance of events brought by certain factors/events/disciplines' being either included or excluded. In terms of producing a fuller analysis of the social, a Foucaultian analysis goes beyond that offered by the social constructivists, albeit that ethnomethodologists also propose that social reality is constructed discursively. For example, Gubrium's (1980) and Holstein's (1992) accounts of the operation of human service organizations identify how human service workers construct or produce the client. Both argue that what is produced is not the *fact* of the client but rather a mediated account determined by the positioning of members and negotiated by them in light of organizational requirements, policies or mandates, and other contingencies. Such accounts are, inevitably, highly selective, emphasizing those dimensions to which the organization and the health workers can respond (which may mean defining as problem behavior that which in a context other than that of patient conferences would go unnoticed). The descriptions offered of clients suppress the selectivity of the details by which clients are constructed. Such descriptions are, Holstein argues, rhetorical. They are organizationally grounded categories, social types, or typifications that orient to the practical tasks confronted within a particular organization or setting (27).

Holstein's account, however, overlooks two critical issues. One is that there may well be competing versions or representations of the client within the organization (or team); the other is the power relations that inform such representations. Such issues raise questions about which representation is advanced, from what (knowledge) location, and with what exclusory (and material) effects.

In contrast to Holstein's analysis, Fox (1994), in his Foucaultian analysis of the competing discourses employed by anesthetists and surgeons, demonstrates how each group, basing its account on (competing) knowledge, represents what constitutes health differently. Each promotes a discursive framework to support a position that produces the patient in very different ways—in this instance with reference to the readiness of the patient for surgery. An inability or unwillingness on the part of the professionals to engage with and resolve the issues informing the different discourses through which patients were represented or produced had potentially serious outcomes for patients.

The second point is that Foucaultian/postmodern discourse analysis directs attention toward the excluded and the marginal. Attending to these areas is particularly valuable because of their capacity to disrupt seemingly smooth social surfaces and accepted wisdom and, in so doing, to create additional, complicating issues to be taken into account and open up alternative discursive spaces that dominant discourses close off. For example, feminists have over the years persistently demonstrated how mainstream accounts of "family" ignore key factors affecting how families operate, how this institution is experienced by its various members, and how, as a consequence, many social policy initiatives are inadequate to the issues they are intended to address. It is, moreover, the small, "petty" issues that can often most effectively demonstrate the workings of institutional power (Rabinow 1996:50).[3] Marilyn Strathern commented on the role of feminist anthropology in shifting discursive boundaries: "It [feminist anthropology] alters the nature of the audience, the range of readership and the kinds of interactions between author and reader, and alters the subject matter of conversation in the way it allows others to speak—what is talked about and whom one is talking to" (Strathern, quoted in Rabinow 1996:53).

In the following statement, I engage, in a context of an analysis of teamwork, with Strathern's commentary on what is required to shift discursive boundaries. Employing postmodern interpretive strategies engaged with the possibilities of paradigmatic shifts enables me to develop a reading of teamwork that is atypical of the literature:

> By focusing on marginalized dimensions of teamwork, this study intends to alter the expectations of readers about key constituting factors of teamwork. It highlights the significance of the complex modes of interaction between organizations and team members and between team members, clients, and families, and it seeks to alter the structure and content of interprofessional discussions in teams by assisting members to rethink how they talk, what is talked about, and how that talk is shaped by context and outcome.

I suggest that this statement and the type of analysis it points to would not have been written by someone operating within modernist discourses and/or using methodologies such as grounded theory, symbolic interactionism, or ethnomethodology.

The third point is that part of the work of this text is to foreground differences in disciplinary knowledge bases, not as that which must be suppressed in teamwork in a desire to reach a consensual position, or regarded as problematic, but as a highly productive dimension of interprofessional teamwork. If a significant element of the rationale for such teams is that clients are most effectively served through a multifaceted approach informed by the knowledge of the different disciplines represented in the team, then a key team task is to display and work productively with those different knowledges and the different representations of clients that they produce (Opie 1997).

Discourse, Representation, and "the Body"

The concept of "discourse" that I am using in this text is grounded in the work of the French philosopher Michel Foucault (Burchell, Gordon, and

Miller 1991; Foucault 1977, 1980, 1981, 1988a, 1988b) and in postmodern feminist scholarship. Within Foucault's work, the construction of a "discourse" is intimately interwoven with issues of power (particularly of the modern state and its institutions) and "knowledge." He argues that all knowledge operates to structure how the world is perceived and what constitutes reality. That knowledge advanced by specific privileged groups not only gains ascendancy, however, but because of its institutionally endorsed power, its representations of how the world "is" are substantially taken for granted. In this process, the privileged knowledge works to *exclude* other modes of knowing. Foucault's writings highlight how knowledge is always positional, always partial, never complete. It may embody "a truth," but never "the truth." Further, the discourses that inform and are informed by such knowledge (a recursive, interactive process) also operate on a meta yet concrete plane to produce, literally and metaphorically, certain types of "bodies." These points, though, require some unpacking.

Central to Foucault's work is an analysis of the operation of power in the modern state. He has argued that a distinguishing feature of the modern (Western) state's power lies in the transition from physical demonstrations of the state's power and control (through the medium of public executions [Foucault 1977]) to more internalized and "less cumbersome" (Foucault 1980:58) modes of control concerned with the production of particular types of (docile) bodies and regulation of behaviors in ways that will benefit the state and its major institutions (Diamond and Quinby 1988; Foucault 1988a and 1988b; Orr 1990). Orr's essay, for example, powerfully links the marketing of the phenomenon of women increasingly experiencing panic attacks with the production of particular types of female bodies, the economic productivity of international pharmaceuticals, and the operations of capitalism. As Rosi Braidotti has noted, " 'Power' thus becomes the name for a complex set of interconnections, between the spaces where truth and knowledge are produced and the systems of control and domination" (Braidotti 1997:60).

These processes of control, then, are no longer exercised only through overt mechanisms of the state. Instead, power comes to be exercised through "surveillance, the perpetual supervision of behavior and tasks, . . . a whole technique of management" (Foucault 1988a:105; Castel 1991). Power in the modern state operates through the internalization of processes of regulation, control, and surveillance by individuals through the development and perpetuation of taken-for-granted behaviors or micropractices (Fraser 1989), with the effect that individuals, as it were, act for the state through their monitoring of their and others' behavior, in order to produce the "bodies" desired by the state. So Petersen and Lupton (1996), in their Foucaultian analysis of the changing discourses in public health in relation to definitions of citizenship, note how the concept "citizen" is expanding to include as part of its definition an increasing number of responsibilities and associated "proper" behaviors, behaviors that require individuals to be constantly vigilant of their actions (not smoking, keeping fit). The state's endorsement of such vigilance is read not only in terms of enhancing the life of the individual but also in terms of the benefit to the state in producing bodies that make fewer demands on health systems. The regulatory implications must also be attended to. At what point do individuals become unable to access certain types of health care because they have refused to control their behavior? Who makes the decision about exclusion and who gets excluded?

As a consequence, postmodern writing investigates how such bodies are written by or inscribed in discourse. This is a considerably more powerful concept than that offered by social constructionists. What it refers to is how actual bodies of individuals are so shaped by social conventions and the micropractices reproduced by discourses that certain physical and intellectual actions that could be performed by them are not regarded as possible. Significantly, however, there is always more than one discourse circulating through a society. To a certain degree, some choices exist about where an individual may come to locate her- or himself discursively and to be discursively located; this process of writing, not just being written by, discourse contributes to changing discursive structures. It should also be noted that discourse is not just about ideology or attitudes or accepted behaviors (micropractices). Changing discourses involves effecting change across all three of these domains. However, the significance of micropractices as very powerful means by which discourses are sustained and changed should not be overlooked.

Theory of Representation

Foucault argues that power circulates through the different disciplinary discourses present in a society and, in that process, power relations are constructed. All discourses generate "truth effects." They purport to "represent" or describe the way the world "really" is and so seek to determine the validity of the ways in which social, economic, and political realities can be ordered and prescribed. Within postmodern theorizing, all accounts are "representations" (Clifford 1983; Hale 1992). This word catches at two dimensions. One is that it is impossible to produce a definitive account of an event. What can be reported or recorded is always incomplete, its incompleteness a result of the positioning of the speaker/reporter. "Representation" signals the break between the object/event/situation and the accounts generated about it. It highlights the intimate connection between language and interpretation, emphasizing how in even seemingly unproblematic and transparent events, interpretation involves selection, exclusion, and weighting of evidence. Language can no longer be understood as a transparent or neutral medium through which meaning can be transmitted. As a result of different configurations of constituent factors (circumstances, actors, observers, discourses), there are always, at least theoretically, alternative and disruptive representations of an event or text. There is no "final" or "real" account. To report on reality, as Calvino (1988) notes, is to engage in distortion. All representations offer at best a partial account of what they purport to describe. (This text, it should be noted, is no exception to this statement.)

The second dimension is that a representation is not just that produced by an individual existing independently of the discourses that circulate in a particular society. Just as it is impossible for the individual person to exist in a social space not structured by discourse, so all representations are socially produced, are part of the means by which different discourses—those that are marginal and are less powerful, as well as those that are dominant—circulate in the social domain and inform and are informed by each other, a point that again highlights the complicit rather than the independent nature of language and its immersion in relations of power. Representations, then, describe particular aspects of the social. The way an event/person/situation is described contributes to the "truth value" of a discourse or discourses, to the way in which discourses construct the social world, to how that construction comes to be taken for granted (its taken-for-grantedness demonstrated in the ways everyday behaviors are structured), and therefore to the power of a particular discourse to sustain a social "truth," a "truth" that operates in part to exclude other modes of representation (Fraser 1989). Or, as Foucault put it, "truth is to be understood as a system of ordered procedures for the production, regulation, distribution, circulation and operation of statements.

" 'Truth' is linked in a circular relation with systems of power which produce and sustain it, and to effects of power which it induces and which extend it" (Foucault 1980:133).

Such "truth effects" have material consequences in the social world. The "truths" of dominant discourses (those that are privileged through their powerful institutional and disciplinary associations) are difficult to challenge by dint of their having entered the realm of the commonsensical and the taken-for-granted. Hence they work to exclude alternative accounts or representations of how that world might be structured.

All this suggests a totally deterministic process. Power, however, is not just about prohibition and exclusion; the existence of power points to the possibility of multiple discourses, multiple sites of operation and resistance. Power is "always already there," but "this does not entail the necessity of accepting an inescapable form of domination or an absolute privilege on the side of the law. To say one can never be 'outside' power does not mean that one is trapped and condemned to defeat no matter what" (Foucault 1980:141–142).

At all times, then, there is more than one discourse available within the social, positing different "truths" and producing different representations of reality. Power is simultaneously controlling and productive.

What, however, might resistance look like? The alternative to totalizing knowledges and their associated discourses is "partial, locatable, critical knowledges sustaining the possibility of webs of connections" (Haraway 1997a:286). Donna Haraway argues that both relativism and totalization claim to see from all positions and deny location, positionality, and the embodiment of the "truths" they assert. In contrast, feminist objectivity privileges "contestation, deconstruction, passionate construction, webbed connections, and hope for transformation of systems of knowledge the taken-for-granted and of attending to 'heterogeneous multiplicities'" (287). Moreover, all discourses are subject to interrogation, identification of the positioning of those who speak them and of how that position restricts vision and excludes alternatives. The questions Haraway poses reflect and extend Foucault's questions about "who speaks?; from what position; who is excluded by that speaking?" She asks, "How to see? Where to see from? What limits to vision? What to see for? Whom to see with? Who gets to have more than one point of view? Who gets blinded? Who wears blinders? Who interprets the visual field? What other sensory powers do we wish to cultivate besides vision?" (289). What is necessary to attend to is not just what is "known" but how any particular field is produced and what representational practices are involved in order to challenge its boundaries to allow alternative or *different* and often subjugated knowledges to enter the field.

Concept of Difference

The concept of "difference" and a positive engagement with difference raise further issues. One, as Haraway (1997a) notes, is the issue of romanticizing alternative or subjugated knowledges. The other is the problematic status of "difference" per se because of its negative connotation. In asking whether it is possible "to think differently about difference" (Braidotti 1997:62) and commenting on the binary structure of Western thought in the context of women as "other," Braidotti writes of "difference as that which is other-than the accepted norm" (62). She goes on to note that difference is associated with the abnormal, the inferior and the devalued.

> If the position of women . . . as logical operators in discursive production is comparable within the dualistic logic, it follows that the misogyny of discourse is not an irrational exception but rather a tightly constructed system that requires difference as perjoration in order to erect the positivity of the norm. In this respect, misogyny is not a hazard but rather the structural necessity of a system that can only represent "otherness" as negativity. (64)

As my account of knowledge-based teamwork emphasizes, positive engagement with difference (between disciplinary knowledge and the different representations of clients that such knowledge produces, and between differently located knowledges) is a critical part of effective teamwork. A key dimension of my argument is that knowledge-based teams regard the generation of different accounts of clients as a necessary, normative part of their work.

"Embodied" Discourse, or Reading the "Body" in the Postmodern

In modernist theory "discourse" is most readily thought of as "speech," and the individual human body is understood to enter and exist in a social space outside of and independent from social institutions, a positioning inextricably caught up in the Cartesian "*Cogito, ergo sum*" ("I think, therefore I am"). In contrast, postmodern theory writes "discourse" (as exemplified in the above discussion) and "body" very differently. Postmodern analysis writes social reality as discursively constructed, defining the bodies of social actors as full participants in the processes of discursivity and representation. What this means is that the postmodern "body" is to be read as a medium of representation, a surface or screen on which institutional discourses and subjective intent (constituted by issues of knowledge/power) are projected. As a result, these locate the individual within specific social sites while their associated micropractices make available certain modes of behavior and restrict access to other modes. "Body," then, becomes a term enabling the conceptualization of these complex processes, so foregrounding issues of social structuration and displacing the conception of the individual as the "founding subject," the supposed origin of meanings and social processes and relationships (Foucault 1981:65). I would then rewrite the Cartesian proposition as "What I, located at this time within this position in the social structure, in this geographical and cultural location, am able to think and act is a result of my inscription in discourse *and* how I act out that position (both challenging and affirming that inscription) in my daily life."

What this proposition emphasizes is that a team member is not an autonomous "I" who makes statements about work or about a client, so bringing to the team certain ideas about clients' issues and what actions can be taken in response to these. It further shifts the ground away from an analysis that is primarily concerned with the management of interpersonal relations between autonomous subjects (individual professionals). Instead, it defines teamwork as a discursive site, a site where discursive/disciplinary differences are demonstrated and enacted by the (discursively produced) representatives of those disciplines. The focus of this analysis (and for teamwork in the postmodern) foregrounds how different discourses and their attendant organizational location are represented by (and by means of) specific individuals.

Teamwork is thus constituted by different representations (embodiments) of, not "*facts*" about, the client and the professional members of the team. Each member of the team, including the client, produces representations of others and is the object of representations by others. This complex of representations provides much of the raw material on which the work of the team is performed, work that is accomplished when team members are physically present to each other and in the thinking and actions of team members between meetings. Key issues in teamwork are how the team enables these different representations to be produced within the process of the team meeting or review and how the team engages with them critically. This requires, for example, that the team is attentive to what members of what disciplines do or do not speak; how input from representatives of different disciplines is attended to; how what has been said may offer a quite different account of a client than the dominant account; and how what has been said could bear materially on the developing care plan. (See part 2 for further discussion.)

A particularly important factor here is how the team attends to and controls for the effect of differential power relations on the relative value of representations about a client by individual team members, including clients. The ways in which teams inscribe clients' bodies through their representational activities may become part of the problem in working effectively with those clients (Opie 1997). Hence, operating in a discourse in which families of psychiatric clients, for example, are described only as "angry" or "pathological" can result in a team's difficulty in accessing alternative but more marginalized accounts that could offer a different approach and allow the team in some respects to define its task and its relationship with that family differently. Understanding teamwork as a discursive site (not as a group of individuals meeting for an hour or so) has the consequence that the analysis of teamwork emphasizes the discursive and organizational location of individual representations, how they intersect with others, and their outcome in terms of structuring the team's work.

Another dimension of the analysis attends to the discursive location of teamwork within organizations (with the attendant practices and outcomes). To write this is to move away from thinking of the organization as providing the context within which teams/groups of individuals who come from different disciplines operate. What is emphasized instead is how teamwork does not exist independently of organizational discursive practices. How each organization attends to or inscribes "teamwork" (how it embodies both professionals and clients in its representations) will crucially affect how teams operate.

A further focus of the analysis is on the bodies (client and professional) inscribed by different models of teamwork. At the beginning of this chapter, I commented on the rhetorical structure of much of the literature on teamwork. This structure relies on an affirmation of an initial brief and generalized proposition about or reference to the value of teamwork. The validity of this proposition/reference is then cast into doubt by what in effect becomes a listing of problems that members of teams typically experience. The value of postmodern theorizing is that it also allows me to engage with how these seemingly relatively simple propositions (such as "teamwork should be great, but it is too often not") can be viewed in a more complex manner. This means that I can highlight what the rhetorical structure, in its accounts of the value and disappointment of teamwork, does not attend to. Furthermore, it allows me to draw a sharp contrast between how both clients and professionals are inscribed in that rhetorical structure, and how knowledge-based teamwork inscribes such bodies rather differently. Working within postmodern theory enables me to write of the literature on teamwork as follows:

> The mainstream literature on teamwork inscribes two types of professional bodies. One, discernible in the idealized representation of teamwork, writes a smooth, untextured, powerful body, contained within precise disciplinary boundaries, unmarked by disagreement or (disciplinary) difference, harmonizing with other, similarly structured professional bodies, and operating in an organizational vacuum. The body of the client, discursively written as the object at which their work is directed, remains offstage.
>
> The second type of professional body, located in the recognition of the problematics of teamwork, is again contained within precise disciplinary boundaries but is marked by conflict and typically unacknowledged differences in power as a consequence of disciplinary location, gender, and ethnicity, its gaze substantially focused on members' relationships. This body is noticeably marked/scarred by such internal tensions, and by the conflicting desire to protect its disciplinary turf and to work consensually. It operates within organizational spaces that are substantially invisible, while those that have become just visible lack other than a generalized, nonspecific structure. Here, too, the professional's expert practices are such that the body of the client and family are represented in terms of passivity, as the marginalized objects toward which work is directed, and where their knowledge is represented as insignificant when placed alongside professional, expert knowledge.
>
> The professional and client bodies inscribed by knowledge-based teamwork are substantially different from the above. Knowledge-based teamwork produces professional bodies that are fluid, flexible, and linguistically competent, able to articulate their discipline-specific knowledge and to play (in the Barthesian sense) with the differences and the implications for practice engendered by different disciplinary positions; at the same time these bodies are not identical in shape, the precise shape of each being a consequence of experience, competence, gender, disciplinary location, and power. Rather than eschewing difference, such bodies recognize difference as critical to their work and seek ways to ensure its production, so directing their gaze not only at the center but also at the margins of the team (what knowledge/issues are not

being produced and why?). The production of such bodies is highly reliant on organizational discourses and elaboration of principles of practice in teamwork, and they inform those practices and discourses.

Knowledge-based teamwork inscribes the body of the client and family as knowing bodies and their knowledges, although different from knowledge collectively held by professionals, as critical to the effective operation of the team. This mode of inscription relocates the client and family away from the team/knowledge margins to occupy a space equal to that of the professionals. Implicit in this relocation, and also important for how professional bodies attend to the knowledge necessary to respond to each situation with which they are engaged, is a recognition of knowledge required by the team as specific to time and place. A powerful example of that specificity, therefore, is cultural difference, because cultural difference is so often represented by different bodies, specifically bodies of color.

Reviewing the Literature

The following is not an exhaustive review of the recent literature on teamwork, and certainly not of that in the burgeoning organizational field. Much of the literature referenced here is specifically related to interprofessional teamwork in health care, and it includes writing from specific disciplinary foci and articles on developing interdisciplinary training programs (for example, Clark 1994; Perkins and Tryssenaar 1996; Roberts et al. 1994; Solomon and Mellor 1992), since the issues to be addressed in such programs are very similar to those faced by teams in the field. In light of the range of literature on teamwork in health care referenced and/or discussed in this text, with its different methodologies and shifts in focus, what is discussed in this review fairly represents the writing in the field.

I have structured this review primarily with respect to two major issues contained within that literature. The first, "representations of teamwork" focuses on the persistently identified tension between teamwork ideals and the mundane realities of practice. The second issue to be discussed, "thinking effectiveness" (since the major rationale for teamwork is that it be effective), relates to dimensions of effectiveness in teamwork. I have structured this discussion with respect to aspects of effectiveness, three of which are easily visible in the teamwork literature and three of which are significantly more marginal. First, I provide an account of the different categorizing of modes of teamwork and their implications for effective teamwork, and I discuss issues of quality of team interaction as it relates to collaboration and member satisfaction, and quality of interaction. I then discuss another three dimensions of effective teamwork that remain marginalized in the mainstream literature but that have a significant impact on the quality of team interaction: the relationship between clients, families, and their teams; the question of organizational support for teamwork; and the production of knowledge work. I suggest that attending to these interactions is critical to the production of effective teamwork.

Representations of Teamwork

Much of the literature on teamwork represents it as occupying an ambiguous position in organizations and among health care professionals and researchers. On the one hand, it is represented as enabling improvements in organizational work. The health care literature suggests that teamwork may increase professional accountability as members' work becomes less "private" and more "visible" as a consequence of discussions or joint work with professionals from other disciplines. Joint work in teams can also contribute to increased job satisfaction, in part because of more frequent use of advanced job skills. Effectiveness may be increased because multiple input into the development of care plans contributes to a reduction in errors (Poulin, Walter, and Walker 1994). The development of interprofessional communication can be stimulating and challenging. An expansion of professionals' cognitive maps contributes to an expansion of knowledge about others' work and its value, while modifying an individual's own practices (Clark 1994; Toseland, Palmer-Ganeles, and Chapman 1986; Solomon and Mellor 1992) and helps members to think more precisely (de Silva et al. 1992); it also requires a recognition of the limitations of one's own "constructions of meaning" (Clark 1994:45) and hence recognition of the value of others' input. Teamwork may contribute to more numerous and more creative programs for clients and prevent professional "burnout," since working in teams enables colleagues to provide more support to each other (Toseland, Palmer-Ganeles, and Chapman 1986). Organizationally, teamwork may permit better use of resources as coordination is improved. Such outcomes imply, with differently articulated degrees of explicitness, the existence within teams of a shared philosophy and goals, task interdependence, equality and equal access to power and decision making.

Unfortunately, teamwork is just not plain sailing. Effective teamwork, as is frequently noted, is honored more in the breach than in the observance. The advantages accruing to members as a consequence of teamwork, and teams' abilities to achieve better-integrated care plans, better interprofessional communication, better service delivery, and more effective use of resources are offset by repeatedly identified and multiple problems. Although an objective of teamwork is to improve interdisciplinary coordination (Saltz 1992), the term *coordination* is not easily defined nor its impact easily assessed (Webb and Hobdell 1980).[4] As a result of professional socialization within their own discipline, members may not sufficiently appreciate the value of different disciplinary inputs. Professional socialization can also complicate power sharing between professionals (Bailey 1984; Griffiths 1997; Mizrahi and Abramson 1994; Salmond 1997; de Silva et al. 1992) and between professionals and clients (Smale and Tuson 1993; Webb and Hobdell 1980). Differences in status, training, and experience may push members toward separateness (Mellor and Solomon 1992). Team members may have to contend with difficulties in communication between themselves and a lack of organizational support, and teamwork may be seen as threatening the maintenance of professional autonomy (Abramson and Rosenthal 1995). Noninvolvement or exclusion of a particular professional group may affect the overall effectiveness of a team's work (McClelland and Sands 1993); equally, the effectiveness of a team may be affected by policies and practices of other organizations and/or teams.

Role blurring in teamwork has been described as inevitable up to a point, and desirable in that taking another's role to a limited degree can help to expand one's skills, but whether the inevitable and desirable occur is affected by members' recognized expertise and professional domain (Toseland, Palmer-Ganeles, and Chapman 1986). Members are not necessarily adequately oriented to teamwork (Abramson 1989). There is an absence of definitions or agreement on what effective collaboration looks like (Webb and Hobdell 1980) and indeed, as I will shortly demonstrate and as others have also commented, an absence of elaboration of the concept "effectiveness" (Whorley 1996). Clients and their families are too easily excluded from involvement in teams' decisions about issues closely affecting them (clients/families) (Abramson 1992; McClain and Bury 1998; Saltz 1992). Moreover, the close association between teamwork and professional benefit detracts from a focus on the client and could result in a definition of the primary objective of teamwork as being to benefit professionals to the exclusion of a focus on how clients benefit from teamwork (de Silva et al. 1992).

Rather than developing fruitful challenge and debate, teams can enforce conformity, and use of a consensus model of teamwork can result in much wasted time and poor decision making (Toseland, Palmer-Ganeles, and Chapman 1986). Gilgun (1988) has noted the general lack of research into decision-making processes in human services teamwork, so that teams' contribution to effective decision making may well be assumed rather than real. Teamwork can be bedeviled by conflict, but avoidance of disagreement can be just as problematic as extensive conflict (Stevenson 1980). Problems also occur because of poor leadership, poor communication of expertise, and lack of clearly defined goals (Saltz 1992). Team goals relating to effective resource use and integrated planning can be compromised by disciplines' unequal access to power as a consequence of professional socialization, gender, and ethnicity (Abramson and Rosenthal 1995; Ely 1995), and such factors can also constrain members' participation in the team, although teamwork relies on member participation (Uhl-Bien and Graen 1992).[5] Teams can become sites of rigid practices and close surveillance of members, thereby contributing to a tense and stressful organizational environment (Barker 1993).

A team's effectiveness may also be affected by practical considerations. Too large a team may inhibit creativity (Bailey 1984); on the other hand, the appropriate size of a team may depend in part on contexts such as "setting, purpose, personalities, frequency of team meetings, etc." (Solomon and Mellor 1992:185), factors that complicate defining an optimum team size. Professional languages can create misunderstandings (Solomon and Mellor 1992). Frequent staff changes may complicate team learning and development, transmission of culture, and sense of mutuality, and the effectiveness of the team may be compromised by a predominance of less experienced workers and ineffective leadership (Solomon and Mellor 1992). Moreover, the style of leadership must be appropriate to the style of team the organization is seeking to build (Uhl-Bien and Graen 1992). In fact, in light of the myriad identified problems confronting teams, one could be excused for being surprised that they get any good press at all.

In effect, the dominant preoccupation of the literature is (understandably) how to bridge this gulf between the ideal of teamwork and its often more complicated and messy reality. However, the literature that is attempting to respond to these multiple difficulties itself poses a problem, with various writers commenting on its failings. Mizrahi and Abramson

(1994) and Sheppard (1992) have noted its exhortatory, prescriptive, and anecdotal nature.[6] McClelland and Sands (1993), Sands (1993), Schwartzman (1986), and Toseland, Palmer-Ganeles, and Chapman (1986) refer to the amount of writing on teamwork produced in the absence of close observation of team practices, and Sands (1993) and Uhl-Bien and Graen (1992) comment on the lack of theoretically informed writing on work. Schwartzman (1986) has noted, too, that much of the work on teams in psychology has been done under laboratory conditions in a context where there was no questioning as to the appropriateness of the orientation of the research, and that such research, reflecting the individualistic culture in the United States, was overfocused on the impact of individuals on groups. In other words, much of the literature may have little to offer by way of "solutions" to the "team" problem, although the problems besetting teamwork are constantly rehearsed.

There are, moreover, further problems that are not identified by these writers, problems in which to varying degrees they themselves participate. First, the structure of the discussion about the possibilities and difficulties confronting teamwork relies on the creation of a dichotomy between the ideal and the real. Such a dichotomy is in itself an issue because it suppresses how the actual production of teamwork at any one site is the result of the institutional, organizational, and professional discourses specific to each site.

Second, as noted earlier, some of the writing is focused on the performance of specific disciplines in a team context. In other words, the argument is about claiming turf and enhancing the visibility and power of specific disciplines (often social work), especially in relation to medicine, in leaner, meaner organizations. Let me, for example, reference two such articles. One (Abramson 1989) discusses how teams could work better; the other (Abramson and Mizrahi 1986) explores collaboration between social workers and physicians and identifies a number of ideal types ("social worker as educator," "social worker as sensitive colleague") and strategies that social workers could adopt to ensure their inclusion in multiple areas of work. Although ostensibly focused on teamwork, the meta-objective of the articles seems to be less an analysis of teamwork per se than attention to the enhancement of the social work role in a team and organizational context. How such attempts at strategic positioning are regarded by other team members, what effect they may have on the day-to-day operation of a team, and, indeed, the validity of identifying particular qualities as peculiar to a specific discipline are not attended to. Such literature tends to inscribe a smooth, generalized, but slightly superior professional body, thereby suppressing differences among practitioners within a specific discipline in skill, experience, and knowledge, differences that if acknowledged would undercut the certainty of the claims.

Third, the solution frequently proposed in both the organizational and the health care literature to the various difficulties that teams encounter is derived, broadly speaking, from a mechanistic model of communication (with exhortations about the need for better communication) and/or from the traditional human relations model. As team members develop more trust, concern, respect, and so on for each other, their performance will improve and members will participate more (for example, Brem 1997; Deeprose 1995; Losoncy 1997; Midgley, Burns, and Garland 1996; Varney 1990).

Fourth, although the question driving the literature is about how to achieve more effective teamwork and how to improve team performance (Moore et al. 1991), the related issues of what constitutes effectiveness in teams and what are the criteria by which a team may measure the effectiveness of its work remain underdeveloped. Schwartzman (1986) has suggested that the focus on evaluation of team effectiveness was typically written from a managerial perspective and that much of the writing in the field at that time assumed, in part, that individuals desire to produce organizationally effective behaviors.[7] It could be argued, however, that the tenor of her question about individual desire and effectiveness do not reflect the substantial changes in the discourses over the last fifteen years within health care organizations, where questions of performance and effectiveness have become increasingly integral to definitions of professional work. For many professionals in such health care systems, the issue of individual desire is likely to be supplanted by such questions as these: Who defines effectiveness? What definitions of effectiveness circulate within the organization? What modes of work do they describe? What modes do they exclude? What gets funded? Given the substantial costs of teamwork and governmental concerns about escalating health budgets, getting value for money is a significant issue for health organizations, and being seen as contributing value for money is a significant issue for health professionals.

Thinking Effectiveness

Ittner and Kogut (1995:158), writing within the organizational literature, have produced a simple definition of *effectiveness*. Contrasting it with *efficiency*, which they define as "doing things right" (hence a focus on order and following correct procedures), they suggest that *effectiveness* relates to "doing the right thing." For example, a team may be working with clients to ensure that most do not stay on a ward beyond the desirable bed days for that client group and that they leave the ward able to return to work. In organizational terms, such a team could be seen as working efficiently. If, however, in the course of their efficient treatment, clients believed they were treated discriminatorily, then the effectiveness of the team becomes questionable, especially if client empowerment is a team objective. Although neatly compact yet seemingly open-ended and offering a nice contrast to its twin "efficiency," this definition nonetheless fails to advance the argument significantly. What the "right thing" is may not be self-evident, each discipline's account of "the right thing" being embedded in different knowledges and discursive practices directing attention to different priorities.

Modes of Interaction: Categorizing Team Types   If organizations desire to establish effective, high-performance teams, then they need to attend to the degree of collaboration expected between members, as this is affected by the model or type of team endorsed by the organization.

The teams participating in the research reported on in this book referred to themselves variously as "multidisciplinary," "interdisciplinary," and (once) "transdisciplinary." Definitions of teamwork in the literature use these terms to describe a hierarchy of types of teamwork centered on progressively more complex knowledge intersections between disciplines, with transdisciplinary work possessing the highest degree of such complexity. A *multidisciplinary* team is characterized by parallel work. Each discipline operates independently of the others. There are infrequent meetings, and the dominant working relationship is one in which one member's contribution is little affected by the input of others. As Gibbons et al. (1994:28) have noted: "Multidisciplinarity is characterised by the autonomy of the various disciplines and does not lead to changes in the existing disciplinary and theoretical structures." This mode of teamwork tends to be seen as the least productive (an issue with considerable organizational implications for those establishing multidisciplinary teams).

An *interdisciplinary* team is characterized by joint activity, collaboration, the beginnings of shared linguistic practices, and shared responsibility (Sands 1993). The outcome is accomplished by interactive work, contributions requiring attention to team process (Bailey 1984), and the development of an action consensus as a way of focusing on task and maintaining group activity.

A *transdisciplinary* team is characterized by integrated thinking based on the sharing of knowledge and greater blurring of professional boundaries than in an interdisciplinary team. Clinically, members are involved in role release rather than role retention as they seek to develop a common knowledge base. Transition to transdisciplinarity requires a shared theoretical base and common language among members as a foundation for consensus building; clarity about targets for intervention and means of measurement; breadth of appropriate interventions; clearly understood program procedures and policies; and systematic observation and feedback mechanisms to assist with team growth and quality assurance (Antoniadis and Videlock 1991). Thus, a transdisciplinary team requires the subordination of the Western cultural values of competition and individualism (Clark 1994), the team's active assumption of members' equality, and substantial organizational commitment to and resourcing of teamwork. Development toward a more complex mode of working, then, is likely to be an intricate process, since the development of a transdisciplinary team would appear to require a long-term commitment of members, correspondingly low turnover of staff, and a stable organizational environment—factors that are less likely to be present in today's health organizations.

These definitions, however, describe "pure" models. In everyday practice it appears to be more difficult to determine whether a team is working in multidisciplinary or interdisciplinary mode. In writing of what was presented as "interdisciplinary" teamwork, Mellor and Solomon (1992:211) asked: "Did the interdisciplinary [meetings] . . . really model an interdisciplinary team approach to geriatric care or was it merely an opportunity for a variety of disciplines to present their perspective—a host of speakers all talking on the same theme but providing parallel statements that never impact on each other?" This question is similar to the one Sands (1993) asked of the team she studied.[8] Equally, teams may well be in a process of transition from one mode of working to another—a state not covered by this terminology.

Furthermore, there are dimensions of the definitions of interdisciplinarity and transdisciplinarity that in the context of this text require further scrutiny. What sort of "process" is Bailey (1984) referring to? There are references to teams developing a "common knowledge base" and "common language" as hallmarks of transdisciplinary work, but it is not entirely clear if these terms are complementary or are being used as alternatives to each other. For example, William Miller (1994), in commenting on the distinctions between multi-, inter-, and transdisciplinary teams with reference to the different ways in which such teams handle input from different disciplines, the extent of questioning and discussion that occurs, the level of collaboration, and the extent to which team members achieve a "sustained common language," wrote:

> Who speaks what language is an accurate guide to which sphere of collaborative [work] is operative at any one moment. When each person consistently speaks in the language of his or her home discipline, then multidisciplinary [work] is occurring. If the members of the group begin using the language of other disciplines, then the group has moved into the sphere of interdisciplinary [work]. When the group repeatedly uses a newly agreed-upon language, it is engaged in transdisciplinary [work].   *(Miller 1994:268–269).*

While Antoniadis and Videlock focus more on the development of a shared theoretical framework (although it is not clear whether this is in relation to a theoretical framework describing the processes of knowledge-based teamwork, or a theoretical framework, say, about the construction of the individual psyche), the transdisciplinary team in Miller's account requires a blurring or merging of disciplinary distinctions, and it is not clear what the basis for the "newly agreed-upon language" might be. His focus is on the elision of difference, not engagement with it. Implicit in his text, then, is a positioning of difference as "other," as negative and as unproductive.

As a consequence of such difficulties, I have eschewed the use of such terminology in this text, instead writing of "interprofessional teamwork" as that involving professionals from more than one discipline. The term *interprofessional* in itself makes no claims about the quality of such work or how it is to be carried out.

Quality of Interaction: Collaboration   My objective here is to recapitulate some of the matters discussed above, but in the context of specific articles that focus on aspects of effective teamwork. The rationale for the deployment of a team centers on its development of appropriate and shared care plans for and with clients to facilitate their achieving or sustaining maximum health gains. Such work requires collaboration, recognition of the interdependence of members' work, and coordination of that work. These attributes of teamwork are central to estimating timeliness and breadth of appropriate input and are, for all the reasons cited above, professionally demanding to develop in practice. Mellor and Solomon (1992:205) noted that, theoretically, interdisciplinary teamwork is carried out by "representatives of the various identified disciplines [who] meet together to assess, treat and order the health and social service care needs of the individual [client]." They quote Beckhardt, who defined an interdisciplinary team as "a group with a specific task or tasks, the accomplishment of which requires the interdependent and collaborative efforts of its members" (205). They then offer two slightly different definitions of collaboration, one by Mailick, the other by Tskuda. Mailick wrote of collaboration as involving "the achievement of some degree of consensus by a group of individuals about a plan of action and its execution"; Tskuda characterized it as the "sharing of planning and action with a joint responsibility for outcome" (205). Mailick's definition emphasizes the achievement of consensus (note the qualification "some degree of," which begs the question of just how much collaboration/consensus is necessary for effective work). Tskuda's definition puts more weight on the need for joint planning and action and on joint responsibility for outcomes, an emphasis that underscores the interdependence of members' work and their equality of power and responsibility. The problem, as Mellor and Solomon have noted, is that achieving interprofessional collaboration is easily stymied without:

- Resolution of differences between disciplines, differences that reflect professional status, and experiences in clinical work, as well as differences among individuals
- Identification of the different meanings that different professional groups ascribe to the same terminology,[9] and
- Management of boundary or "turf" issues by members.

These factors suggest that effective collaboration depends in part on a double process: the ability of members of traditionally less powerful disciplines to clearly articulate discipline-specific knowledge and to have that knowledge accorded status by other members located within more powerful disciplinary discourses (Abramson and Rosenthal 1995). What is absent, though, from Mellor and Solomon's discussion is a more focused account of how teams might better manage the differences arising from the different knowledges of their members and how teamwork that affords equality to its different knowledges might be conducted. Moreover, the interdisciplinary team that they observed took four years to move to a point at which members were able "to raise questions, to challenge the nature of the interdisciplinary team modelling and to critique themselves and others in their interdisciplinary performances" (211); *and* the team's ability to do this appeared, from their report, to rely on "friendships and group camaraderie" (211). Given that it might be assumed that professional accountability requires an evaluation/critique of work, the team they studied took a very considerable amount of time to achieve these necessary outcomes/changes.

Quality of Interaction: Member Interdependence   The need for some clarification of criteria informing "effectiveness" is highlighted by research such as that of Poulin, Walter, and Walker (1994). This study reports on a survey of one thousand gerontological social workers working in what were said to be interdisciplinary teams. The focus of the survey was on respondents' levels of satisfaction with the working of their teams. Leaving aside what appear to be contradictions in the data in the context of the actual working of the teams, which the authors do not address (such as that 78 percent saw input from other disciplines as a highly positive feature of teamwork, but nearly 50 percent thought there were problems in cooperating with other workers and a similar percentage also thought that the existence of professional subcultures made it difficult to hear input from other disciplines), there is no discussion of the possibility that reported satisfaction with teamwork (78 percent) cannot necessarily be equated with effectiveness. What, then, are other possible criteria for evaluating effectiveness?

In discussing the question of effectiveness in transdisciplinary teamwork, Antoniadis and Videlock (1991:158) refer to Shea and Guzzo's work on group effectiveness. Shea and Guzzo (Guzzo 1986:48) have conceptualized group effectiveness as mediated by three interrelated factors: "task interdependence," "outcome interdependence," and "potency." Task interdependence is the extent to which the task requires cooperation from the group. Not all tasks require the same degree of interdependence, but high interdependence requires high levels of coordination and cooperation. Antoniadis and Videlock suggest, then, that a clinical team requires "multiple opportunities to interact" in order to achieve high levels of task interdependence and build "consensus" (58); "outcome interdependence" refers to the degree to which rewards are dependent on group performance. Shea and Guzzo argue that the greater the group rewards, the more these work to promote interdependence. "Potency" is the recognition that "knowledge about past performance is an influential force in shaping beliefs about future effectiveness" (Guzzo 1986:49). Antoniadis and Videlock have also suggested that potency involves "the team's belief that they have the skills and environmental supports to accomplish the tasks" (159).

Antoniadis and Videlock (162) suggest therefore that (transdisciplinary) teamwork is mediated by professional and environmental factors. They define the factors that foster effective work in the clinical environment as: a strong theoretical base, clear intervention targets, appropriate clinical tools, effective procedures and policies, feedback, prescriptive supervision and training, and validation of members. Relevant clinical factors include role release, the possession of a common knowledge base, the presence of trust and respect, risk taking, and clinical competence.

The criteria that are of particular value seem to me to be those relating to "potency," with its emphasis on skill, its foregrounding of the organizational role in effective work, and notions of members' interdependence. What is absent, however, is any clear demonstration or discussion of what "brainstorming" or "interdependence" actually looks like and how the team, having shared information, then works with that information. In other words, key terms used here to describe elements of teamwork themselves require unpacking rather than being assumed to be self-evident.

Guzzo (1986), writing in the organizational literature, outlined three additional criteria for evaluating effectiveness. He labeled these "ultimate effectiveness," that is, group outputs, and the overall satisfaction of members; "healthy social interaction"; and "intermediate effectiveness," that is, the "quality of the group interaction process as it performs the task at hand." Evaluating the effectiveness of the group interaction process requires, therefore, "assessments of the level of member effort, the extent to which resources are applied toward task accomplishment, and the appropriateness of strategies used by a group to accomplish its task" (Guzzo 1986:46). Such criteria are, I suggest, problematic. I have already noted the dubiousness of equating member satisfaction with effectiveness, while other criteria ("healthy interaction" and the several elements in his definition of "intermediate effectiveness") are not transparent and require further definition. Interestingly, though, Guzzo comments on the problems of equating quality of interaction with effectiveness, suggesting that what constitutes effectiveness is highly contextualized. He notes, for example, that if a group is established to make a decision, then its effectiveness rests on the quality of its decision making. Decision making requires the team to have "performance strategies for group decision-making" (56) in place. These strategies include an "intelligence phase," a "design stage" involving the development of alternative solutions, and an agreed process governing how decisions are to be made (56–71).

Foregrounding Marginalized Dimensions of Effectiveness

The elements relating to effective teamwork that I discuss below shift from discussions of (very substantially) untheorized aspects of teamwork or of effectiveness to focus instead on three interdependent dimensions of teamwork. Although present in the health care literature, these dimensions have typically remained marginal in discussions of the constitution of effective work. One, focusing on the orientation of team members toward their clientele and the differently located and therefore differently informed knowledge that the team accesses and compiles in its formulation of care plans, directs attention to the centrality of clients and families in teamwork (Saltz 1992; McClain and Bury 1998) and focuses on how the team accesses and incorporates into its work the knowledge that clients and family members hold about relevant issues. Another begins a discussion, continued in the next chapter, of the organizational contribution to effective teamwork, while a third addresses issues of knowledge work.

Quality of Interaction: Clients, Families, and Their Teams   The development of teamwork can be described as a response to the dual, interactive ethical and organizational demands of Western health care. Teams' ethical responsibilities to involve clients and their families in decision making are reflected in the long-standing concern reported in the medical anthropology and medical sociology literatures about disciplinary fragmentation of clients' bodies and the predominance of a medical focus with the resultant exclusion of attention to clients' life-world and associated social and emotional needs. The exclusion of such domains, it is also argued, may become more compromising when clients are those with long-term and chronic conditions, and the inability of medical science to intervene curatively means that the condition has to be managed in the course of everyday life. For these reasons, the social and emotional dimensions of the illness and its impact on the individual and his or her available support networks, and not just its medical sequelae, are highly significant issues for teams to attend to, as is accessing and working with clients' and families' understandings of their situations and concerns—a process that highlights teams' accountability to their clients. Moreover, close involvement of clients in decisions affecting their care has a positive impact on post-discharge outcomes (Abramson 1992), a factor in which health care organizations as well as clients and teams have an interest.

Part of the rationale for teamwork derives from assumptions about increased benefits to clients. The tendency has been, therefore, to describe such benefits largely in terms of service provision, and it has been assumed that teamwork will result in clients' various needs being more fully attended to, but there has been little attention to how the relationships among clients, families, and teams are played out. However, Abramson (1992), McClain and Bury (1998), Ovretveit (1993), and Saltz (1992) have commented on the importance of teams closely involving clients in decision making and seeking to empower them, with Saltz suggesting that the extent to which a team empowers its clients is a hallmark of effective work. McClain and Bury and Saltz have noted that working to include clients as team members can result, for example, in an expansion of team responsibilities (for instance, clients' participation in goal setting may involve the team in client education—to which I would add that the clients may have an "educative" role in relation to the team as well). Similarly, Clark has quoted Schön's comments that the reflective practitioner seeks to "discover the limits of his [*sic*] expertise through reflective conversations with the client" (Clark 1994:41). Both of these comments reposition professional knowledge and rearrange power relations between practitioner and client through the challenging of familiar knowledge hierarchies and positioning of individuals.

"Empowerment," then, can be read in this context as requiring traditionally dominant health professionals to take account of the different (here, clients') knowledges surrounding an event and to ensure that those knowledges adequately inform decision-making processes. An empowering process therefore decenters professional knowledge and emphasizes lay knowledge as significant in informing decisions in health care. It acknowledges multiple perspectives, rather than assuming a taken-for-granted commonality of interest between clients and professionals; for instance, the introduction of patient charters in the United Kingdom and users' codes of rights in Aotearoa/New Zealand represent in part attempts to realign roles in areas of health care provision. The desired repositioning of professional knowledge is not easily attained, however, even in those disciplines that claim empowerment of their clientele as one of the hallmarks of their profession (Smale and Tuson 1993), and the development of meaningful empowering practices is complicated in the case of some client groups, such as committed psychiatric patients.

The significance to clients and families and teams and organizations of the clients' and families' involvement in decision making suggests that this is an important dimension in evaluations of teams' effectiveness. Arriving at viable modes of working with clients and families and repositioning them as central participants in teamwork requires the development of appropriate processes and procedures; these procedures require ongoing evaluation, as there is often insufficient attention to maintaining the processes intended to give substance to the form (E. Miller 1993). Developing and critiquing team procedures and practices pertaining to client empowerment goes beyond being only a team decision; it also refers to organizational endorsement of such work and organizational appreciation of its implications in terms of training, resourcing, and caseloads.

Quality of Interaction: The Organizational Dimension in the Production of Effective Teamwork Much of the health care teamwork literature contains few or no references to the role of organization in the development of teamwork. Introducing this dimension moves beyond writing teams as closed systems and acknowledging teams' need to have and to manage access to resources and interface with external organizations (Ancona 1990; Roberts et al. 1994). A central tenet of my argument in relation to effective work is that teamwork cannot flourish without what Winnicott has called (with reference to sustaining maternal practices) a "good enough" environment (Stacey 1996; Mankin, Cohen, and Bikson 1995). Effective teamwork is not an end in itself. It reflects an organizational requirement for the production of certain types of work that bear on organizational effectiveness (Katzenbach and Smith 1993; Mankin, Cohen, and Bikson 1995). The literature therefore addresses the organizational requirement for particular team practices and objectives and emphasizes the need for organizational resourcing, input, and nurturing of teamwork at the macro and micro levels. It notes the importance of an organizational interest in team design, elaboration of team goals, and the provision of access to training and resources necessary for the team to undertake its tasks (Abramson 1993; Antoniadis and Videlock 1991; Mankin, Cohen, and Bikson 1995), and the development of procedures, policies, lines of accountability, and standards (Briggs 1980). It suggests that organizational expectations about performance are critical and that effective teams require established and common goals since, as Katzenbach and Smith (1993:21) have argued, too often teams "accept goals that are neither demanding, precise, realistic, nor actually held *in common.*"

Ovretveit (1993) also has addressed the question of team performance and organizational expectations in the context of his commentary on the organizational investment in the degree of collective responsibility that a team assumes. (His commentary reflects elements of the earlier discussion about different types of teams in relation to the mode of teamwork an organization wishes to achieve). He has suggested that the extent of integration in a team affects whether the team operates as a group of individuals, each making his or her own decisions (in effect operating as a multidisciplinary team) or whether "each person's decisions are governed by collective policies and decisions" (Ovretveit 1993:84). This distinction has considerable organizational implications, in addition to affecting the orientation of the team gaze. Do "members of a team share a responsibility as a collective to serve the needs of the client population [or do they] each provide separate services, with the team merely coordinating the care of individual clients?" (Ovretveit 1993:85). If the former, then developing and maintaining collective responsibility requires policies about teams' intervention and involvement in decisions about members' work, especially about closure of cases. For example, accepting a client for longer-term work needs to be a team decision, made after a review of the individual's situation, the team's workload, and the rationale for continued involvement; in turn, these factors need to be placed against team priorities and reflect "needs analyses, and not just past practice" (Ovretveit 1993:93). The decision is not one for the individual practitioner alone but one for the team in thinking through how such work would affect its objectives and resources—hence the organizational investment in such decisions. Decision making involves ensuring that "the team influences the practitioner's decisions," though "ensuring that arrangements for each stage are agreed and defined by team decision criteria," and that there is "team guidance and policy about practice" (Ovretveit 1993:94).

Teamwork also highlights the need for operational channels of communication across (flatter) organizational hierarchies responsive to members' differently sited knowledge. Writing in 1976 on effecting innovation in a psychiatric hospital, Eric Miller addressed the critical need for staff on the job to "have the requisite knowledge and authority themselves to examine [their task] critically and to seek new and more effective ways of performing the task; and they may indeed need to question the accepted definition of the task itself" (Miller 1993:219). This resonates, nineteen years later, with Whiteley's (1995) identification of the wastage inherent in organizational maintenance of strong hierarchical boundaries, and her contrast between older-style organizations, in which the workers' role was to "do," and newer models, in which workers participate in development and change planning.

Onyett, Standen, and Peck (1997) have emphasized the significance at the micro level of the role of team managers in the development of information systems; the exercising of proper authority over the team; the development of adequate structures for operational management; the acknowledgment and response to members' training needs and to the team's macro-level conditions, including ensuring a clear mandate for the team from the funding agency and investing sufficient power in the management role to establish agreements among the disciplines concerned about operational policies. Here, the team manager acts as an important point of mediation and pressure between the team and the organization. In practice, however, the situation is more complicated. These writers state that the currently small amount of research on the managerial role in mental health teams points to the difficulty managers have had in "supporting a structure and atmosphere conducive to innovation." Despite stated objectives to the contrary, their managers focused more on "control and efficiency" (Onyett, Standen, and Peck 1997:45).

Quality of Interaction: Doing Knowledge-Based Teamwork   Describing teamwork in the context of the management of knowledge is not an entirely new approach. For instance, Clark (1994) has written of the importance of interdisciplinary programs' moving beyond divisive disciplinary boundaries to collaborate across knowledge domains:

> Knowledge is *created* in the collaborative interchange; it is *discovered* in the process of experiencing the interaction among members of the group. Thus, the outcome . . . is more than the sum of its individual contributors, and the learning team or collaborative (*sic*) is the source of new knowledge and insights (39).

Equally, Northcraft et al. (1995:71), in writing of effective teamwork, have stated:

> *Effectiveness* refers to an organization's ability to accomplish its core goals, purposes, or mission. In terms of effectiveness, cognitive variety is the wellspring of creativity. Creative solutions to difficult problems are

more likely to emerge if a variety of problem restructurings can be brought to bear. It is a multiplicity of perceptions that produces creativity, and the emerging appreciations that come from cognitive cross-fertilization provide insights into complex problems. . . . Discussion of diverse opinions and perspectives allows diverse individuals to pool information and combine ideas, and also can help clarify, organize, and even prioritize ideas.

The authors go on to note the ways in which task specialization may promote efficiency but can work against effectiveness. They note how "some apparently counterproductive redundancy in skills and task assignments needs to occur to allow cross-fertilization of ideas . . ." (72) and write of the team task as one of achieving a "negotiated integration" (76) (a process, however, complicated by social or gender differences between members).

How, then, is such knowledge work to be achieved? Clark has defined collaborative learning as being achieved through processes of "positive interdependence, face-to-face interaction, personal responsibility, collaborative skills, and group processing" (39) and through the elaboration of core disciplinary assumptions and recognition of their limitiations. "Recognition of the limitations of one's own construction of meaning . . . becomes the common ground for dialogue and discussion, ultimately leading to the emergence of a new plane of group-based meaning, identification and value" (Clark 1994:45; Nonaka and Takeuchi 1995). McKenzie, describing how the value of cross-functional teams lies in the "development of a comprehensive and in-depth view of any situation . . . through the pooling of knowledge and information" (McKenzie 1994:3), has defined effective team behaviors centering around task accomplishments such as "initiating," "seeking information," "clarifying," "summarizing" and "consensus testing" (9).

These and other texts (such as Atkinson 1995) support the thesis of the significance of knowledge-based work in teamwork. This text, however, takes the issue further. It foregrounds the importance of attending to differences between differently located knowledge domains in the production of effective teamwork, and it writes of the engagement with difference as a key team activity. Difference and difference effects are not something to be brushed over. The strength of the team lies in recognizing the existence of, articulating, and positively engaging with discipline-based differences and their implications. This emphasis goes beyond, for example, the recognition of the limitations of knowledge constructions of any particular discipline. On the basis of close analyses of team discussions or reviews of clients, I have developed a map of the structure of an effective knowledge-based team discussion that does not encourage prescriptiveness, that allows for a more fluid, flatter, more purposive, and more elaborated process than that suggested by McKenzie (1994); this map, moreover, encourages attention to members' representations of clients/families and the implications of such representations in structuring how the team comes to think about its work.

Knowledge-based teamwork requires members to go beyond information sharing per se. It also requires engagement with differently located information and attention to the outcomes of such engagement. Thinking of teamwork in this manner allows me to posit the following definition of the work of a knowledge-based team:

> An effective team is one that attends to and works with the different knowledges of clients and their situations available to it through discipline-specific accounts and accounts of clients and families (which may also differ from each other). The work of the team requires the engagement with such differences (rather than their eliding) to ensure, as clients' circumstances evolve, the continued elaboration and revision of team goals and care plans. The ongoing development of effective work will focus primarily on evaluations of teams' processes of knowledge production and creation. The organizational discourses inscribing teamwork are also critical to the effectiveness of that work.

The objective of this text, then, is to foreground the organizational discourses describing and informing teamwork, the recognition and engagement of clients' and families' knowledge, and knowledge work and knowledge production as highly significant in the production of effective teamwork. Each of these dimensions is, in slightly different ways, concerned with boundary issues and therefore with issues of inclusion, exclusion, and power: Who constitutes "the team"? What is the organizational role in the structuring and shaping of effective teamwork? What knowledges does a team access and how does it engage with these productively?

The significance of advancing these elements, as they are elaborated in the course of this book, is that they provide valuable and observable qualitative elements against which teams can review, critique, and develop their work. Further, defining teamwork as knowledge-based work in itself engages in a qualitative shift, relocating teamwork and team development as moving significantly beyond the achievement of smooth interpersonal relations. The focus therefore shifts from the production of a group of self-aware individuals (therapeutically) attending to the quality of interaction within the team to the discursively produced team that is self-consciously alert to its practices of knowledge management and to how its ability to work with knowledge determines the team product: the elaboration of necessarily contingent care plans. These issues are explored in greater detail in the remainder of this text.

3

The Teams and Their Organizational Locations

The conditions for the production of effective teamwork are not restricted to ensuring adequate professional training and the production of competent professionals. These are germane factors, although the notion of training is a highly complex one, raising issues of degree, intensity, focus, and appropriateness. What attention to such factors excludes, though, is the importance of the organizational environment in which teamwork is practiced. All teamwork is produced within an organization. My argument is that rather than relying on generalized rhetoric about the value of teamwork, organizations concerned with the production of effective teamwork are necessarily attentive to the conditions under which such work is produced and to what organizational policies and practices are required to support that production (an issue to which I return in some detail in chapter 9). My objective at this point is to discuss the specific difficult organizational environments in which the teams involved in the research conducted their work, environments that were themselves the products of particular international discourses.

This chapter is intended to work simultaneously across two planes. One plane is the contextual or the local. I therefore provide an account of the six multidisciplinary teams in three services at three different sites that were involved in the research, and I outline aspects of the particular organizational settings in which these teams operated. I first comment briefly on some of the more recent changes, driven by neoliberal discourses, in health policy in Aotearoa/New Zealand. Second, drawing attention to the implications of reading "organization" in light of postmodern theory, I take up John Law's (1994) writing on organizational narratives to provide an account of the various competing narratives about their work that were circulating within these teams. Such narratives are themselves discursively structured, and members' articulation of this or that narrative is a consequence of their different and at times contradictory locations within the range of health care discourses that are in play at any one time. Third, in order to foreground the association between organizational discourses about teamwork, team micropractices, and the production of effective teamwork, I discuss three mundane aspects of organizational work bearing on the support and development of these teams' work: the production and focus of job descriptions, the provision and content of orientation programs, and training in teamwork.

The local, however, is never entirely local, having wider implications and points of reference. The neoliberal discourses (and their associated new managerialist practices) that have so markedly structured political, social, and economic life in Aotearoa/New Zealand over the last fifteen or so years are also to be found in other countries (for example, the United Kingdom and the United States, along with Canada and Australia), although these countries have not embraced such policies at the same time or with the same degree of intensity (Taylor 1990; Smyth and Cass 1998). I do not assume that the organizational practices and narratives I discuss are to be found in identical form at all sites in all geographical locations. Such generalizations cannot be made in qualitative research. What this mode of research does allow, however, is the extrapolation from specific instances of a set of propositions about how a particular phenomenon or event may be conceptualized or reconceptualized. The Aotearoa/New Zealand data provide access to a range of organizational factors that need to be taken into account in relation to the development and production of effective teamwork; moreover, the fact that the discourses driving aspects of organizational practices are to be found internationally, and are therefore not peculiar to Aotearoa/New Zealand, heightens the relevance of the principles bearing on effectiveness discussed in this text to contexts beyond this country. Equally, this does not mean that the application of any such principles can proceed without taking into account the peculiarities of local conditions and local factors.

The Teams

There were several reasons for deciding to involve teams that provide services to those with physical and psychiatric disabilities and to older people whose health was in various ways deteriorating. Much of the work with those with longer-term disabilities, and with some older people, focuses on habilitation, rather than rehabilitation. Clients' conditions may improve only gradually, stay much the same, or deteriorate. Although many health professionals regard the chronically ill and the elderly as unrewarding groups with whom to work, their needs are often complex and require more than a medical response, their illnesses and disabilities being as much a social and emotional event involving the management of the everyday as they are a medical event, and their care needs to be coordinated over a number of different disciplines.

In addition to these more general reasons for deciding to approach teams working with these groups, a 1995-1996 Aotearoa/New Zealand health priority was that people with chronic illnesses should receive services through multidisciplinary input and that better linkages should be developed between care provided in hospital and that provided in community settings. In recognition of the ways in which conventional modes of service delivery and interaction with professionals have disempowered and/or infantilized these clients, another health priority focused on the development of more empowering services. Clients should "be more involved in decisions about the services they receive and will have more service options available to them" (Ministry of Health 1995:10), and services should achieve a high level of acceptability through focusing on "respect for and empowerment of people and on peoples' autonomy and participation" (10–11). Following the publication of the Mason Report (1996), mental health services became a health priority.[1]

The teams participating in the research project, then, were located within services for people with physical disabilities, people with psychiatric illnesses, and older people (hereafter called the disability, psychiatric, and elderly teams). Within each service there were two administratively separate teams, one taking primary responsibility for inpatients, the other for community-based clients, although the majority of members in each team were members of both. I undertook fieldwork with both teams in each service at all three sites—with the elderly and disability teams in 1995 and with the psychiatric team in mid-1996. Table 3.1 provides a summary of the main features of these teams.

The Disability Service

The disability service was responsible for providing a regional service for people with physical disabilities. At the time of the fieldwork, the inpatient

Table 3.1 The Teams in the Study

	Disability Service	Elderly Service	Psychiatric Service
Numbers in Teams	*Inpatient team:* 13 members, 6–10 present during fieldwork *Community team:* 12 members, 6–12 present during fieldwork	*Inpatient team:* 8 members, 7–8 present during fieldwork *Community team:* 10 members, 8–10 present during fieldwork	*Inpatient team:* 13 members, up to 17 people attended meetings during fieldwork *Community team:* 11 members, 9 generally present during fieldwork
Client Group	*Inpatient team:* Provided AT&R services, respite care, and long-term care (18 patients) *Community team:* Responsible for about 500 clients	*Inpatient team:* Provided AT&R services for 10 patients and respite care for 3 patients. There were 3 continuing-care patients who were only reviewed every three months (not part of study). *Community team:* Needs and financial assessments for home care services/financial assistance by state	*Inpatient team:* 16 longer-term severely ill psychiatric patients *Community team:* Responsible for 60–70 clients who had been on the unit but had been discharged into the community. A number of these were on supervision orders
Meetings	*Inpatient team:* Weekly meetings Clinical review: 60–90 minutes Business meeting: 30 minutes Family meetings: 20–45 minutes *Community team:* Fortnightly meetings: 30 minutes	*Inpatient team:* Weekly meetings Clinical review: 60 minutes Family meetings: 20–45 minutes *Community team:* Weekly meetings Review meeting: 45 minutes	*Inpatient team:* Weekly meetings Clinical review: 90–180 minutes Irregular family meetings *Community team:* Weekly meetings Clinical review: 30–40 minutes Fortnightly/alternating meetings: Staff: 60 minutes Community staff support meeting: 60 minutes
Physical Surroundings	Both teams met in unattractive surroundings on ward (hot, noisy, crowded)	Both teams met in a room on the ward. It was quiet, comfortable, and had a pleasant outlook.	*Inpatient team:* Large room on ward, noisy, a lot of coming and going of staff during meeting Patient interruptions. *Community team:* Small, hot room

team, working out of a city-based hospital, was responsible for eighteen patients. These included assessment, treatment, and rehabilitation (AT&R) patients, respite or intermittent care patients, and long-stay and therefore very seriously disabled patients. The second and third patient categories, however, were shortly to be shifted out of the service because of changing definitions of the service's "core work."

The Inpatient Team   The members of the team, in no particular order, were as follows: two occupational therapists (OT), a speech language therapist (SLT), a doctor (DR), a rehabilitation specialist (RS), a senior medical clinician (SMC), the clinical nurse specialist (CNS), who was also the unit manager, a nurse (N), a social worker (SW), a psychiatric registrar (PR), a nursing service coordinator (NSC), a dietitian, and a locum physiotherapist. Between six and ten members normally attended the weekly meetings, which were about an hour and a half long. Students attended as observers from time to time. As a consequence of competing engagements in other services and pressure of work, the rehabilitation specialist and the senior medical clinician attended the meetings on alternate weeks; the dietitian, who had started to attend meetings partway through the fieldwork, left the meetings after discussing clients with whom she was involved; the psychiatric registrar (who was rotated on a six-month basis) attended meetings intermittently and briefly; and the responsibility for representing the nursing perspective on the team was divided between two nurses during the time I was on-site. Because of other, short-term commitments, the unit manager came to very few meetings during the period of the fieldwork. The only men on the team were the rehabilitation specialist and the senior medical clinician.

The inpatient team had been established more than a decade before by a clinician who "believed in teamwork," and it had retained a positive reputation in the hospital over this period. There were, however, dissenting (sotto voce) voices within and beyond the team who believed that trading on its reputation had prevented the team from reviewing its work more dispassionately. The majority of members were experienced health professionals (seven had had more than eleven years' experience in their fields).[2] All but one had worked on more than one team. Two of the original members were still with the team, and seven had been members for two or more years. The rehabilitation specialist, the senior medical clinician, and the OT responsible for the AT&R clients had joined the team most recently (within the last two years). The unit manager (a nurse) was the team leader but did not chair the inpatient review meetings. Responsibility for chairing these meetings was rotated among the nonmedical staff, a practice that reflected an ideological stance about the significance of other than medical input as well as practicalities about the fact that doctors did not always make the meetings. Responsibility for taking minutes was also rotated through the nonmedical staff.

Only the doctor and the CNS had (tiny) offices on the ward. The two OTs and the speech language therapist had offices close to each other and to the ward. The ward itself was located in an older part of the hospital, the location reflecting, so a number of staff considered, the marginalizing of their clientele within the health system. The ward's corridor was crowded with wheelchairs, bath chairs, and other appliances, and the team meeting room generally had to be reorganized before each meeting because it also was used as a storage area for equipment. The room was small, crowded, and hot, the furniture tatty and not especially comfortable. There was no soundproofing, and discussions were punctuated by many sounds from the ward.

The inpatient team generally held three meetings per week. The clinical review meeting lasted sixty to ninety minutes. It was followed by a thirty-minute business meeting chaired by the resource manager. This meeting addressed a range of service and organizational issues, highlighting advocacy issues for the client group,[3] sharing information about and discussing key policy issues, and directing members' attention to relevant events within the hospital. The business meeting was often followed by scheduled meetings with patients and their families. Those family meetings that I observed and audio-taped lasted twenty to forty-five minutes.

The Community Team   The community team comprised most of the members of the inpatient team (excluding the dietician, the inpatient locum physio, the registrar, and the medical clinician). The other members were joined by a community-based physiotherapist and a community-based occupational therapist (neither of whom attended every meeting). The team was responsible for more than five hundred people living at home or in sheltered accommodation. It met on alternate weeks for about thirty minutes. From six to twelve people attended the three community meetings at which I was present. Typically, the discussions focused on administrative issues, such as allocation of respite care beds, and on policy and communication issues within and beyond the hospital. There was general agreement that the structure and focus of the meeting were unsatisfactory, and the team was intending to review this (and did so shortly after I left).

The Elderly Service

The service consisted of an inpatient team, which provided an assessment, treatment, and rehabilitation service for older people who had been admitted to the hospital, and a community team, which mainly focused on assessments of eligibility for home services and for residential care, including assessing older people's eligibility for state funding for residential care. Both teams operated out of a hospital, located in a small provincial town, that served a large rural hinterland. The weekly inpatient meetings that I attended ran for an hour, during which time the team reviewed the care of ten rehabilitation patients and three intermittent care patients. As with the disability team, this team scheduled times most weeks to meet with families and patients. These family meetings lasted between twenty and forty-five minutes. The community team meeting lasted forty-five minutes and was immediately followed by the inpatient team meeting.

The Inpatient Team   This team had been established for about two years. It consisted of a charge nurse who was the team leader (CN), a doctor (DR), a house surgeon (HS) who was rotated regularly (the one working on the team at the time of my fieldwork had just joined the team), a social worker (SW), a speech language therapist (SLT), occupational therapists (OT) (sometimes two attended), and a physiotherapist, totaling a core team of seven to eight people. Nurses joined the team, usually on a rotational basis, in order to present the patients for whom they were the key worker for that day. Most of the team brought considerable experience in their particular fields to their work, and most had had experience on other teams. However, the OT who was officially the team member was a recent graduate and had very little team experience, and the experienced language therapist and physiotherapist were both recent immigrants to Aotearoa/New Zealand and so were new to the team and the service. The social worker did not hold a social work degree, although she had related qualifications. As on the disability team, there was a significant gender imbalance, with the only men being the doctor and the house surgeon. At various points during the fieldwork, OT and physio students observed the meetings. Members were cautiously optimistic about the quality of the team's functioning.

The inpatient beds were in a relatively new, purpose-built rehabilitation unit. The team met in the nursing staff room, a bright space that looked out onto a paved area with flowers (often tended by patients as part of their rehabilitation). Since the room was situated slightly away from the main body of the ward, the absence of background noise was quite remarkable in contrast to the noise that the disability and psychiatric teams had to contend with during their meetings. The speech language therapist, OT, and physiotherapist had rooms close to each other on the ward, a factor that contributed to a high level of interchange between them, and the social worker, who was housed in an old nursing home about a hundred yards away, was often on the ward. A number of the nonmedical staff frequently ate lunch together.

The Community Team   The community assessment team had ten members. The doctor, charge nurse, social worker, language therapist, OT, and physiotherapist from the inpatient team were joined by two community-based social workers (neither of whom had professional qualifications and both of whom were on leave for most of the fieldwork), the assessment coordinator (also an unqualified social worker), and the nurse assessor. The team met in the same room as the inpatient team did.

The team had been in existence for about eighteen months, but as a consequence of bitter personal and professional conflict its membership had changed substantially about seven months before I began the fieldwork. It had lost its service coordinator and much of its sense of direction. Team morale was very low. The charge nurse had been asked to act as leader by the service manager, and she had agreed to do so reluctantly, since she did not consider that this was an appropriate extension of her role. She was given no extra resources with which to do the job. The nurse assessor, who had recently joined the team, worked part time, had had no orientation to the team and no specific training in assessment, and, after some months in the job, was still very tentatively feeling her way. As noted above, the OT had only recently graduated. This was her first job and her first experience of teamwork, in which she had received no training. The social workers, with differing degrees of vehemence, were opposed to the thrust of most of the health policies and, as part of their oppositional stance, defined their work as advocating for their clients against an uncaring system. The way they went about this advocacy tended to position some clients as victims and sometimes contributed to the team's difficulties in working more effectively.

All members were extremely critical of the way the team functioned. The service manager, from whom they had sought assistance, was part of the team that was negotiating the hospital contract with the regional funder and, as a consequence of being off-site for months, had been unavailable to provide much help or direction. The only training provided for the team had been more than a year ago, and at the time few of the current team were in place. Members collectively felt that they lacked the time, the commitment, and in some cases the knowledge to make this team work better, and several were resentful that seemingly pointless meetings took time away from "real" work—that is, their work with clients. Some members considered that the level of team functioning was such that the team was a "paper" team only, the rationale for its existence being to secure the service contract for a financially strapped organization.

The team was further beset by organizational and policy contradictions. Many of the clients were referred for home help services and did not require input from the health professionals, nor (at that point) ongoing work, so few of the team members had any connection with them. Overall, there appeared to be few shared clients among the team. This lack of shared work was further accentuated since the speech language therapist, the OT, and the physiotherapist did not carry community-based workloads and, being new to the service, lacked the local knowledge about many of the clients that some of the "older" team members had. These factors restricted their input at team meetings. They attended the meetings as representatives of their disciplines because the team met at a time when the doctor could attend, although the community-based OT and physio staff could not be present.

As disciplinary representatives, the physiotherapist and the OT were to provide input from their community-based colleagues about clients who had been assessed, and they were also to take relevant information about clients from the team back to those colleagues. The former objective was complicated, since no agenda was circulated before the meeting, and therefore no one knew which community-based clients would be discussed. Thus the representatives were unable to consult with their colleagues about specific issues they ought to be aware of and/or raise. While the speech language therapist was more willing to attend the meeting than the OT and the physio because she wished to educate her colleagues about her work (her solo position having just been established), this objective was in part frustrated because of the lack of development of the team's discussions.

The team's work was further complicated because of difficulties having to do with its contracted annual volumes or numbers of assessments. Not only was there considerable skepticism about how the decision about volumes had been arrived at initially (the team members and the service manager regarded the number of assessments able to be carried out by this team as far too low in relation to local knowledge of levels of need), but just before I started the fieldwork at this site the government changed the regulations regarding service provision for older people. As a consequence, while many more older people than before were entitled to apply for home support services and therefore have their needs assessed to determine need levels and actual entitlement, the funding to provide the service and the contracted numbers of clients that the service had been allocated to assess had not changed. In light of the hospital's acute financial crisis, staff were repeatedly instructed that under no circumstances were they to undertake any work not covered by the contract. The result was an ever-increasing waiting list. In an attempt to respond positively to the situation, the team defined degrees of need so as to target clients with higher support needs. This strategy, however, created a further problem since, in order for the funding system to work, the provider of the home-based services required a client mix that included clients with lower, not just higher, service needs. Referring only clients with higher needs, requiring a higher level of services, meant that the provider was facing a considerable financial shortfall.

The Psychiatric Service

Following Ken Mason's (1988) first extremely critical review of Aotearoa/ New Zealand's mental health services, the hospital had sought to attract highly qualified staff to work in a multidisciplinary service to provide quality and comprehensive care for a particularly challenging group of psychiatric clients. The major objective of the teams providing care for this group was to rehabilitate sufficiently those patients who had been committed to a locked inpatient unit so that they could move back into the community. In addition to the sixteen patients in the inpatient unit, the service provided ongoing care and follow-up for between sixty and seventy clients in the community. Because of the nature of its clientele, the work of this service was highly demanding, both in the actual work with clients, many of whom had very complex, long psychiatric histories, and in relation to the service's charged political role, which required that issues of public safety be balanced against the legal rights of those clients on the locked unit. Not surprisingly, much of the team's work was concerned directly and indirectly with issues of risk management.

At the time of the fieldwork the service was housed in two buildings a few minutes' walk from each other. This setup was about to change, as the clinicians were to move to a refurbished building at the other end of a sprawling and busy campus, a move described by the clinicians as simply administrative and as having no impact on the nursing staff on the unit. The nurses, though, believed the shift would have a potentially significant negative impact on nursing and clinician relationships and on the level of support the clinicians would be able to provide.

The Inpatient Team   The weekly review meetings I attended generally lasted for two or two and a half hours. One lasted nearly three hours. A number of the members considered the time spent in the meeting excessive, but, as with all the teams, there was no forum in which issues of team functioning and performance could be discussed. The meetings were held in a large room in the inpatient unit. The chairs were placed along the walls on three and a half sides of the room, creating a large empty space in the middle. Team members nearly always sat in the same place. None of the meetings I attended started on time, and clinicians' tardiness was a source of largely unspoken (but bodily expressed) frustration for some of the nursing staff.

The team included thirteen members: two senior psychologists (SP), a consultant psychiatrist (CP), two senior social workers (SSW), a social worker (SW), a psychiatric registrar (PR), two clinical nurse specialists (CNS), the charge nurse and unit manager (UM), the deputy unit manager and senior nurse (DM), a part-time OT, and a counselor. In addition to this core group, nurses joined the meetings in rotation to present the clients they were responsible for on that day. A new psychology intern who had just joined the service observed rather than actively participated in the meetings, and a nurse adviser also attended two of the seven meetings at which I was present. During the fieldwork, one of the psychologists and the part-time OT were on leave for three weeks. This team was much more balanced than the other teams in terms of gender. The social worker, a senior psychologist, the consultant, both of the registrars, one of the clinical nurse specialists, and the counselor were men.

The team members were all experienced professionals. None had had fewer than two years' experience as a health professional, and five had more than twelve years' experience. Most members had had experience in other teams. There was a general consensus that this team worked better than those because it was less medically dominated and there was less overt tension (there was no team discussion of the covert or overt tensions). Although several members had been on the team for some years, the team's personnel had undergone a number of recent changes. One of the senior social workers had joined the team within the last nine months; the other (a founding member of the team) had over the last eighteen months significantly reduced her working hours as a result of accepting part-time employment elsewhere. The hospital had been employing overseas consultants on short-term contracts, a practice that the other team members regarded as highly disruptive and often professionally problematic because these psychiatrists came from professional cultures that differed radically from that in Aotearoa/New Zealand. The consultant who took up his (permanent) position shortly after I started the fieldwork was a New Zealander who had worked previously with the team. The registrars were rotated every six months.

There had been considerable recent turnover among the experienced nursing staff, a factor that was commented on mainly by the nurses, although the changes also affected the clinicians, who benefited from nurses' familiarity with clients and their ability to contribute knowledgeably to discussions. A further point complicating the nursing input to the team's work was that the inpatient unit was part of a psychiatric training program. This meant that very inexperienced trainees, often with a minimum of psychiatric input before their ten-week placements, were involved in presenting and (in theory) discussing clients.

In addition to the clinical meetings and the legally mandated reviews, case conferences and client reviews (involving clients and, where appropriate and possible, families) were held at scheduled times over the year. The development of these regular review processes was described as contributing to the quality-assurance dimension of the service. All clients had a management team, and from time to time that team was asked to bring a recommendation for action to the larger team. No formal reporting-back procedures seemed to be in place, however.

The Community Team The community and ward teams had substantially the same personnel as the other teams, a factor that team members emphasized contributed to the continuity of clients' care. The two senior psychologists, the consultant psychiatrist, one of the senior social workers, the social worker, and both psychiatric registrars were joined by three court officers, and a (male) community nurse, who had very recently joined the team. Although the team officially had eleven members, nine attended the meetings at which I was present (two were on leave). The meeting was scheduled for an hour but generally lasted between thirty and forty minutes. The team met in the somewhat run-down building (initially built as nurses' accommodations) where the clinicians worked and in which some of the senior nurses also had office space. The room was an awkward shape and was often hot; if all the team members attended, the space was very crowded and uncomfortable.

The community review meetings were followed on alternate weeks by an hourlong staff meeting, the ostensible purpose of which was to enable consultation and advice about service-related issues between line staff and the executive group. Team social events were also arranged during this meeting. This was the only one of the three services that had such events.

The business meeting alternated with a community team staff meeting. The objectives of this meeting were (1) to provide a form of debriefing for outreach staff whose day-to-day work provided them with little support, (2) to give feedback to the clinicians about clients on whom these staff had written reports, and (3) to serve as a forum for discussion of the complexities of the Mental Health Act. These meetings were very unstructured, and the discussion in the ones that I attended centered almost exclusively on the act and its interpretation. Two members (male and female) commented independently of each other on the unsatisfactoriness of the meetings and their failure to meet a prime objective: the discussion of the emotional impact of the work on staff and provision of support. One of these members believed that unresolved gender issues within the team made any discussion of the very real emotional stress of the work impossible.

Although funding to this service had recently been somewhat reduced because of other priorities in mental health services generally, it appeared to have been less affected by the restructuring processes than the other services involved in the research. The senior members of the service believed that they enjoyed an increasingly positive relationship with the funding authority in terms of negotiating a better contract. The detailed statistical evidence that the service had collected about the range and extent of their work and the development of management and accountability processes meant, they thought, that elements of their work not funded in the recent past were now more likely to be funded, and they outlined plans for a significant expansion of the service. While there had been problems in attracting psychiatric consultants (this was a national problem, not just a local one), and a number of nursing staff had left as a result of downsizing and natural attrition, the clinical team was viewed as having attracted highly qualified staff. In contrast to the other teams in the study, staff in this service were encouraged to attend relevant courses and conferences, and the manager stressed that, contrary to previous practices, allocation of funding to attend conferences was influenced by the training and development needs of particular staff rather than by status.

Although the recent development of the service and plans for its future were described very positively by senior staff, their perceptions were not shared by all team members, some of whom continued, as did staff on the other teams, to be concerned about the nonexistent or very low levels of resourcing allocated to key professional demands of their work, were less certain than their senior members that these activities would be more adequately funded, and were unhappy about the possible implications of some of the management-driven changes. There was agreement that some of the imported management practices were beneficial, but a few team members thought that some of the planned further changes were not, as was claimed, neutral in their implications for professional work, that clinical/administrative boundaries were not as clear-cut as was suggested by the manager and the senior clinicians, and that the "real" objective of some of the proposed changes was to increase the focus on professionals' accountability in an environment where professional issues and concerns about how that work could be more effectively produced tended to be regarded with suspicion, because of distrust of the highly ideologically driven restructuring of the health services.

The Political and Policy Context in Health Care

The Aotearoa/New Zealand health system has undergone several major restructurings over the last twelve years in response to a variably performing economy, concerns about cost-effectiveness of service delivery in public institutions, and a profound reworking of the relationship of government and state, a reworking informed by successive governments' active endorsement of neoliberal economic theory (Boston et al. 1991; Holland and Boston 1990; Kelsey 1995; Salmond, Mooney, and Laugeson 1994). As Emy (1998:23) has noted, "Neoliberalism tends to conceptualise the relations between state and society, or state and economy, in antagonistic terms or as a kind of zero-sum game: scope for one detracts from the other."

One of the key elements in the restructuring processes has been the concept of new managerialism. Orchard (1998), writing about similar developments in Australia, has argued that over the previous two decades a case was made for bringing management principles to bear on various sectors of the economy, particularly to the public sector, which was defined as inflexible and in need of reform. These reforms have involved, in conjunction with public choice theory, a redefinition of the role of government, devolved management, and different approaches to budgeting, which have led to a focus on measurement, outputs, and close management of financial responsibility. It would be foolish to suggest, at least in the Aotearoa/New Zealand context, that much richer information about the production of public services, identification of their points of inflexibility, absence of client choice and, accordingly, the exploration of alternative modes of service delivery, and greater transparency in public service accountability were not needed. However, the longer-term social consequences of neoliberalist economic policies, particularly in the area of redistribution of wealth away from the less advantaged, is locally and internationally of major concern (Emy 1998). Equally, the new managerialism has been strongly critiqued in relation to issues for which it has been most valorized, that is,

> the narrowing of the intellectual perspective for the management of public institutions to questions of outputs, products, the measurable; and capacity for centralised control, authority, and integration. Inappropriate private sector models of management were applied to the public sector. Despite the important efforts to decentralise service delivery, the new managerialism was centralist in its stress on control over finance. The tension between these approaches was unsustainable in the long term. The new approaches also essentially denied the essentially political nature of government activity. The stress on measuring and products meant an overemphasis on the quantifiable, single-purpose outputs while denigrating claims of worth and effectiveness made on non-economic grounds.   *(Orchard 1998:117–118)*

Throughout much of the last fifteen years in Aotearoa/New Zealand there has been almost daily public debate about the outcomes of the reforms in relation to service availability, accessibility, quality, and the rising health costs to individuals and families, in addition to continued concern from 1991 to 1999 about the conservative government's unstated agenda of privatization of the health system. My intention, however, is not to dwell on the validity of the rationale of the restructuring as it has affected the health care system or to attempt to evaluate the degree of its success, but to identify some of the key changes in the organizational environments in which the teams worked.

Following an initial process of change to the health care system introduced in 1988 by a Labour government, the subsequent National government embarked on a more radical restructuring (Upton 1991). The principal changes to the health system were as follows: the creation of a funder-provider split; the creation of four regional health authorities with government appointees, replacing fourteen elected area health boards; the definition of health care as a business and the introduction of competition among the regional health authorities (a position subsequently modified); an attempt to define publicly available "core" health services[4]; the introduction of competitive contracting for services to increase professional accountability and define services' core work; and, concomitantly within the developing managerialist ethos and as a result of redefinitions of hospitals' "core" work, the introduction of changing patterns and ethos of professional work.[5] Some of the ongoing consequences of the restructuring have been frequent laying off of staff and constant internal restructuring within the hospitals, and in many hospitals staff morale has declined substantially.

The contracting process relied on population-based allocation of funding for services, but informed decisions about appropriate volumes of work to be funded were, at least for some years, complicated by the absence of relevant detailed comparative statistical and other data. There have been ongoing and significant differences between service providers and purchasers with regard to the representation of a service's work and what work was to be funded, and the adequacy of funding levels if the service was to be effective. Service specifications have tended to exclude (and therefore not to fund) areas of work that professionals regard as important (such as report writing to other agencies with whom their clients frequently interface).[6] A key concern for many professionals is the degree to which their attempts to provide input for decisions about funding have been regarded by management, in line with public choice theory, as self-interested and therefore suspect.

One of the outcomes of the contracting environment has been an emphasis on development of standards and a concern with quality outcomes. For example, a policy document by the Ministry of Health (1995) suggested that improvements in quality could be achieved through use of time quality management (TQM), accreditation, peer review, audits, practice guidelines, training, and innovation. There is nothing extraordinary about this list, although it does move on from the substantial earlier focus on consumer satisfaction surveys that the hospitals were constantly undertaking, a method of evaluating professional work that is now seen as very limited in the adequacy of feedback that can be achieved and problematic because it suppresses significant issues of client relationships with service providers.[7]

The ways of achieving quality outlined in the ministry's document are, however, open to critique. Each mode is itself open to interrogation and critique: Who monitors the peer review practices? What is the quality of training offered by accredited organizations? What criteria are employed to evaluate a role and who controls the task definition? When do guidelines become prescriptive rather than facilitative? And so on. Further, the regulatory gaze is internal. There are no references to input based on differently structured, differently located knowledge, such as that from client/consumer organizations, with whom the regional funding authorities were not obliged (only encouraged) to consult. There is no account of how innovative developments occur within demoralized, chaotic, financially strapped organizations nor any reference to the organizational conditions necessary to sustain quality work, and organizational responsibilities in the development of innovative work are not mentioned. As has been noted elsewhere, innovation is "not a well-controlled process" (Mohrman and Mohrman 1993:93). It relies on "the availability of slack resources, redundancy of effort, trial and error, experimentation, freedom from constraints and specified ways of doing things, autonomy, and the ability to be playful"; equally, "long-term orientation, resource support, organizational vision, management support, proximity to decision makers, interfunctional networks and teamwork, learning connections with the external environment, and incentives for risk and experiment" constitute necessary organizational conditions supporting innovation and improvement (Mohrman and Mohrman 1993:97).

The Provision of Culturally Appropriate and Safe Services

My noting of the absence of reference to other than professional knowledge, however, does require some qualification. Aotearoa/New Zealand's inclusion in the British Empire was not the result of war (although war between settlers and Māori, the indigenous people, or *tangata whenua,* broke out soon after) but occurred in 1840 as the consequence of the signing of the Treaty of Waitangi at Waitangi by Governor Hobson, as the representative of the English Crown, and by five hundred Māori chiefs. The actual objective of the treaty has been in dispute for the last 160 years. Major factors contributing to this dispute are that not only were there different versions of the English text in circulation, but the Māori and English texts were not exact translations of each other, and the meaning of each text is quite different. The English and the settlers claimed that the treaty ceded sovereignty to the Crown. In contrast, "the Māori text predicates a *sharing of power and authority* in the governance of the country between Crown and Māori. The English text is about a transfer of power leaving the Crown as sovereign and Māori as subjects" (Williams 1989:79–80, my italics). As a result, Māori and Pakeha[8] regarded the treaty in quite different lights, with Pakeha "ignoring . . . the Treaty because it was not viewed as of any constitutional significance or political or social relevance," while Māori placed "continuing reliance on Treaty promises and continuing expressions of great loyalty to and trust in the Crown" (Richardson, J., cited in Williams 1989:76; Orange 1987).

Following the signing of the treaty, Māori were dispossessed not only of their lands but substantially of their language and culture. Continued petitions by Māori over the next more than one hundred years to various English monarchs for justice and restoration of rights written, as they understood it, into the treaty were unsuccessful. Rising Māori discontent during the 1970s resulted in the overwhelmingly Pakeha governments' very belated acknowledgment of their obligations under the treaty and the official recognition of Aotearoa/New Zealand as a bicultural nation.

The last two decades have seen a something of a reworking of the status of Māori in Aotearoa/New Zealand. Defining Aotearoa/New Zealand officially as a bicultural nation recognizes the relationship between Māori and government as one of partnership. It has also been understood that the differential (and lesser) access by Māori to health care services (as a people Māori have significantly poorer health than other ethnic groups in New Zealand as measured by most public health statistics) has been partly the result of structural inequity and partly the result of many Māoris' regarding mainstream health and welfare services as culturally unsafe—that is, they were monocultural, suppressing Māori health practices, the collective structure of Māori society, and issues of Māori spirituality. Their "unsafeness" meant that many Māori were reluctant to use Pakeha health care services. In 1988 Irihapeti Ramsden produced a text on what she called "culturally safe practices" in nursing, arguing that the distinctive needs of Māori arising from cultural practices very different from those of Pakeha required the development of practices in mainstream health care services that actively recognized and engaged with these differences (Ramsden 1988). Further work in this area led to the articulation of Māori principles of health (Durie 1994; Public Health Commission 1994–1995), and there have been similar moves in the welfare/social work arenas (Rangihau et al. 1986; Ruwhiu et al. 1999).

As a result of this work, current Māori and mainstream health policies and other documentation consistently emphasize the need for culturally appropriate services to ensure that Māori health care needs are properly attended to and that Māori feel safe in accessing health care.[9] However, although a number of *iwi* (Māori from local areas, or tribes) are now funded to provide health care principally to their people, service provision is still dominated by Pakeha providers and the extent to which mainstream service providers have significantly modified monocultural practices is debatable.[10]

Of the teams in the three services participating in the research, only the psychiatric team had a high proportion of Māori clients, a factor reflecting the disproportionate representation of Māori in the mental health and prison systems. The hospital in which the psychiatric team was located employed Māori nurses and cultural advisers and funded a Māori health service, but the psychiatric community team had only one Māori staff member (employed in a relatively low-status role and institutionally marginal), who believed that the service's response to Māori issues was at best token, instancing his employment (one Māori on a team of eleven) as an example of that tokenism.[11] During the inpatient team's team reviews there were references to patients' involvement in Māori mental health services and there were occasional very brief reports brought back from those providers by one team member about patients' progress. Māori mental health staff did not attend any of the meetings at which I was present, and it was difficult to see/hear where any nuanced knowledge about these clients held by Māori service providers was other than very superficially incorporated into the team's discussions. It may have been that some team members consulted extensively with the Māori health service. My point is rather that if they did, then the information they acquired did not appear to be easily accessible to all team members.

The teams in the other two services had no Māori staff and few Māori clients. Several of the disability team members thought the service was probably not seen as relevant to Māori because the service structure was not responsive to significant cultural issues, and this was reflected in the low number of Māori clients.[12] Statistically, a team working with older people would not expect to have an equal proportion of Māori and Pakeha clients, since Māori life expectancy remains lower than that of Pakeha.

The Teams' Organizational Narratives

The reading of *organization* employed in this text goes against the grain of modernist readings of *organization* as a stable, rational entity, conceived of as "purposeful, goal-oriented action, encapsulated within routine, recurrent reproduction of social action, social relations and social structures" (Clegg 1990:26). Instead, postmodern theory writes *organization* as constituted by a range of competing discourses, each grounded within its own parameters of rationality; each with the objective of advancing its own interests (Fox 1994), making a final account of an organization impossible as "organization itself . . . is chronically incomplete"(Law 1994:249). The implications of this position are several. It highlights the extreme complexity of large organizations and the difficulty of assuming that there are shared goals, or that goals and objectives articulated by one sector will complement, not contradict, those articulated by another sector. It highlights, as noted above, how more than one discourse will be circulating to inform the work of that organization, so that staff informed by their different discursive positioning will bring different accounts of how the work of the organization could be constituted, thereby placing the organization in a position of always trying to assert control and having that control persistently challenged.

In order to discuss further the relationship of the services and teams to their organizations, I am employing Law's concept of organizational narratives. Law, referring to Cooper and Burrell's (1988) work, writes of an organization as "a multidiscursive and precarious effect or product," chronically reproducing itself through "uncertain processes." Such processes include the production of a "grand narrative" purporting to tell the character of the organization (Law 1994:250). Law therefore addresses how organizations continue to try to assert control through their generation of a grand narrative; how the conversation of individuals within that organization *"embodies and performs multiple narratives"* (261); and how these competing, and also inevitably incomplete, narratives generate organizational impasses.

Law has identified how several types of narratives can exist within one organization, resulting in the production of "juxtaposed narrative fragments" (255). For example, a "cowboy" narrative addresses issues of "struggle and qualitative change" and has, he suggests, an element of the "heroic" about it; a "civil servant" narrative emphasizes "accretion and quantitative change"; an "enterprise" narrative describes an opportunist and pragmatic agent, focused on pulling it all together; an "administration" narrative highlights smooth functioning, "ordered hierarchical structures" focused on rules and "rational divisions of labour," is committed to due process, and emphasizes the potential of all, rather than the heroics of a particular group or individual; a "vision" narrative is elitist and creative; and a "vocation" narrative focuses on issues of self-motivation and embodied skill (Law 1994:253–256). He emphasizes how organizational narratives are always incomplete, noting that no single narrative can offer a complete account of the organization; each narrative is strategic and advances the interests and concerns of those who articulate it.

Three of Law's terms are useful in describing the narratives circulating in these teams. I am also, however, adding to his list by identifying additional narratives: those of "embattlement," "failure," "survival," and "increasing maturation." These different narratives existed on occasion contradictorily within the same team. They arose from the different and competing discourses of health care circulating within the health system. How an individual member defined his or her work affected the discursive positioning and the narrative of care that he or she produced. These additional narratives were evident both in comments that team members made in the course of the interviews I conducted with them about their team's work and its relationship to the wider organization and in more informal comments that arose in discussions.

The grand political narrative at the time of the research about the changes to the public health system in Aotearoa/New Zealand was one of being on the cusp of a success but nonetheless (disappointingly) still requiring yet more restructurings to confirm that the whole service, not just a few hospitals, was properly efficient, competitive, and focused on its core business. Although admitting that things were still often not easy (one person was somewhat more skeptical than the others about what had been gained as a result of the multiple restructurings of the health system), nonetheless the dominant organizational narrative underpinning the content of the service managers' interviews with me was largely positive. This (celebratory) narrative described the positive gains of the current focus on organizational efficiency. It was rapidly evident that by no means all team members uniformly subscribed to this organizational narrative, but neither was there a common team narrative running across the teams or even within individual teams. The fact that eight identifiable narratives were generated by various team members highlights the diversity of the narratives that circulated at these sites, all of which offered competing propositions about members' relationships to the dominant organizational narratives and to their clients. What was also interesting was that some members subscribed (at least in part) to more than one (competing) narrative.

What follows is an account of these narratives. The key details have been set out in table 3.2 in order to highlight their main features. In the elderly service, members persistently commented on the difference in functioning between the two teams and produced quite different team narratives in relation to each team. This did not happen in the other teams and, accordingly, I have not defined community team narratives separately in the other two services.

The Disability Team's Organizational Narratives

Embattlement   I have defined the disability inpatient team's dominant narrative (dominant in relation to the numbers who articulated it) of its relationship to its organization as one of embattlement, in which was embedded a subnarrative, vocation. I am using the term *embattlement* to describe a narrative that refers to several factors, operating either individually or in concert, in relation to actual or impending unwelcome loss or change of work focus; inability to agree on how work is to be produced or managed; and perceived organizational indifference to concerns about the implications of the proposed changes to the service. *Vocation* refers to what Law calls "embodied skill" (256). These narratives were in competition with a narrative of enterprise that was also circulating within the team. This last narrative was, however, more organizationally powerful, although it had fewer subscribers.

The hospital's decision to move away from providing long-term care and respite care beds in favor of developing the assessment, treatment, and rehabilitation aspects of the service was going to result in considerable changes in the orientation of the team's work. In particular, it would result in the literal loss of many clients with whom a number of the staff had had a long-term relationship, a relationship reflected in the frequent references to the team as constituting part of clients' families. The issue, though, went beyond this loss of long-term relationships. A number of staff believed that the hospital's focus on efficiency and cost management would result in the devaluing of the kind of small human gestures on which (some) members of the team prided themselves. They were concerned, with some justification, that one outcome of the restructuring of the service would be that very severely disabled clients were placed in residential settings with minimal staff and that those staff would lack the kind of collective and individual experience and knowledge about caring for people with disabilities that was held by team members. They foresaw a reduction in the supportive work in the community with clients and their informal caregivers that had hitherto been offered by team members. None of these "human" issues were thought to be of concern to the hospital administration, especially at a time when the hospital was struggling financially and there was a possibility that it would close.

The narratives of embattlement and vocation, then, inscribed a particular type of professionalism wherein effectiveness was in part characterized/marked by attentiveness to individual relationships and the production of nuanced care based on long-term knowledge of many clients with whom the team had been in contact for years, even though such care had to be provided within the service's substantial budgetary constraints. These narratives also contained an element of the heroic, demonstrated in references to the team's heyday, when the team had had a highly regarded leader.

Enterprise Numerically weaker in relation to numbers of supporters, but organizationally supported and more powerful, the enterprise narrative was advanced mostly by a minority who had joined the team more recently and who had not had the long-term associations with long-stay clients enjoyed by "older" members. This narrative, though, was also subscribed to intermittently by a few of the older members who considered that the team had become too self-congratulatory and less effective and efficient over time and that it needed to reevaluate its modes of working. The enterprise narrative reflected a managerial discourse of opportunity, development, and efficiency. In highlighting the service's limited resources it stressed the need for prioritizing work and streamlining the team's discussions. In defining the enterprise narrative, Law (1994:255) writes of

Table 3.2 Teams' Organizational Narratives

| | **Team Narratives** | | |
Teams	*Embattled*	*Enterprise*	*Marginalization*
Disability Team	Dominant narrative. Focused on what many members saw as negative impending organizational changes to work in relation to clients and the nature of professional work, and recognized divisions in the team over these changes. Also incorporated a narrative of "vocation" addressing attentiveness, long-term relationship with clients, and a "heroic" narrative in relation to team's well-regarded past. Emphasized the value of a "supportive" team. Overall, focus was relational.	Subordinate but organizationally endorsed narrative, though strongly subscribed to by more recently arrived team members, and intermittently and partially by some of those who also subscribed to the "embattled" narrative. Focused on ending respite/long-term care services; attention on assessment of AT&R clients, prioritizing of resource allocation, more efficient use of skilled staff, need to review how the team worked. Critical of what was seen as (some) members' overintrusive relationship with clients. Also incorporated vocation narrative but in context of production of skilled professional evaluation/assessment/input. Performance-focused.	A highly marginalized narrative produced occasionally by a very few long-term members with strong links into community. Critical of lack of focus on community clients and of the amount of resourcing given to those who came onto the ward, in contrast to those in community, many of whom refused to use the respite care program because of its lack of resources. Focus on marginalization of those "less needy" clients in the community and their difficulty in attracting resources in the current environment because of focus on targeting. Concerned about equity issues.
	Enterprise narrative (to better survive in— or beyond—the organization)		*Embattled narrative*
Psychiatric Team	Dominant narrative, and particularly heavily subscribed to by two senior (male) members of teams' management group. Considerable emphasis on incorporation of other similar services, and new developments, relocation of clinicians, the desirability of the team's further embracing new managerialist principles to make service more efficient. Focus on core inpatient client group for more effective use of skills/resources; shed ongoing responsibility for community clients. Focus on performance, success of service; hopeful. Narrative did not reflect any of the criticisms of the team advanced by some of those articulating it.		A marginalized narrative, produced particularly by one less-senior (woman) team member. Focus on how administrative efficiency was changing nature of professional work but without seemingly understanding the nature of that work and the reasons for those practices; included concern for ongoing quality of care for community clients. Critical of dominance of efficiency argument. Critical of team and teamwork and lack of opportunities to review team performance. Senior inpatient unit staff member believed that the clinicians' relocation would further weaken already weak links between clinicians and nurses, to client detriment.

Elderly Team

	Maturational narrative	Narrative of failure	Survival narrative
Inpatient team	Sense of team coming together, collective sense of purpose; substantial adherence to proposition that attempts to make team more efficient working; a sense of control in relation to their work. Subscribed to by all members.		
Community team		Articulated by all members. Significant organizationally related problems affecting the operation of the team, political changes to system with no regard for resourcing, a key member's inexperience and lack of training, past hostilities, and lack of leadership from absent manager make team impossible. Clients and client needs marginalized by team, system, organization. "It shouldn't be like this, but it is." Emotions of defeat and frustration rampant.	Highly marginalized narrative rarely articulated. "If we muck up, then the clients will get an even worse deal. We have to try to make the system work for them. Also don't want to lose our jobs, which we could if the hospital does not get the elderly assessment contract renewed." Focus on professional self-interest and need to avoid even further marginalizing the clients.

its opportunistic, pragmatic, and performance dimensions, wherein the desirability and possibility of change are assumed and opportunities must be seized. Its emphasis on performance, he suggests, introduces a moral dimension because performance will be rewarded by good organizations.

The enterprise narrative contained an implicit critique of the team's relationship to its clientele as overidentified and excessively emotionally involved. It focused on how reevaluating the direction of the team's work would enable it to use specific members' specialized skills to better effect because it would concentrate on clients who were better able to respond to therapy, and the more immediate commencement of rehabilitation (currently constrained because of the resources going to respite- and continuing-care clients) would enhance clients' chances of a fuller recovery. It would require more careful, professional, nuanced assessments (herein accessing a vocation narrative but with a slightly different slant) to ensure that clients who were unable to benefit from the service would be moved, thus protecting resources for those who could benefit.

A discourse of professional opportunity and development, client benefit, and targeted use of resources is very attractive. It nonetheless raises issues that have long been of concern to disability advocacy groups in the context of constructions of the (disabled) body. A significant line of inquiry that Foucault has followed is how particular discursive practices are intended to produce docile bodies—a concern reflected in much of the medical sociology literature. One of the implications of the enterprise discourse—contradicting the rhetoric about client empowerment and partnership that circulates in health policy documents—is that it relies on docility. Within the helping professions, people who do not get better, who challenge in this and other ways professionals' sense of their competence, who seem ungrateful for assistance, or who appear unable or unwilling to accept their condition are all too easily open to attributions of negative (moral) qualities or behaviors (Opie 1997). To ensure that a service meets its output targets and does so within its financial constraints requires cooperative, docile patients who will "deal" with their disability rationally, follow advice, and act in conformity with instructions. Patients (or their families) who do not respond in this way may easily be construed as a threat to the viability (indeed, the survival) of the service because they do not rehabilitate sufficiently quickly or they become too resource-heavy. Beyond this, there are questions about the level of resourcing available to clients whose condition is not going to change and may well deteriorate, and there are questions about professional input and persistence over time in working with a client whose condition does not conform to clinical pathways.

Marginalization   A third, highly marginalized narrative was also circulating in the disability team. Those who articulated it were older members who had very strong links to community clients and who articulated at different times both of the above narratives as well. This narrative was critical of the extent to which targeting meant that many "less needy" but nonetheless very disabled clients had considerable difficulty obtaining services and assistance. They saw the ward as resource-hungry and believed that the increasing focus on rehabilitation raised considerable, but undebated, equity issues.

The Psychiatric Team's Organizational Narratives

Enterprise   The dominant psychiatric team narrative was also that of enterprise, but with a more intensively expansionist dimension than was present in the disability team account. The discourse was of the marketplace and administrative efficiency. Rather than being caught up or held down by the (failing) parent organization, the service was actively seeking to move away from that organization through its expansionist desires. This narrative drew on an inscription of writing professionals as highly competent, an emphasis that could, and did, complicate any critical evaluation of practice.

Whereas the disability service was being more organizationally pushed toward a redefinition of its core business, most of the senior staff in the psychiatric service were much more actively seeking change. This in part involved a reevaluation of the service's responsibilities to clients in the community, with an emphasis on the desirability of handing them on more quickly to local community mental health teams than had been the practice in the past, in order to focus the available resources on very needy inpatients.

Embattlement   Given the team's knowledge of the instability of the community teams and the lack of training of some of their staff, however, a few members, introducing elements of the embattlement narrative, were concerned about the quality of service their community clientele would receive and about an apparent organizational emphasis on moving the clients on in order to allow the service to concentrate on its changing definition of its core business to maximize its expansionist desires, regardless of the quality of the available community services. Parallel to this concern, and part of the narrative, was the anxiety discussed above about the subtle and not so subtle changes to professional practices and relationships with clients embedded in a focus on administrative and organizational efficiency.

The narratives generated within both teams, then, operated substantially within a binary, and therefore oppositional, structure. Each narrative placed concepts of efficiency and effectiveness in opposition to each other. The "embattled" narratives could be said to be located in a discourse of relationship between client and professional. In contrast, the more opportunistic, enterprise narratives emphasized administrative efficiency and professional competence and rigor in focusing on a core task. While their emphasis is considerably different, these positions are not necessarily totally unrelated. An exploration of points of connection and overlap, however, would have required detailed discussions of the differences in the way the team wished to position itself in relation to its client population, the differences in the definitions of effectiveness accessed by each narrative, and the different resultant modes of inscription of professional work and desired outcomes for clients. Undertaking such work was substantially complicated by the organizational imperatives (which could not be ignored) pushing the teams in particular directions, the absence of forums for team discussions, and the definitely not-to-be-underrated complications in discussing issues of service provision when the position adopted by some was in contradiction to powerful dominant organizational and political discourses.

The Elderly Team's Organizational Narratives

The Community Team's Narratives of Failure and Survival   The narratives at play in the elderly service teams were substantially different from those of the disability and psychiatric teams. The dominant narrative in the community team was a narrative of failure, a term referencing a perceived lack of organizational interest, inimical administrative arrangements within and beyond the hospital that affected teamwork, and an absence of resourcing. These factors seriously compromised the team's ability to discharge its role. This narrative wrote professionals as being "at sea," caught up in (organizational) whirlpools and personalities and unable to be effective in the discharge of their responsibilities. Such a narrative left little room for attention to the client. There was, however, an emerging, although highly marginalized, narrative of survival. This narrative accessed personal self-interest (job retention) and professional competence (offering an improved service to clients); it was demonstrated in the team's attempt to define priorities for service; rather than remaining at the whirlpool's center, the team was trying to edge its way to less turbulent, less dangerous waters, and there was a suspicion of hope that they could come through.

The Inpatient Team's Narrative of Maturation　The elderly inpatient team's narrative was one of increasing maturation. It described a growing sense of members' professional competence reflecting a collective sense of purpose, members' reasonable degree of confidence in the effectiveness of their teamwork and in their improved administrative systems that allowed them to track client care plans better, and a belief that they could further improve their work (although the team lacked a forum for review of that work). Within this narrative, effectiveness was written both as involving nuanced care and attention to relationships and as having to respond to, but not be entirely driven by, organizational concerns about efficiency. This narrative, then, opens up a reading of efficiency as enabling a dynamic interchange between organizational imperatives and professional practices, so that the objective of efficient practices is to support and extend professional input into client care (the raison d'être of a hospital) rather than the pursuit of efficiency as an end in itself.

Let me recapitulate briefly: All of these narratives are located within international discourses of need, targeting, professional autonomy and accountability, and effective and efficient resource allocation. Each discursively inscribes professional and client bodies differently, although there are likely to be degrees of intersection, and each places clients and professionals in different relationships to each other. Each may well have (organizationally) unintended effects, or effects that a service within an organization may conclude are no longer its responsibility, given its changed core business (for example, the quality of care provided by others for clients for whom that service is no longer responsible). As these teams demonstrated, health care organizational imperatives—imperatives not always subscribed to by health care professionals—are likely to generate different narratives in teams (and throughout health organizations) as to who the client is and how their role in relation to that client is to be discharged. These narratives are significant in that that they continue to foreground the fact that the answers to these questions are not self-evident or neutral but instead are highly political, a fact that neoliberal economic theories (like all dominant discourses) seek to obscure and deny.

What is the value in identifying these narratives? First, as I have just noted, a team is less likely to deliver quality care if its narrative is one of failure, and the identification of such narratives ought to be of organizational concern. Second, identifying organizational narratives provides access to points of both energy and resistance. An effective organization needs to attend to both points, for each provides different vantage points from which to assess how the organization conducts its work and what is suppressed by dominant narratives within different sections of that organization. For instance, the embattled narratives raised significant and legitimate questions, based on members' experiences, about the availability of both specific professional skills/knowledge beyond the teams and quality care in the "community"; equally, the enterprise narratives, also concerned from a different vantage point with quality, foregrounded issues of focus and efficient use of scarce resources (people, skills, knowledge) *and,* in the disability team, raised questions about the adequacy of the physical environment and resourcing of the ward for the provision of respite and long-term care. Third, the narratives highlight the political nature of all decisions informing service provision. Such decisions are too often presented as the result of an "objective" assessment of need. Finally, identifying current narratives may result in strategic realignments and the production of a further narrative or set of narratives, with different power effects.

It should also be noted that such narratives are quite likely to be unstable because they are produced and sustained by specific organizational conditions. Several months after I had completed the fieldwork, a brief discussion with one member from the elderly inpatient team suggested that, as a consequence of external factors (organizational changes, budgetary cuts, uncertainty about the service's future, and staff departures and transfers), that team's narrative had shifted significantly from a narrative of maturation to one of survival.

The Organizations and the Support of Teamwork

At the beginning of this chapter, I wrote of the necessary intersection between the production of effective teamwork and supporting organizational practices and policies. My objective in this section is to discuss how, moving beyond the managerial rhetoric about teamwork's significant contribution to the provision of quality health care, the management practices within the three organizations supported and contributed to the development of teamwork. To do this, I have selected three mundane but necessary areas relating to teamwork in order to evaluate how teamwork was organizationally supported at these sites. My evaluation focused, then, on how the organizations represented teams and teamwork through the accounts of teamwork provided in job descriptions, in the formal and informal orientation processes, and in the training in teamwork made available to team members. Overall, the evidence suggested that as an activity teamwork was very much taken for granted and that organizationally and professionally teamwork was a largely undeveloped domain.

Job Descriptions and Teamwork

In the organizational literature, job descriptions are understood to have three main objectives: to inform prospective employees of their role, to enable organizations to set goals, and to inform subsequent performance reviews conducted with individual employees. At all three sites the job descriptions, with the exceptions of those where a job had been relatively recently advertised, were some years out of date, as the organizational practice was to revise descriptions only when a job was to be readvertised.

In their predominant focus on key professional discipline-specific activities of each role, the descriptions reflected the organizational placing of members as primarily responsible to their discipline rather than to the interprofessional team. There were brief references to teamwork at the end of the list of employee responsibilities, where it was stated that employees were expected to attend meetings and, in a somewhat bland and unelaborated clause, "make a contribution" to the work of the team. There was no reference in the descriptions to roles that members would be expected to carry out within the team, such as facilitation of family meetings, a role that one or two more recently employed junior members were shocked to discover they were expected to perform (their training and experience had not prepared them for such work). Apart from one remembering that she was asked if she could defend her point of view and stand up for herself if challenged, none of the relatively recent appointees could remember clearly what had been discussed about teamwork in their interviews.

There is clearly a limit to what can be included in a job description. However, the minimal organizational articulation of teamwork in documents outlining professional roles and responsibilities suggests that while the discipline-specific role was understood as a professionally complex activity, the role of "team member" was not seen as requiring anything approximating the same degree of organizational focus or interest. As a consequence of remaining unarticulated and with few organizational expectations attached to it, the concept "teamwork" appeared to be correspondingly difficult to discuss with potential team members.

Orientation Programs

While the job description establishes the parameters of the work, the objective of an orientation program is to instruct new employees in the operation of a service's work and provide an understanding of how their work intersects with that of others. Though orientation programs officially existed at all sites, team members' comments suggested that these programs addressed primarily service protocols, procedures, and general hospital policies. In order to more fully understand the work of other team members, new team members spent about half an hour with each colleague, discussing that person's role and how it might intersect with their own. As two workers pointed out, though, there is a difference between familiarizing oneself with practices in other disciplines and addressing how the team, not its individual members, works.

In contrast to the orientation to discipline-driven work, orientation to the teams' ethos and modes of working seemed nonexistent. No site had developed protocols or had procedures in place to which new members could be directed. At one site, new members were told about the strength of the team and quality of the teamwork; at another, one member said she was given the rundown by her supervisor about the team power structure, consisting of an account of various members' personalities. At one meeting at which I was present, someone described the team's work to a new member as "telling each other about clients" and "discussing services." While this rather empty account does suggest a narrative and interactive structure to the discussion, it does not attend to the possibility of multiple narratives about specific clients and how their intersection might generate productive work.

Given the absence of a more substantial articulation of teamwork by the organizations and by team members, it was not surprising to find workers replicating these very limited accounts during the interviews I conducted with them. For example, a nurse said that new members "have to be sort of educated into the/ what is expected and/ get used to the . . .

that kind of discussion" (see appendix for explanation of transcript conventions). A unit manager's fifteen lines of commentary on this subject ranged from specifying members' responsibility to make a contribution about client issues in the context of a supportive team environment ("nobody's going to actually jump down their throats" because "everyone's entitled to have a say"), to making a principled statement about team equality, to noting that when team members had not contributed the result was an undesirable disciplinary/personal dominance where "the strongest members of the team who have most to say" take over. A psychiatric registrar, in commenting about her continued lack of clarity about her role in the team (after six months) said in relation to my question about what she had told her successor:

> Oh I/ I've/ told her all about it um but um/ but no I sort of didn't talk much what her role in/ in actually these meetings is. I mean I/ I sort of narrowed it down to basically just be there for the patient discussion and um/ have any input and whatever. I pick up or look at . um sometimes there have been patients that I have been asked to see and I just get a better view of them {from hearing what others have to say} than from notes.

On one plane, these comments provide a simple descriptive and somewhat reductive account of teamwork: it requires physical presence, input, listening to others' statements, and it is (variously) problematic; on another plane, they raise a substantial number of questions and issues. For example, the nurse's comment suggests that teamwork requires more than simply information exchange; equally, however, she does not elaborate on the peculiarities of this "kind of discussion" or the "education" required to achieve a better mode of teamwork. Her subsequent comment, that nurses' orientation to the team's work was achieved through attending meetings and seeing what happens, did not engage with what was "seen," how this was interpreted, whether what was seen was "good teamwork" and what the parameters of such work might be, or how, when, and with whom such perceptions were critically appraised.

The unit manager's comments focused on information exchange, where the objective was to share information about the client, an objective that suggested a rather mechanistic conception of communication and did not address how conflicting accounts were to be managed; equally, informing her commentary was a persistent (but here lightly touched on) tension embedded in the notion of the supportive team. When is teamwork about being supportive, and thus ensuring that people feel okay? ("If you feel uncomfortable in the team you should identify that with someone who's got some responsibility to the team"). When is it about challenging assumptions, goals, directions—that is, concentrating on the professional work produced by the team? The comments of these speakers, then, raised significant questions about the nature of teamwork: What does a "good" team in action look like, and what is the nature of the team product? Is teamwork just about exchanging information, and if so, to what end? Alternatively, is it also about developing an agreed, collective account, making sense of differences in perspectives rather than suppressing them, and thus enabling the team to formulate an overall plan taking such differences into account? If so, how is this to be done?

The psychiatric registrar's remarks repeat the concept of teamwork as informational and as narrative ("telling"). She was there to listen and to "view," but there was no implied obligation to critique and evaluate what was heard, or to produce what she "viewed" for others' inspection. Her account contained significant lacunae if teamwork is to be understood as involving the development of care plans and attention to points of intersection and overlap of members' work.

These texts, then, both in what is remarked on and in what goes unsaid, begin to map what might be involved in an orientation program about teamwork. They point to the organization's role in ensuring that teams have a developed philosophy (known to members), protocols, some procedures (which are open to revision), and, especially important, an agreed account of how the team produces effective teamwork and assesses its effectiveness. Developing and revisiting these dimensions require the allocation of organizationally legitimated time. Protocols assist in establishing the rules of the game, in providing points of reference to which appeals can be made, and in relation to which changes can be made. They may set out the specific dimensions of some key roles, such as that of team leader, define teamwork not just as supportive but as questioning and challenging professional input and assumptions and the rationale for this, establish rules as to how this may be done, and define acceptable team behaviors. Procedures establish how a team goes about its work—how it runs clinical review meetings, makes policy submissions, runs family meetings, and critiques its work in the context of an agreed account of how an effective discussion may be structured. Knowledge of what is expected of them is critical for new members, as participating in some procedures may well call for additional training; correspondingly, the organization needs to be aware of members' training needs so that they get the training to ensure that they are able to act as effectively as possible in a team setting.

Training in Teamwork

The team members in the study had had minimal training in teamwork before and after they joined these teams. Of the forty-odd professionals whom I interviewed, only four social workers, the two psychologists, the counselor, one OT, and the three psychiatrists had had any teamwork training in their professional courses. That training had focused on group dynamics. There was a very limited amount of in-service team training and, given the straitened financial circumstances of the hospitals, this was not surprising, for training requires an organizational commitment of resources (Mohrman and Mohrman 1993). Nursing staff were unable to take part in team training days, although they were team members, because of safety considerations.[13] The training that was provided addressed members' interpersonal relations, ensuring that people had "fun" and teams were seen as "supportive," with the trainers (and two team leaders) favoring the use of the Myers-Briggs personality tests. There were no discussions in the training sessions about how the teams actually conducted their work, whether members were happy with existing practices, or how they might be changed. One social worker commented, "What we actually needed was the guts of what this team was to do and how it was going to do it and what role people were going to have in that and what their responsibilities were going to be."

What was most significant was that none of the training focused on or facilitated discussion of or changes to aspects of their work (all bearing on effectiveness) that some members considered were poorly managed. These included difficult team behaviors (such as constant interruptions and persistent inaudibility) and team processes, such as defining the objective of reviews and discussing ways of structuring discussions, including whether all clients should be reviewed at each weekly meeting, and time management of the discussions of each client. Nor did the training allow for attention to how specific roles, such as the leader's, might be developed in light of a general rejection of the model of an authoritarian (medical) leadership. Good feelings generated during infrequent training days rapidly dissipated once the team returned to the realities of everyday work, while new staff joining the teams subsequent to the training had inevitably missed out on what was intended to be a strengthening exercise. I would suggest that team training sessions that do not actively focus on how the team may both recognize and then produce effective teamwork that meets carefully defined organizational objectives may well not advance those teams' abilities to work effectively.

The teams that were involved in the fieldwork were all located in complex, unstable organizational environments. While the grand political narrative, informed by neoliberal economic theory, was of increased efficiency, improved services, and greater choice, the fieldwork presented a less rosy picture of often very run-down working conditions, high staff turnover and loss of some valued staff, poor morale, and concerns about some of the implications for marginalized clients of progressive redefinitions of services' core business. It was not surprising that the team narratives were about the direction and shape of the service, and that this preoccupation complicated the production of other organizational narratives about teamwork and its more effective production. At none of the three sites was there other than minimal organizational attention to teamwork and reliance on received wisdom about what teams have to offer, and staff had received no or little training (and that questionable in its focus) in how to perform in teams.

Under these conditions it was not surprising that the work I observed was in various ways often problematic; equally, however, these same (often problematic) practices have enabled the articulation of an alternative paradigm of teamwork, a paradigm that foregrounds the interconnectedness of members' work and emphasizes teamwork as a knowledge-based activity. Before moving into the analysis of transcripts of team meetings presented in part 2, however, I will discuss the theoretical and methodological issues associated with carrying out the research and developing the analysis.

4

Researching the Interprofessional

Theory/Site/Practice

Simply by sailing in a new direction
You could enlarge the world.
                              —Curnow 1974

A key objective of this text is to take a familiar mode of service delivery in health care (teamwork) and, "by sailing in a new direction," map the contours of an alternative paradigm, offering a different account, a different conceptual land (sea) scape in which to locate "teamwork." Journeying, however, requires a map, and it is for this reason that the trope of "journeying/mapping" permeates the text. However, exploring new conceptual territories is not without its own hazards. Mapping describes both a time-consuming and uncertain process (producing the map recording the passage to an unknown destination) and a powerful act of definition and of (territorial) possession (enabling others to follow, shifting boundaries, laying conceptual claims).[1]

The first section of this chapter, "Setting Out," employs the (anthropologically) familiar (and now suspect) metaphor of traveling/journeying in order to establish some of the theoretical and methodological issues embedded in the research. The next section, "Theoretical Sites: Textual Motion," draws on Barthes's (1986) account of "text" and "intertext," an account that plays with the notion of texts not as stationary but as in movement (traversing), foregrounding rather than closure (the definitive reading), the openness of all texts, interwoven as they are by myriad different elements, where readers, bringing different textual histories to a particular text, will produce different accounts, allowing different interpretations and different foci to develop. This in turn leads into a discussion of "strong objectivity" and its implications in terms of defining teamwork as knowledge-based work. The next three parts in the section move between theory and method. How one theorizes the object of study affects data collection and processes of editing transcripts. Hence, the first of the following three parts in this section, "Interprofessional Practices: Defining 'Teamwork,'" focuses the research on the "work" of the team; the next, "Collecting Teamwork," describes what data were collected as a result of this focus; the third, "Working with Transcripts," is an account of methodological and theoretical issues associated with working with transcripts, particularly the theoretical issues associated with editing oral texts.

The third section, "Undertaking Qualitative Analysis: Fleshing Out the Text," takes Eco's (1985) elegant commentary on writing one of his books as its starting point. My objective in this section is to attend to how the analysis progressed. "Moving from Looking to Observing" attends to some of the methodological issues associated with attempting to analyse teamwork. "Thinking Narratively/Working Knowledgeably" is a discussion of the processes by which the concept "narrative," a key theoretical concept informing this research, was developed over time.

Methodological accounts can be thought of as heroic narratives, typically designed to demonstrate how the researcher overcame the at times seemingly intractable problems that research projects tend to generate and establish, by recounting the facts of the research process, the validity of the research findings. Hence the attention to factors such as the number of sites where fieldwork was conducted, the number and categories of respondents interviewed, how data were recorded (factors attesting to the breadth, range, and degree of data triangulation); and how those data were then processed. The danger of such accounts is that what comes through is (at best) technical proficiency; what gets obscured, particularly in accounts of analytic processes, is first, the centrality of theory, and second, any discussion of the process of developing a particular theoretical approach.

Inevitably, this account too can be seen as producing its own heroic claims. In the writing of this methodology, however, my objective has been to attest to the uncertain processes of moving outside of familiar terrain, setting my account of my identification of a key dimension of the research (effective teamwork as knowledge-based work) and the implications of that for data collection and production of transcripts in the context of

Eco's (1995) text on the interplay of the constraints of (historical) facts and the possibilities, within those facts, of creativity.

Setting Out

Sleepless, in a hotel room facing onto a Los Angeles motorway, with a never ceasing roar of traffic throughout the night, I wrote:

> In the old days, ethnographers made real journeys. They crossed geographical boundaries, moved into different locations. Malinowski's (1967) diary tells of preparations and planning: the collection of the necessary paraphernalia—tents, insect nets, insect repellents, food; of slow steamers, magical seas and verdant landscapes; of welcoming canoes and disappointing natives. But these days, as Geertz has remarked, the "Other" is just as likely to be down the hall. Ethnographic (or in this instance sociological) voyages are not necessarily a trip into the exotic or the unknown. My plans were more mundane. I did not have to get in supplies for a year, but there were complex negotiations about car usage involving prioritizing of family activities, and pressure to be back on time. The organizational and ethical lights guarding the sites for investigation flashed endlessly/repetitively stop/go/ stop go/stop/go/ st..o..p/go. In starting down another research highway I experience a sense of déjà vu, weariness, disbelief that I am repetitively/ obsessively relocating myself in organizational chaos and stressed bodies in an (ephemeral) pursuit for a desire for continuity in a research career, for a valorising of complexity. Making my (sociological) trip "down the hall" has not been without its moments of (especially) psychological preparation.
>
> On the face of it, my journey is not from the familiar into the unfamiliar. My desire is not to capture the unfamiliar within familiar frames or to regulate and constrain its luxurious landscapes and curious habits to produce scientific, ordered and recognizable conceptual gardens. Instead, my desire is to defamiliarize a familiar dimension of a professional landscape, map marginalized discursive sites and, following their fainter lines, re-work some of the sites/sights within that landscape. I have visited this territory before, albeit some years ago and in a different role, a member of that which I now intend to observe, a verb of which I am mindful is not without its own complexities.

To look, see and observe are different ways of using the organ of sight, each with its own intensity, even when there is some deterioration, for example, to look without seeing, when someone is distracted, a common situation in traditional novels, or to see and not notice, when the eyes out of weariness and boredom avoid anything to tax them. Only by observing can we achieve full vision, when at a given moment or successively, our attention becomes concentrated, which may just as easily result from a conscious decision as from an involuntary state of synaesthesia, whereby what is seen pleads to be seen once more, thus passing from one sensation to another, arresting, slowing down the process of looking, as if the image were about to be produced in two different places in the brain, with a temporal discrepancy of a hundredth of a second, first the simplified sign, then the exact design, the clear, imperious definition of a thick handle in polished brass on a dark varnished door which suddenly becomes an absolute presence.   *(Saramago 1996:146)*

The smoothness of the highway is seductive. Signposts point me towards familiar destinations, the feet-high painted letters on the rock cliffs bordering the road promise truth and salvation through adherence to this route. But my still uncertain gaze is caught by the small clump of kaihikatea in boggy ground edging a semi-concealed and unsealed turning on the left with no signs indicating destinations or distances.

And, as with ethnographers, I too have my concerns about the "natives" I will encounter on this poorly defined track. How fully will they describe the corner of the organizational and practice world which they inhabit and which concerns me? Will they disappear at the critical moment? Will they want to talk beyond the one encounter we negotiated with some difficulty, given their stress levels and work demands? How much time do they have to engage in such "unproductive" activities, busy as they are? What (metaphoric) alternatives do I have to tobacco and what are the ethics of plying such trade? Where will I hang out? Will this faint track bring me to any recognizable point of arrival? Will I get bogged down or simply circle back into the self-evident, the repetitious? In what spirit will others regard my "discoveries"?

This, then, is an account of another journey—a trip involving observation and analysis, not so much of the bodies marked/scarred by the effects of physical and psychiatric disabilities and of aging, but of the

intersection of professional bodies and professional discourses surrounding, intersecting, interpellating these bodies. The organizational
rhetoric of "holistic" care and effective practice is inscribed in the
humanistic discourse of attention to the "whole" body, a discourse pen-
etrated/contradicted/constrained by more dominant discourses of economic rationality (prioritizing, allocating, bed days, budget constraints,
core business) in their "clean," "objective," and "neutral" language.

So what happened? Let's get on with the tale. The field trips were relatively uneventful.

This account ended here, its last word uncomfortably stranded because
I realized I could not support such a claim. I have no detailed idea of what
most of those who took part in the research thought about what I was
doing or of the questions I asked, although the ways that individual interviews with team members developed allow me to make some guesses, both
positive and negative. The research quickly raised inevitable complications
of power even before I arrived on-site. At one site, in an act of organizational and professional silencing by a more dominant discipline, no members of one discipline whose work was critical to the team were included
on the list setting out the names and professions of all team members that
was forwarded to me. There were problems of entrée at the same site. My
initial visits to discuss the team's participation in the research and my
arrival to begin the fieldwork were cause for puzzlement. No one seemed
to know I was coming, although I have a copy of the letters in my files confirming meeting times to discuss the project and, later, the agreed starting
date. And then, it seemed that despite all the discussions of how I intended
to go about the fieldwork, a key member had not agreed to my taping
meetings. Should I interpret this as "resistance" (which immediately and
unhelpfully personalizes the issue) or as a response to organizational over-
load, or as part of an ongoing struggle around disciplinary status within
this particular group of clinicians? Or, even more simply, had the letter got
lost in the post?

Nor, as I struggled with different aspects of the project, was the fieldwork uneventful for me. Indeed, there were points at which I wondered
about how I could write up the research at all. It was one thing at the
research proposal stage to write of the focus of the research being on *teamwork*, emphasizing that the content of the teams' discussion was not the
focus of the research, but how they structured their discussion was. It was
another to be confronted some months later with the "reality" that I had

somewhat suppressed: that teams' talk is often of intimate (how recognizable, and by whom?) details of people's lives and bodies, and that my
analysis depended on the reproduction of sections of these intimate texts.

Theoretical Sites: Textual Motion

Within postmodern theory a "text" is more than a play, a novel, a poem. A
text is that which opens an interpretation of the social so that a billboard, a
film, a car, a medical file, a transcript of an interview, or a discussion all
offer ways of analyzing particular aspects of social/cultural situations. A
text is not constituted by claims of definitiveness and filiation. Its objective
is not to put down roots but to be engaged in motion, through encouraging not just reading, but stimulating writing and, in its turn, the generation of a new text. A text is also an "intertext." Barthes (1986) wrote that

> *the Text is experienced only in an activity, in a production.* It follows that
> the Text cannot stop (for example, at a library shelf); its constitutive
> moment is *traversal.* . . . The text . . . practices the infinite postpone-
> ment of the signified, the Text is dilatory . . . The Text is plural. This
> does not mean only that it has several meanings but that it fulfills the
> very plurality of meaning: an *irreducible* (and not just acceptable) plu-
> rality. The Text is not coexistence of meaning, but passage, traversal;
> hence it depends not on an interpretation, however liberal, but on an
> explosion, on dissemination. The plurality of the Text depends, as a
> matter of fact, not on the ambiguity of its contents, but on what we
> might call the stereographic plurality of the signifiers which weave it
> (etymologically, the text is a fabric): the reader of the Text might be
> compared to an idle subject . . . : this fairly empty subject strolls . . .
> along a hillside at the bottom of which flows a wadi (I use the word to
> attest to a certain alienation); what he [*sic*] perceives is multiple, irre-
> ducible, issuing from heterogeneous, detached substances and levels:
> lights, colors, vegetation, heat, air, tenuous explosions of sound, tiny
> cries of birds, children's voices from the other sides of the valley: . . . all
> these incidents are half identifiable: they issue from known codes, but
> their combinative operation is unique, it grounds the stroll in differ-
> ence, which cannot be repeated except *as difference.* This is what hap-
> pens in the Text: it can be Text only in its difference . . . [it is] entirely
> woven of quotations, references, echoes: cultural languages . . . ,

antecedent or contemporary, which traverse it through and through, in a vast stereophony. The intertextuality in which any text is apprehended, since it is itself the intertext of another text, cannot be identified with some *origin* of the text: to seek out the "sources," the "influences" of a work is to satisfy the myth of filiation; the quotations a text is made of are anonymous, irrecoverable, and yet *already read*[:] they are quotations without quotation marks.   *(Barthes 1986:58-60)*

Texts are not closed but are constituted by heterogenous (cultural/ social/other) elements. Any text is generated by a particular, a unique combination of such elements. A text (itself the result of the intersection of those intertexts on which the writer has drawn) is open to multiple readings. Each reader brings a different textual history to inform their readings, histories that lead to different points of engagement with the text, different points of emphasis, different weighing of implications. There is a link here to the Derridian notion of *différence,* a concept highlighting both difference and differral/slippage of meaning. There is (theoretically) no closure. There is always the possibility of another "explosion."

To write this is not to collapse into an unreflexive relativity, where one argument, one position is as good as another; nor it is to posit the "objective" (in the scientific sense of the word) validity of the reading I advance about teamwork in this text. I draw here on Donna Haraway's commentary on Sandra Harding's concept of "strong objectivity."

Strong objectivity insists that both the objects and the subjects of knowledge-making practices must be located. Location is not a listing of adjectives or assigning of labels. . . . Location is always partial, always finite, always fraught play of foreground and background, text and context, that constitutes critical inquiry. Above all, location is not self-evident or transparent.

Location is also partial in the sense of being *for* some worlds and not others. There is no way around this polluting criterion for strong objectivity.   *(Haraway 1997b:37)*

The account of teamwork presented in this book, however theoretically well informed and supported by the data generated in the fieldwork process, is necessarily an account that results in the exclusion and marginalization of issues another reader may desire to reposition; it is *"for"* knowledge-based practice and, being for that, it does not focus on issues of members' transference, their interpersonal issues, or the psyche of individuals, offering instead in the context of postmodern theory a radically different analysis. This text (or any text) cannot claim definitiveness. Its intention is "dissemination": the objective is not to attempt to lock "teamwork" into a rigid new paradigm but to explore the (organizational and practice) implications of realigning the field, restructuring the view, recognizing that such realignments will contribute to subsequent rewritings and different realignments.

What, then, of the identifiable intertexts informing the analysis of teamwork developed here? This text is constructed from a range of data: individual interviews with health professionals and managers, recordings of various modes of teamwork, and organizational documentation. It is contextualized by the literature on teamwork and by my (now distant) clinical experience as part of a small multidisciplinary team in the Child and Family Clinic in Wellington, Aotearoa/New Zealand. It draws on feminist/postmodern theory, with particular reference, as has been discussed, to Foucault's theory of power/knowledge, and, in chapter 6, to Deleuze and Guattari's (1983) theory of lines. I have drawn on postmodern/feminist strategies of reading, with particular attention to issues of connections across unfamiliar domains (Braidotti 1997), positionality (Haraway 1997a and 1997b), and marginality (Nicholson 1990; Soja 1996).

Interprofessional Practices: Defining "Teamwork"

The primary focus on the study was on the observation and audio-taping of how teams went about or produced their work (the process of discussions and the outcomes of those discussions) and analysis of that work. I understood "team meetings" as those significant formal occasions when most members of the team gathered for a specific organizationally endorsed purpose: the sharing of information about clients' situations and the formulation of ongoing plans informed by working knowledgeably on information pertaining to clients. Such a focus could appear to exclude what other commentators (for example, Saltz 1992; Whittington 1983) have defined as significant dimensions of teamwork, that is, the production of joint work between two or more team members. Joint work, however, is just that. It is work carried out between two health professionals, who may or may not be members of the same team. Certainly such work may be facilitated by teamwork, and unsurprisingly, team members did consult each other to varying degrees outside of the meetings. Some members (generally in closely related disciplines) relied extensively on each other's expertise and input to assist and augment their work. The critical *team* issue, though, is whether and how that joint work (as with work carried out by individuals and irrespective of where the decision to undertake it was made) is subsequently brought back into the team. Feeding back issues pertaining to work done between meetings brings that work into the collective knowledge held within the team about a specific client and therefore informs its ongoing discussions and review processes. The work of "the team" lies, therefore, in the process of its meetings, making that work simultaneously process, output, and outcome. It was for these reasons that I did not attempt to observe joint work between team members. My interest in relation to any joint work that was undertaken was not the fact that it had occurred but instead how it was reported on and how such reports entered the team discussions.

Collecting Teamwork

In light of my definition of teamwork and my interest in knowledge intersections, it was obvious that just talking to team members about their perception of teams, or observing teams, or recording occasional team meetings would not provide adequate data with which to develop my analysis. The focus of the study required the audio-taping of a number of consecutive team meetings, as this would enable me to track how discussions about clients developed over time, while undertaking the fieldwork at different sites would provide rich comparative data. I observed and taped, then, eight inpatient disability team meetings and six at the other two sites, as well as five community assessment team meetings run, respectively, by the elderly and psychiatric teams. I taped one community team meeting run by the disability team and then took detailed notes of two subsequent meetings. I decided not to tape these because they were almost overwhelmingly concerned with administrative issues and because of the team's intentions to change the meeting's structure. I attended and taped a elderly community team meeting at which members were developing criteria in relation to determining what clients should be allocated a priority status. I attended a highly emotionally charged meeting involving all hospital staff at this site in relation to management's negotiations with the funding authority over the contract, the outcome of which was a further re-restructuring of services and consequent loss of jobs in a town where the hospital was the main employer. I observed and audio-taped three case conferences run by the psychiatric team at which a subgroup of the inpatient team met to develop or refine a plan or to attend to specific problems the team was experiencing with a client.

Because of policy and service emphases on client and family empowerment and because it constituted another significant occasion to view teams in action, I observed and audio-taped ten meetings between members of the teams and clients and their families. Rather than relying on reports of what took place on such occasions, analysis of professional practice and of team/client/family interaction is particularly necessary because of the complications of reworking relationships in which power has been held predominantly by one group and in which part of what is required is the active inclusion of clients' and families' typically marginalized knowledge, knowledge that may well be different in its focus and orientation from that of the team. Transcripts, then, provide evidence, in a way that verbal or written reports provided by professionals and clients and families cannot, of team micropractices (and hence of the perpetuation of particular discursive relationships) of which both teams and families are likely to be largely unaware because micropractices are taken for granted and are therefore not easily open to identification and analysis by those involved in their perpetuation.

Team members made the decision about which family meetings I should attend, and they made the initial approach to the family and client about my being present. All but one of the meetings I observed and taped were run by the disability and elderly inpatient teams, where family meetings were a regular dimension of the work, generally being held at the point when a client came onto the ward and at his or her discharge. In some cases, meetings were also held at about midway through a client's stay.

The psychiatric teams had a different perspective on family meetings than did the other teams. Clients did not always want contact with family, and the teams also did not always believe family involvement would lead to a therapeutic outcome; further, the size of the service's catchment area meant that family meetings could not always be arranged, although other means of family involvement were organized. During the fieldwork the inpatient team held only three meetings with families. I did not participate in these, as it was felt that my presence would make already very difficult situations even more so. I did observe two interagency case conferences run by the community team where clients failed to show, and one team conference (also run by the community team) involving a father and his son (the client).

I decided early in the development of the research proposal that I would not seek commentary from clients and their families about the effectiveness of the teams working with them. In light of my discussion in chapter 2 about positioning clients and families as central to teams' work, this seems somewhat quixotic, if not downright contradictory. Why this seeming discrepancy? While I had no doubt that clients could comment on their experience of the work of individual members of the team, this commentary could not provide me with information about the team's work, work with which clients/families would have significantly less contact because it was largely conducted "backstage" (Atkinson 1994:118), where clients and family were not present. Taping family meetings, however, provided valuable evidence of the management of knowledge and power issues between clients/families and teams, as well as raising questions about the degree of empowerment (an objective in two teams) achieved through this process.

I interviewed and audio-taped the forty-odd team members and the three service managers at three sites about issues relating to teamwork. These interviews lasted from sixty to ninety minutes. Because the objective of the research was to focus on the "doing" of teamwork, rather than discussions about members' representations of how their teams operated, I have not drawn as extensively on these data as I have on the transcripts of team meetings.[2]

I reviewed a range of related documentation across all sites, such as minutes of team meetings and family meetings, some clients' files, staff job descriptions, and copies of service philosophies.

Working with Transcripts

The transcripts of the team discussions provided a very rich set of data with which to work. Their transcription, however, was complicated at times on two sites by invasive environmental noises—vacuum cleaners in action, water heaters being filled, trolleys passing the door of the meeting room, steel buckets being dropped, shouting, and, on the locked ward, the door to the meeting room being locked and unlocked as members came and went during the course of the meeting. I have not marked these noise factors on the transcripts because simply noting the presence of noise is very different from having that noise as a constant in the background. In addition to these noises, the team members contributed to the problem of the tapes' audibility by rustling papers, talking simultaneously, interrupting, laughing, and chatting with each other.

The audibility of some members whose voices trailed off or spoke very softly was also a problem. Transcribing the speech of two members in particular presented considerable difficulties, and one of these was largely inaudible during the meetings, not just on tape. I have indicated the sections (and their approximate length) that were inaudible. The audibility factor at times contributed to a certain incoherency in the transcripts and occasionally complicated the analysis. For instance, the minutes of one meeting refer to a decision that the psychiatric registrar see a client, although there was no reference to such a decision in the transcript of the previous team meeting. It was not therefore clear where or when or by whom this decision had been made.

In order to illustrate the analytic issues I have addressed in this text, I have typically presented lengthy segments from the transcripts, the length itself an important part of demonstrating the flow of the discussion and the moments of elision, elaboration, and the presence or absence of disciplinary intersections. I have not undertaken significant editing of these segments, and what editing I have done has largely focused on changing key details about clients in order to preserve confidentiality. I have not removed all hesitancies, repetitions, and so forth. One of the outcomes of my practice is that the transcript data presented here may need to be read slowly.

Atkinson (1995) has argued that readers may assume speakers' incompetence if oral texts are not substantially edited. I have presented aspects of my research on teamwork to local and international professional audiences, illustrating the issues I was discussing with segments of quite heavily edited transcripts. Nonetheless, conceivably because it provides an immediate and obvious explanation, these audiences focused immediately and almost exclusively on the issue of professional competence despite my identification of factors that complicated this oversimplistic reading. In my experience, then, editing the transcripts has not affected audiences' assumptions of professional incompetence.

Furthermore, I consider there to be sound methodological reasons for not engaging in substantial editing of oral transcripts, and my position is supported by Tedlock's commentary on the importance of recognizing the peculiarities of spoken texts as often "*good speaking* rather than *bad writing*" (Tedlock 1983:6, his emphasis). A failure to formally recognize the differences between oral and written texts has meant that the act of transcribing interview data has been conceptualized as "straightforward transposition from acoustic signals to graphic signs" (Fabian 1993:86).

What is lost in the production of such "straightforward" writing is not only the performative dimensions of the text and their implications but also elements of intelligibility and readability, since all these textual elements depend on "culturally and historically specific situations" (86). Even more ironically, such transcription practices result in the suppression of evidence that would enhance the very phenomena that the researcher is intending to analyze. In place of a richly textured and contoured oral account, the researcher (and later, the reader) typically works from or reads an impoverished representation of the informant's speech.

The production of an enriched text is, moreover, subversive of the ideology of literacy because it acknowledges the interrelationship of oralization and reading, rather than privileging the latter (Fabian 1993).[3] Anthropological research into textuality, orality, and transcription practices therefore challenges "our 'scriptural' societies" (de Certeau 1984:131), where privileging writing at the expense of the oral has contributed to literacy's association with the unambiguous and with objectivity. In contrast, orality has been associated with a lack of scientific rigor and progressiveness, and with primitiveness and magic. The power relations inherent in such characterizations have been remarked on in the links made between the subordination of oral cultures and the foregrounding by imperialist powers of literacy as a means of maintaining distance (Fabian 1993), and the association of literacy and the construction of official languages as part of the process of colonization (Bourdieu 1991).

Maintaining a focus on the oral nature of transcripts recognizes that team discussions are not constituted by well-formed sentences. They are necessarily messy. They do not always proceed in linear fashion, but loop back on themselves, or move off in several different directions. Thoughts and sentences are not always finished. Speakers do not necessarily express themselves elegantly. Some statements are ambiguous. Teamwork is indisputably conducted as an oral exercise, and it is this oral "text" of which team members (and researchers) must make sense. Writing/editing out all these factors may well hide dimensions of teamwork that bear on teams' abilities to engage in effective work.

Undertaking Qualitative Analysis: Fleshing Out the Text

Umberto Eco wrote *The Name of the Rose* because "I felt like poisoning a monk. I believe a novel is always born of an idea like this: the rest is flesh that is added along the way" (Eco 1985:13). Fleshing out the novel requires an initial idea, and after that there is a certain logicality, a certain inevitability. "*Rem tene, verba sequentur:* grasp the subject, and the words will follow" (24). The work begins to generate its own internal demands. Eco writes:

> I realized the novel had to include things that, in the beginning, had never crossed my mind, such as the debate over poverty and the Inquisition's hostility towards the Fraticelli.
>
> For example: why are the fourteenth-century Fraticelli in my book? . . . I needed an investigator, English if possible . . ., with a great gift of observation and a special sensitivity to interpreting evidence. These qualities could only be found among the Franciscans, and only after Roger Bacon; furthermore, we find a developed theory of signs only with the Occamites. . . . It is only between Bacon and Occam that signs are used to acquire knowledge of individuals. . . .
>
> But why does everything take place at the end of November, 1327? Because by December, Michael of Cesena is already in Avignon. (This is what I mean by furnishing a world in an historical novel: some elements . . . can be determined by the author, but others, like the movements of Michael, depend on the real world. . .).
>
> But November is too early. I also needed to have a pig slaughtered. Why? The answer is simple: so that the corpse could be thrust, head down, into a great jar of blood. And why did I need this? Because the second trumpet of the Apocalypse says . . . I could not change the Apocalypse, after all; it was a part of this world. Now, it so happens (I made inquiries) that pigs are not slaughtered until cold weather comes, and November might be too early—unless I situated the abbey in the mountains so there would already be snow. . . .
>
> The constructed world will then tell us how the story must proceed.
> *(Eco 1985:26–27)*

Key elements in this account are its elegant and fluid movement between concept and the (carefully researched) necessary historical detail that imposes its particular constraints on the structure of the novel; equally, there is space for interpretation and creativity.

There are, I think, fascinating parallels between Eco's account of the writing of his historical/fictional world and the writing of a postmodern text in a qualitative study. Researchers, as did Eco, have to contend with unchangeable elements of the "real world." These include the fieldwork location (data collection can happen only here, and not there, and consequently certain, possibly generative, comparisons will remain unmade); the nature of that site with its attendant social, political, spatial determinants; and its relationship to the wider social/political environment. Once collected, the quality, quantity, and range of the data are unchangeable. They then become factors to be worked with as best one might, so bringing into play researchers' conceptual and theoretical horizons, horizons that structure their reading strategies, encourage attention to certain phenomena, assist in the production of different complexities of analysis.

Eco decided to poison a monk. I decided to explore the concept of effectiveness as it was demonstrated in interprofessional team discussions. Here, then, the "real world," in the shape of changing discourses in the context of health care delivery, inserts itself into the research design and the production of the subsequent text. Other "historical" and "real world" facts were provided through the transcripts and in the documentation, staff training in teamwork, their experience, how they conducted their meetings, the organizational environment in which they worked, and so on. These were things that could not be changed. They provided the environment in which teamwork was produced; equally, these "facts" were available for analysis and the products of these facts (in general terms, what was said and how it was said) provided the necessary spaces for analysis and interpretation, although I was not at first certain how such spaces might look. It was one thing to arrive at the first site feeling quite dissatisfied with the typical analysis of teamwork, another to have a more fully developed plan of how I was going to flesh out an alternative teamwork narrative.

Moving from Looking to Observing

The "fleshing out" necessarily took time. In the first week or so at each site a lot of my energy was taken up trying to make sense of my surroundings. To use Saramago's (1996) terminology, this initial period at each site was spent looking, rather than observing. I found it difficult at first to move beyond the commonsensical and the obvious, such as marked differences of opinion over possible courses of action, brief sarcastic or angry statements or a member's negative body language in reaction to a colleague's comments. From time to time there were opportunities to ask one or two members about their interpretations of specific incidents or interchanges involving different team members, and sometimes their commentary highlighted the different discourses (personal relationships as opposed to attempts to improve effectiveness) in which teamwork can be reproduced. Other comments addressed the lack of protocols and the lack of space and time to review the team's work (since the points of difference had related to how the team worked), but offered no elaboration of what the focus or conduct of such a review process would be.

All discussions are contextual. My observations/analysis about the teamwork I looked at and then began to observe had to take into account clients' past histories and previous team decisions and actions made in relation to those histories. Although at one site client histories were extensively documented, it was not always easy to determine team input into the work with specific clients, as many files had remarkably little information on what any (or some) team members' work objectives were; nor was it always clear which members had been involved with that client in what capacity over what period of time. As a transitory newcomer to the team, I was always going to be significantly less well informed than team members about the complex backgrounds of each case (although it at times became apparent that my lack of knowledge about issues relating to a client and his or her situation was shared by other, much longer-term team members).

My lack of contextualizing information about each client was further complicated at two sites where, although the team review provided an "introduction" to each client, most of the clients were well known to the team (if not always to individual members). As a result, the "introduction" provided a minimum of information about that client's current issues. Trying to make sense of complex information, including terminology and abbreviations with which I was unfamiliar (and found it difficult to ask about because I didn't want to appear stupid), complicated attending to the "process"—assuming, of course, that I knew what the process was to which I should be attending.

While gaining some knowledge of clients' situations was possible, although not always easy, in the early stages of "looking" at the teams' work, I caught myself "faulting" the team, or some members, for not pursuing what seemed to me to be "self-evident" lines of action, then realizing I did not know what had been done in the past and with what effect. My attempts to catch up on what specific work with clients had been undertaken in the past was made harder by workers' typically rapidly dispersing after meetings. Nor was it easy to understand what some disciplines' objectives were in their work with clients. At one site, my requests for information about what work was actually in progress tended to get translated into accounts of clients' psychopathology or another discipline's problems of client management. I often felt frustrated and very much at a loose end, particularly at two of the sites, where my contact with team members outside of the meetings, except for when I was interviewing them, was almost nonexistent.

To make things more difficult, a number of members were openly anxious about being interviewed. What could they say about teamwork? The team meeting was just a weekly meeting they had to attend.[4] Others, conscious of their lack of training in teamwork, were concerned about appearing ill informed. I often felt that interviews were not going well but worried that an attempt to focus the discussion more sharply would result in the respondent's feeling insecure and becoming more hesitant, while seemingly well-flowing, focused, and expansive interviews looked much less so when I reviewed the transcripts. As I got further into working over the transcripts of the team discussions, I began, tentatively, to define how it might be possible to think about the constituent factors in effective teamwork. I tested these ideas out with the research advisory group. I also tested them out in the course of my interviews with four or five team members, either by offering a statement about what I had observed and what seemed to me points of omission and asking for comments or by asking about the interviewee's understanding of the implications of team responses. The reception to these questions and observations varied from the uncomprehending (which meant that matters could be taken no further), to a rapid endorsement of the issues I was concerned about and their further elaboration, to, occasionally, a denial of the validity of my observations. When this last happened I went back to check the transcripts, which bore out my representation of what had happened. What this suggested, though, was not just a simple issue of whether I was "right" and the other "wrong," but that their assumptions that the team operated in certain ways made it more difficult to note how the team's actual practices quite often did not conform to those expectations.

Thinking Narratively/Working Knowledgeably

Finding a way of thinking more analytically, and not just descriptively, about the texts generated by the fieldwork was not a simple task. As I became a more expert reader of this project's data sets, I came increasingly to focus on the transcripts of team reviews (and much less on members' commentary on teamwork in the interviews I conducted with them) as that which provided rich evidence of how effective teamwork is structured by issues of narration, knowledge, and difference. What follows is an account of my attempts to engage analytically with the texts of the team reviews, and the process of moving the twinned concepts "narrative" and "knowledge work" to center stage.

Once the tapes had been transcribed, I reviewed the transcriptions for accuracy and to remove identifying features about the site and the clients. In part, this involved using the Replace function on my word-processing package to remove members' initials, replacing them with initials relating to occupation. At the end of each global change, the computer ran a little dialogue box stating the number of changes made. This indicated (roughly) the number of occasions each person had spoken in the meeting. In a context where the literature and members stressed "contribution" as a key factor of team effectiveness, this offered a crude method of quantifying the considerable variation in members' levels of contribution.[5] However, the contextual/textual data highlighted problems of equating input with significance or quality. For example, in one team, the most prolific speaker often said "least," her frequent input contributing on a number of occasions to a decrease in clarity and focus, rather than the reverse. Moreover, in any team, not all members are equally involved in the care of all patients. They may therefore have had nothing to "contribute" in relation to their discipline's specific input into client care over the course of several discussions. Recognizing these factors led me to think initially that this process had simply been a waste of time; further reflection led me to see that in rejecting this mode of analysis I had begun to discriminate more than I had been able to at first about that to which it was important to attend. The points raised above allowed me to conceptualize teamwork as *less* about the presentation of the work of each member and *more* about engagement from diverse perspectives with the knowledge about the client held by different team members.

Determining Effectiveness in Teamwork   I worked with the texts of the meetings in a variety of ways, each contributing over time to conceptualizing effectiveness and to the refinement of the analysis. The recording of sequential meetings permitted the collation of discussions over several weeks about individual patients so that I could track, for example, how discussions developed over time and the aspects of care that were emphasized, while also noting what did not get attended to, what discipline's input was never included in minutes, how teams used the minutes, and the significance of introductory statements about each patients. Collating all introductory and ending statements about each client at two sites helped in the identification of the idiosyncratic features of the ways the teams presented the clients to themselves.

During the first round of fieldwork I met with the three project advisers.[6] I selected reviews of clients to discuss with them, the criteria for selection being that the reviews were either those where the team had engaged in lengthy and unresolved discussion(s); cases where the team agreed that nothing needed to be said, but a diffuse discussion happened anyway; cases where the discussion appeared to be inconsequential; and those where members' discussion of their work resulted in work-focused interchanges between members. In a situation where team members were by and large enthusiastic about their team and its practices and where I was still very much beginning to develop my analysis, it was extremely helpful to have the advisory group's commentary (all are skilled professionals with substantial experience in teamwork and skeptical about many of the claims made about teams) as their endorsement of my interpretations confirmed that there was some substance to my observations (that is, I had not just got myself stuck and was unable to see wood for trees).

My initial working definition was that the purpose of teamwork was to advance clients' care through some undefined process of laying out different perspectives represented by different disciplines. My first readings of the transcript were focused around very simple questions: "What is going on here?" "What are they trying to do?" While offering an initial way into the data, such questions too easily generated descriptive accounts. Over time, the questions driving the analysis changed, becoming "What does an effective discussion look like, and what makes for its effectiveness?" These questions imply some degree of structure and a process of development of the discussion. They generated two more: "How does the team go about its discussion?" "What is the result of the discussion?" These questions were significantly more task-related, addressing outcomes and highlighting purposiveness. Placing these questions against the selected texts resulted in identification of a number of issues that recurred persistently throughout the transcripts. These included:

- Teams' nonengagement with seemingly significant information;
- The general absence of questions about the direction and purpose of members' individual work;

- The general absence of questions about the direction of a discussion and of statements summarizing the position the team had reached when a number of different issues about a client and interpretations of her/his behavior had been produced;
- Difficulties in responding to competing representations of clients, and the (powerful) adoption of moral attitudes toward some clients, and the outcome of this in relation to progressing the care of the client;
- The persistent failure by one team to discuss patient requests, despite the fact that deciding how to respond to these requests was said to be one of the main objectives of the team meeting;
- The lack of critique or evaluation by teams of their work, including an absence of evaluation of meetings with clients and/or families that were generally agreed to have gone badly;
- Lack of an identified purpose for reviewing a client and, alternatively, the purpose of extremely brief "reviews";[7]
- The place of narrative in teamwork;
- A general absence of definitions of team goals; and
- The lack of a clearly defined organizational role in the production of teamwork.

Determining factors affecting effectiveness in a team discussion was a somewhat complex process. It is one thing to see what is "wrong," another to develop an analytic framework that allows for the development of an account of teamwork that goes beyond the itemizing of problems and the elaboration of prescriptive statements intended to produce significant improvements in a team's mode of operation (e.g., Moore et al. 1991). I shall comment on two issues. The first has to do with my relationship to the data, to the analysis I wished to develop, and the ease with which a more simplistic analysis could have been produced. I have noted earlier the importance of moving beyond a simplistic reading of these teams as just demonstrating professional incompetence. Nonetheless, it was extremely easy to adopt a moral, condemnatory attitude toward team members because of the ease with which the contribution of organizational and professional discourses and practices in the production of compromising team practices can be overlooked/suppressed. Studying transcripts away from pressures of meetings is a luxury generally unavailable to team members. As I reviewed the transcripts, I had to admit how much as a "looker" and even as an "observer," and in the absence of any obvious structure for each discussion, I had been too caught up in the minutiae of the discussion. My subsequent ability to distance myself from those minutiae and attend to the structure of the discussion was possible only *because,* from the privileged position of researcher, I could review transcripts in detail in the context of a particular theoretical position.

The second point relates to the complex processes attendant on the development of an analysis. Part of the research contract with the teams had been that I would produce an account about the teamwork at each site, relying only on the transcripts of the team reviews. Writing what turned out to be substantial reports for each site at the completion of each phase of fieldwork materially assisted in the development of the analysis, as the obligation to write the first site report forced me to engage analytically very early on with the transcripts of team discussions. The reports to the other two sites provided an opportunity to revisit the analytic positions I had reached in the context of writing the first report and contributed to the development of key articles and conference papers reporting on the research. Completion of these in turn further refined my argument. Beginning to develop an analysis relies on an ability to determine certain generative (even if at times very basic) questions; equally, asking these questions excluded attention to others.

Achieving analytic refinement requires pushing conceptual boundaries and keeping key concepts in motion, thus avoiding too early a closure. For example, I first used the word *narrative* to refer to a process I had identified in the disability team's transcripts. Members produced (with varying degrees of elaborateness) stories or narratives about clients. My initial relationship to these narratives was ambivalent. In fact, it is probably more true to say that my attitude was somewhat dismissive, for I regarded the narratives, which were at times seemingly directionless, as largely unnecessary. I placed them in the context of "woolly thinking." I agreed with a medical team member who wished to cut short the meetings and valorized qualities of quickness of discussion and economy of information, all hallmarks of medical reviews of patients (Atkinson 1995). I also, however, regarded my position as unsatisfactory. Economic discussions that disposed of contextual information could well generate other problems. I did not resolve my paradoxical positioning toward team narratives in the compilation of my site reports, and was not fully aware of my contradictory positioning until later. Initially, then, I used *narrative* as a simple descriptor, as a means of referring to the different accounts of clients that team members brought to the reviews. A second, and more analytic, phase of my engagement with the concept of narrative developed in relation to attending to the implications of the representations of clients generated in such narratives, with particular attention to the relationship between effective teamwork and the team's management of its representational processes (Opie 1997).

After I had finished the fieldwork, I began to write what was to become, in terms of research outputs, a key article on team narratives (see chapter 7). This required me to attend more closely to the theoretical discussions of narrative than I had when I had used the term in the context of writing the site reports. Postmodern theorizing of narrative as contingent, fluid, and open provided the necessary theoretical sophistication that allowed me to fully take account of the structure/shape of the teams' narratives of their clients and required me to rework my reading of the data. The more complex explanatory framework of reading "narrative" made me engage more than I had been able to earlier with the positive implications for teamwork of such open, contingent narratives, and realize the need to theorize the "shape" of team discussions. The value of these critical conceptual shifts was that they assisted me in defining effective teamwork as constituted in part by a focused, interrogative, semistructured interplay across narrative lines. That is, narrative was necessary to the production of effective interprofessional teamwork, making both the production of and the engagement with team narratives critical team processes. My serendipitous reading of Nonaka and Takeuchi's (1995) book on knowledge work and teamwork suggested an association between narrative production, information transfer, and knowledge creation; moreover, this book reiterated my understanding of the crucial organizational role in the development of effective, knowledge-based teamwork.

Just as Eco did not expect to research the Inquisition in writing his novel about a monk's poisoning, neither did I expect, at the outset of my project, to arrive at the significance of knowledge and narrative in the production of effective interprofessional teamwork. But having done so, I found that other things flowed on.

Part Two

Displaying Teamwork

The major rationale for teamwork is that teams produce more effective work; at the same time there is a substantial absence of discussion based on close analysis of transcripts of team reviews about the shape and features of this supposedly effective work. The analysis produced here is not intended to result in a *prescriptive* list of conditions or factors against which the effectiveness of teams can be universally and authoritatively measured. Teamwork is a dynamic outcome of the intersection of professional and organizational discourses and objectives, the range of disciplines represented in a team, the organizational settings in which members work, and the team itself. Precisely how these extremely complex elements intersect will vary in relation to different geographical, cultural, and legal spaces, and within those spaces teamwork is also played out in the context of organizational and practice cultures. A team in the United States operates in different legal and cultural environments than does a team in Aotearoa/New Zealand and, as some members in the study emphasized, such environments inform very different assumptions about interprofessional relationships, authority, and team practices. The objective of part 2 is to engage with the concept of effectiveness, placing it against analyses of members' transcripts, team discussions (including sequential discussions of two clients running over several weeks), and family meetings in order to provide points of reference against which teams can review elements of their performance.

In chapters 5 and 6 I have quoted from a number of interviews with various team members. I have not identified the speakers of these quotes nor their sites because none of them had raised the critiques they developed in the course of our interview with their teams, and identifying their profession and/or site could mean that they would be identifiable by knowledgeable local readers. I have also not attempted a detailed gender analysis of members' discussions of issues surrounding teamwork; indeed, undertaking such an exercise would be somewhat complicated by the heavy predominance of women on the teams in the study. There are, however, two points I wish to make in this connection, which suggest the need for a fluid reading of gender. First, given the discourses that locate women within the affective domain, it was hardly surprising that a number of the women, although not all of them, spoke affirmatively of the emotionally supportive functions of teamwork, whereas very few of the men did. Second, the most detailed and extensive critiques of teamwork per se and of the functioning of their specific teams were largely developed by a few male respondents. Similar, but less detailed, critiques were developed by very few of the women. The critiques advanced by these respondents included reference to the problems associated with foregrounding personal rather than professional relationships among members because personalizing critical comments complicated teams' abilities to deal with the issues. However, a (male) counselor emphasized that members should be aware of the porous boundaries between personal issues and professional performance and that, without a space in the team to discuss and (therapeutically) work on personal issues, these issues could contaminate the team's effectiveness. This comment therefore wrote the team as a site where professionals engaged in their own therapeutic work. This model of teamwork was expressly rejected by one woman, who considered that it left team members open to abuse and misuse of power.

In developing the analyses I have presented in chapters 5 and 6, I have drawn almost entirely on the inpatient teams' work because, at all three fieldwork sites, significantly less time was allocated to the community team discussions (at one site, one member saw this as an informal reaction to the length of the inpatient meetings), and the discussions of clients were correspondingly generally extremely truncated. The result was that the texts that the community team reviews produced mostly lacked the richness and complexity of the reviews of the inpatient teams. The problematic issues, however, that occurred in the inpatient teams' discussions were replicated in the community teams' reviews of clients.

5

Mapping Effectiveness
Achieving a "More Subtle Vision"

Thinking Teams/Thinking Effectiveness

This chapter begins with a discussion of the accounts of effective practices identified by team members, and it draws attention to the general absence of agreement on these practices, an issue that has considerable significance for the production of effective work. The second part of the chapter, "Difference Patterns and Increasing Subtlety of Vision in Team Practices," moves, however, in a somewhat different direction. Basing the discussion on an analysis of the transcripts of a small number of team members, and employing Donna Haraway's (1997b) concept of "diffraction," I intend here to foreground how, within knowledge-based teamwork, close attention to difference and the effects of difference is critical to the production of effective teamwork. Casting teamwork in this framework, and drawing on commentary in these texts also allows me to demonstrate how familiar, taken-for-granted concepts such as the "supportive team" can be inimical to the production of such work and to link the development of effective teamwork with a specific type of leadership role.

Having drawn attention to the differences among members about conceptualizing effective work, I address first the two areas in which there was substantial agreement about how effective work was defined. First, a number of team members defined effectiveness in terms of organizational criteria relating to efficiency. These criteria reflected aspects of the work that were stipulated in the teams' contracts and on which they were audited, with a particular focus on recording outputs (critical to service funding). A number also commented on how effective practices relied on the development and periodic review and revision of team protocols and procedures. They were referring here to the development of forms for recording case plans, the stipulation of time frames for the completion of a piece of work, the institution of more regular review mechanisms, the definition of shared team objectives and audits of team decision-making processes, the development of documentation for the client (for example, complaint procedures and information sheets for clients and families about the service and inpatient procedures) and better team documentation (shared files, goal sheets, and so on). Although team members suggested that the introduction of factors such as these would increase effectiveness (and some thought that with respect to some of the factors mentioned above that had already been introduced, effectiveness had improved), no one spelled out how these changes would be implemented (as in the case of improving decision making) or why more reviews would necessarily result in improved quality of discussion and decision making.

Second, members agreed that effective teamwork depended on organizational resourcing and that absence of resourcing at all points of the services compromised the effectiveness of members' and teams' work. There were frequent comments about the lack of on-site team training and some criticisms of the focus of the little training that had been offered, the difficulty in including nursing staff in any training days, and the lack of focused orientation programs. Most members commented that the lack of resourcing affected the teams' effectiveness because there were insufficient resources in the community to which they could refer clients. The effectiveness of joint work was also seen as compromised by a lack of resourcing within the team. For instance, one member spoke of how she had discharged her role "effectively" by carrying out within the team's stipulated time frame the assessment requested by a nursing colleague of a client who had severe swallowing difficulties and was unable to feed herself. The assessment highlighted the need for nurses to place very small quantities of food in the back of the client's mouth and to ensure she had fully swallowed each mouthful before offering her another spoonful. However, this particular application of teamwork (the evaluation of a client's problem by one discipline and the discharge of the recommended practices by another) was rendered ineffective because of limited organizational resources. The recommendations could not properly be put into effect because there were insufficient nurses available to offer the client the necessary undivided attention during meals.

These areas of agreement aside, my dominant impression of members' accounts of teams and teamwork was of their differences: in emphasis on the value of teamwork, in evaluations of their teams' performance and effectiveness, and in the degree of complexity brought to those evaluations. That members produced such different accounts about the functioning of their teams is not in itself remarkable. What it points to is a general proposition about members' apprehension of teamwork: that each member can be said to apprehend or "know" the team differently as a consequence of the ways his or her perception is shaped by different disciplinary knowledge and focus, by past experiences, by the status accorded her or his discipline by other team members, and, not necessarily synonymously, by the individual's standing in the team.

My analysis of members' heterogeneous representations or accounts of what constituted effective teamwork suggested that the accounts fell into three categories: the unproblematic, the more constrained, and the distinctly dubious. Those falling into the "unproblematic" category provided enthusiastically unqualified comments by a relatively few members (not restricted to "soft" disciplines) about their team's effectiveness. In these accounts, discipline-specific differences and difficulties relating to how the team actually performed its work were either absent or marginalized. The particular value of the team lay in the support it provided to members, a mode of representation locating teamwork specifically within the interpersonal domain and less within a framework where the rationale for teams had to do with their effectively furthering organizational objectives. Comments offering a "more constrained" view of teamwork addressed more the organizational constraints to effective teamwork: differences over team processes, lack of training and proper orientation procedures, lack of opportunity to discuss these factors, and lack of resourcing. These speakers (the majority of those interviewed) frequently differentiated between the positive rhetoric of teamwork and their often less satisfactory experiences as part of current or past teams.

The "distinctly dubious" commentaries offered considerably more qualified accounts of the value and effectiveness of their team's work and, with varying degrees of complexity, spoke of teamwork as a highly complex process, operating across linguistic, organizational, interpersonal, and interprofessional domains. As will be demonstrated later in this chapter, the speakers who particularly contributed to this representation of teamwork highlighted the substantial difficulties of effecting the necessary changes in team and practices in order to achieve the more subtle team behaviors that they outlined as necessary to producing more effective work. Their comments took the discussion of effective work well beyond the prescriptive lists of organizationally desired, goal-centered behaviors and the achievement of outputs, which was the way members generally assumed that the organization evaluated their work.

The first point, then, was that there was no consensus on what constituted effective team practices. The second was that there was no consensus about the effectiveness of specific practices. Members on each team disagreed about the effectiveness of routine procedures that were common to all sites, such as how the statement about each client leading into the team's review of that person should be developed and its objective, the objective of the meeting,[1] and the consequences of changing organizational imperatives. One team leader, for example, spoke very positively about the administrative requirements that had resulted in her developing "goal sheets" (sheets recording patients' goals/desires for the outcome of their treatment to assist in achieving outcomes that were client- as well as staff-driven), saying,

> Everybody's quite clear about what they are doing and they are quite clear about what the outcome's going to be/ they feel like they've succeeded because they know we've met it and I think that they/ it's ended with people turning over a lot more quickly too/ which is good for staff too.

Having to ensure that her staff completed goal sheets had changed her behavior in ways that she thought made her more effective as a leader. She had become more "aggressive" in requesting goals, especially from the social workers, whom she saw as insufficiently accountable. The comments of a social worker on this team, framed by her different location in the team and different disciplinary focus, provided a less enthusiastic account of the value and implications of the goal sheets and goal-setting practices. She believed that the recorded staff goals tended to focus on nursing objectives, therefore insufficiently reflecting the goals of other disciplines. She drew attention to how the members of the team erroneously tended to equate a goal or goals that were discipline-specific, or a goal articulated by the client alone, with the *team* goal, thereby treating these very differently focused goals as synonymous. In contrast to this position, she defined a team goal as one that reflected the overall direction of the team's work as defined by the different disciplines' goals *and* therefore framed the ongoing work of the *team*. Furthermore, she commented that goal setting in itself could become problematic in light of managerial tendencies to equate goal setting, discharge, and efficiency and that sometimes there were complex reasons for an intended discharge date's not being achieved. She was concerned that, within a stressed organization, the focus of the team gaze on meeting goals could result in the clients' being marginalized.

The ways in which members differently conceptualized their work highlighted their different positioning in competing health discourses, each producing very different accounts of the focus of the team's role and its work, each therefore producing different criteria for evaluating effectiveness. Let me briefly return to the competing narratives of their work that the disability inpatient team produced. At the time of the fieldwork, long-stay clients, whose health was deteriorating (even if slowly) made up half of the inpatient population at any given time. Staff who had had a long-term association with these patients foregrounded the team's effectiveness in delivering quality, compassionate, and humane care to a socially and medically marginalized group. An alternative representation of the team's work was critical of the often lengthy (and arguably sometimes intrusive) discussions about these clients during team reviews. This representation supported the organizational case for a closer definition of the service's "core business," privileging the team's rehabilitative work as its "serious" effective work. A third (barely visible) representation was of the inpatient service generally as absorbing an undue proportion of scarce resources for a relatively few clients at the expense of the large numbers of disabled people in the community.

The significance of these different representations of the team's "real" work was that each laid claim to the most "effective" use of scarce resources. Equally, none was ultimately "true" (although one representation had significantly more organizational weight behind it, which reinforced the perception of its "truthfulness"). Each was a discursive construct, producing different accounts of clients' needs, highlighting how "effectiveness," as is "need" (Fraser 1989), is an unstable, slippery, political, social, and economic construct.[2]

Similarly, individual members' interpretations of their contribution to a discussion could highlight very different understandings of the effectiveness of their individual work to the overall effectiveness of their team's work. The elderly community team debated the continued driving of a client who had quite advanced Alzheimer's disease. An untrained social worker, asserting that the client drove infrequently and traveled only minimal distances (factors that were disputed), opposed suggestions that the team approach the police about canceling his license. She later defined her role as that of advocate and her intervention as "effective" because her opposition to the course of action endorsed by the rest of the team made the team recognize its ageist tendencies. Another member of the team complained to me that the social worker's behavior was in effect compromising the "effectiveness" of the team because in her desire to ensure that this client was not "harassed" about his disability, the social worker had tried to discourage her colleague from undertaking the assessment of the client requested by the doctor. While the social worker, who considered social work to occupy a marginal role on the team, had defined advocacy as a key discipline-specific goal, others on the team, then, not only thought the intervention inappropriate (hence justifying not attending to her commentary) but saw this goal as ill-informed and as inhibiting the team's arriving at a more informed overall evaluation of the situation, which was necessary to the development of their plan for and with this client and his family.

Just as there were different perceptions about the constitution of an effective team, so too were there differences about the constitution of an effective discussion. In the context of one team's very unstructured discussions, the medical staff on the team commented that working on a large team resulted in dissipation of energy and the production of "speculative" and "uninformed" remarks about issues pertaining to clients from members not involved in the care of those clients. "Knowledge" in this context referred to immediate knowledge of a client's situation and problem as a result of work with that person. Those doctors, then, saw smaller teams constituted of members with clearly defined responsibilities for specific clients as being more effective. They also wanted more discussion of medication issues and better time management through the allocation of specified time slots for discussion of each person. Such changes, they argued, would contribute to "fuller" and more effective (because more focused and less garrulous) discussions. Atkinson (1995) has commented that medical teams define effective discussions as constituted by qualities of focus, precision, structure, and linearity. Commentary such as this highlighted the interactive process in discursive production and emphasized the workings of disciplinary power in attempting to define and control team membership and the right to contribute to a discussion. The doctors' advancement of "actively working with the client" as the criterion for participation in a discussion was to them a self-evident proposition favoring the medical staff. It demonstrated their inscription within one discourse, while in their articulation of the criteria for team membership, they actively reinforced that discourse, a process that was intensified by their designation of another team member's input to discussions about clients with whom he was not directly engaged as "speculative" (and therefore unnecessary).

A contrasting account of an effective team discussion produced by this nonmedical colleague foregrounded the very dimensions that his medical colleagues wished to eliminate. The representation of an effective discussion that he produced as a consequence of *his* location within his discipline was that an effective discussion included not only the elaboration of issues pertaining to clients' circumstances (hence rewriting, from another discursive space, "garrulousness" as contributing to nuanced knowledge) but also the value of speculative interchange as better encouraging an interplay of information and perspectives from different team members.[3] This account of effective teamwork directly challenged the notion "uninformed comments" because it recognized that the value of the (possibly not) "uninformed" comment is not always its reliance on facts (this person is fully knowledgeable about all that has happened to this client) but the possibility of its raising questions about and engaging with (different) issues confronting the team in its work with that client, thereby challenging and further developing a particular discipline's and the team's knowledge about its client.

In the account proffered by this nonmedical team member of factors contributing to an effective team discussion, a larger team, rather than being an inevitable encumbrance to decision making, has the potential to make available to the team a range of different perspectives to inform decisions and to require the team to think more critically about issues that it may be taking for granted. What this highlights, then, are three critical factors contributing to a more effective discussion in an interprofessional team: access to members' differently positioned knowledge, which enables the generation of a range of both competing and complementary accounts of the client; the different accounts and questions that (potentially) team members are able to ask about the development of a team member's and the team's work with the client as a result of their different discipline-related perspectives; and the ways that the team works with these different knowledges about a client.

Difference Patterns and Increasing Subtlety of Vision
in Team Practices

In developing this association between the identification of difference patterns and engagement with the disciplinary differences within teams as relating to increased subtlety and effectiveness of their work, I go beyond the limitations of the concepts of "reflective practice" (Fook 1996) and "reflexivity" as constituting elements in effective professional work. Both words derive from the humanist tradition; both, as noted earlier, locate improved practice as a result of individuals' self-awareness and self-consciousness about the production of work (Myerhoff and Jay 1982); both then foreground the (autonomous) individual as the site of improved practice, a focus that excludes attention, in a team context, on how discipline-generated competing accounts of the proper focus of work to be undertaken are managed and on how the agreed team goals (to which members contribute) drive individual practice.

A consequence of conceptualizing practitioners as autonomous individuals is that critiques of the work they perform can too easily be open to interpretation as personal criticism because it defines the individual rather than that person's location within discipline-specific knowledge and associated practices, as the primary source of authority. Such an approach may well seriously inhibit a member's or members' efforts to raise questions about the nature and effectiveness of the team's operations. Instead, defining professional behaviors as the discursively structured outcomes of their particular disciplines assists in depersonalizing a critique. It also foregrounds differences between accounts of a client provided by different team members as both inevitable and desirable because each discipline draws on differently structured knowledge, is informed by different assumptions, and has different modes of responding to a problem.

For example, a number of members in one team commented to me about their annoyance at a social worker's lack of input to team reviews. Their tendency was to represent her behavior as a personal affront and as involving a deliberate refusal to share her information with the team. This notion of a deliberate withholding of information was strengthened by the very minimal notes in the social work section of patients' files about the work she was doing. There was, however, an acknowledgment that in one-to-one situations with more senior staff the worker did talk more fully and helpfully about her assessment of patients' situations. Nonetheless, the dominant account of her performance in the team setting drew on a not uncommon representation of the uncertain value of social work per se.

The social worker herself produced a rather more complex account of her behavior, underscoring her interpellation in discourse and how that structured the presentation of her work to the team. A key tenet within social work relates to the maintenance of client confidentiality. She was aware that she worked in a setting where gossip was rife (a factor also confirmed by some other members of the team). Knowing how much to say and when to say it was therefore a constant problem, given her professional commitment to this value position. She assumed, erroneously, that other team members were aware of this constraint. A further complicating factor in the dominant representation circulating in the team about the "silent and unhelpful worker" was the fact that a review of the minutes of the team discussions against the transcripts of the team meetings indicated that when she did comment on work she was doing with clients or on issues relating to those clients, her comments were never recorded and so became inaccessible to the team. Here, then, the marginalization of social work in medical settings was being played out and (unintentionally) perpetuated by current team practices. Her "silence" was not just an issue for her individually to attend to reflectively or reflexively. Instead it raised significant questions about different disciplines' and the team's management of the question of client confidentiality and the effects of those differences in a context where clients' privacy was a constant issue, and it raised questions about the team's minutes takers' decisions about what was important and should be recorded.

Donna Haraway, in her invigorating discussion of Boyle's invention of the vacuum pump and the lacunae of much of Western scientific epistemology, is critical of the term *reflexivity*. In the context of a discussion of Woolgar's epistemological critique, she writes of his "relentless insistence on reflexivity, which seems not to be able to get beyond self-vision as the cure for self-invisibility. The disease and the cure seem to be practically the same thing, if what you are after is another kind of world or worldliness. Diffraction, the production of difference patterns, might be a much more useful metaphor for the needed work than reflexivity" (Haraway 1997b:33–34).

She takes this notion further: "Diffraction is a mapping of inference, not of replication, reflection, or reproduction. A diffraction pattern does not map where differences appear, but rather maps where the effects of difference appear. Tropically . . . the first invites the illusion of an essen-tial, fixed position, while the second trains us to a more subtle vision" (cited in Soja 1996:116).

If I place this quote against the account developed above about the social worker's and the team's management of client confidentiality, then in the context of the production of a more diffracted practice, two things would happen. First, a question about her silence would not remain unasked. Nor would such a question be stated only as "What stops this person from providing a fuller account of her work?," although that could well be a starting point for, say, the leader to take up. A more diffracted practice would recognize the contextual and discursive nature of all behav-ior. The team's inquiry would both address its own processes in relation to confidentiality and go beyond eliciting fairly general statements about dif-ferent professions' relation to this ethic, for such a general focus would at best provide an outline only of "fixed" positions.

A more diffracted practice would require the team to focus on the out-come of this inquiry for its work, identifying the breadth of the team, the different concepts of confidentiality circulating among team members and the different ethnic groups with whom the team worked, and the ways in which such differences could be properly managed. Discussion of these factors would also need to be placed alongside the actual practices around confidentiality that existed at that site and how, as a result of its work, the team sought to redefine its practices around confidentiality. Diffraction, then, incorporates the issue of self-awareness, with its internal/inward focus, to emphasize simultaneously the outer-directedness of a "diffracted" gaze and to highlight the association between effectiveness and positive engagement with the inferences of difference.

One aspect of a diffracted process, developed in subsequent chapters, focuses on how team members engage with the different knowledges rep-resented in (and beyond) the team.[4] The focus of this chapter, however, works with the concept of diffraction in relation to developing, evaluating, and changing mundane ways of conceptualizing teamwork. I suggest that effective teamwork is embedded in attention to difference and to the effects of that difference—in other words, what it becomes possible to say when not just the fact of difference is acknowledged but also its implica-tions are engaged with. A team wishing to review its effectiveness and explore different practices must, however, first self-consciously entertain the possibility that its current practices and assumptions may be constrain-ing. Only then will it be in a position to attend to the possibilities of working differently. Qualitatively, diffracted practices are suggestive of fluidity, lightness, and openness (Calvino 1988), in contrast to what can be powerful discursive constraints working against changing practices. Such constraints are all too real in the absence of professionals' awareness of their own discursive production, the lack of organizational knowledge and expectations about teamwork, and the absence of mechanisms for reviewing team practices.

Producing More Diffracted Work: Assessing the Constraints of a Supportive Team Ethos

The texts from which I build this account of the possibility of production of diffracted practice were marginal in more than one sense of the word. First, the texts were produced by seven or eight speakers, each of whom believed both that his or her commentary would be regarded as heretical by the other members of the team and that consequently the issues he or she raised would be extremely difficult to insert into practice although, contradictorily, all were members of disciplines with high professional status. Second, despite the fact that the majority of these speakers were representatives of disciplines with high institutional status and two of them held senior positions within their services, their status and that of their disciplines *within* their teams were not uniformly highly valued by all members.

The particular value of these texts is that they provide reasonably extensive, thoughtful commentary on the need for changing team practices and, with different degrees of directness, they collectively point toward some of the initial qualities necessary to the production of a more diffracted practice: a certain disenchantment with current practices, a questioning of the familiar and taken-for-granted, a preparedness for uncertainty, and a need for speculation and attention to implications of what is known, in order to arrive at a "more subtle vision."

They also attest to the complications in so doing. My interviews with these respondents provided them with occasions to voice doubts that they could not voice within the team setting. One said:

> The more I seem to talk about this {in the interview context} the more I
> I think we have to actually review what we are doing (mm) and and
> *again*/ because this is a process that's been done before (*softly*) and *again*
> actually/ *formalize* and operationalize aah . what the roles are within
> that meeting because . . in the three or four meetings now that I've been

at I've had a sense that . . that (*sigh*) that things are just kind of drifting and decisions aren't . (mm) so much being made (*louder*) and/ I, it's started to take, take some definite shape with me. I *initially* thought that it just reflects the patient population that we have at the moment but I'm not sure any more (*softly*) and that I think it's an area that/ it's a meeting that will need rejuvenation.

Collectively, these texts attested to the ease of going along with (and thereby blunting one's critical tendencies) rather than challenging the team's culture and practices. They underlined the perceived difficulties in breaking familiar flows and inserting different practices. These speakers assumed that presenting a critique of their team's work to that team would result in other members' distress and anger and in their being ostracized, and one considered that to do so would possibly result in having to seek alternative employment. To speak was to risk marginalization, if not exclusion—powerful reasons for remaining silent, although to do so meant the loss of opportunities to build alliances with (silent/silenced) others who had similar concerns.

Changing practices is not easy. It involves thinking differently about the management and production of familiar processes. The problem confronting these team members was how to introduce the possibilities of alternative practices and critique of current practices without such efforts being defined by other team members as "unsupportive" or self-interested. The ease with which such accounts can be produced foregrounds the necessity of rethinking much more critically how the concept of "support" is used in teamwork and the extent to which the conventional notion of the "supportive team" may inhibit the production of more-effective team practices.

In a difficult work environment and in the context of demanding work, it was hardly surprising that a number of team members stressed the value of a supportive team. In these texts, "support" was typically associated with actions such as the affirmation of the value of members' work and effort in a difficult work environment. At first blush, the following quote from an interview with a nurse manager could be read in this context.

I think, yeah, I think *there are areas of frustration* with me with the multi-disciplinary team in that um . sometimes I feel that ah, they don't have a clear appreciation of what it's like to work with a client 24 hours a day, and *I don't believe* that the nursing staff get the recognition that they deserve . and *if they do* that's normally because in that forum I will *say,* "Sally, you're doing a *really good* job with this client" and *then* the MDT will come forward and say, "Oh well yes you are, Sally" but *it normally comes from me* and that makes me angry *and I also believe at times* the multi-disciplinary team comes *in* and they have expectations—you know this needs to happen and this needs to happen, this needs to happen and *it all relates* to resourcing and *they don't have an appreciation of the amount* of time that it takes to resource these things and the amount of *energy* it takes to manoeuvre people around. So those/those will probably be the most . frustrating things for me (mm) in the MDT and that if we *book* a case conference like we did with P13 last week and then all of a sudden we only had one person turn up for that case conference that to me is just not on in that *I ensure* that the nursing staff *do their reports/* do their presentation and then we have people drift in with nothing and I mean *basically* those reports are supposed to be out a week in advance so that we don't *waste* time talking about the reports. People will have *already* read them and we're there to do the business and ah/ that doesn't happen.

In this extract, the speaker seemingly accesses a highly conventional notion of support that refers to the need for sensitivity to and respect for others, team recognition of the value of others' work, doing the necessary preparation in time, and, overall, attending to the quality of interpersonal team relations.

Let me, however, in the context of interrogating the notion "support," take the argument a step further. As it happened, the question of the rescheduled case conference came up in the following team meeting in an angry exchange between this speaker and another speaker, with the former refusing to change the date for another conference to suit the second member. Since she gave no reasons for her insistence that the date not be changed, it was easy for others, as she was well aware, to personalize the issue (speaker as typically "difficult"/business as usual). Taking this approach allowed other team members to continue to ignore how their joint behaviors contributed to and were the outcome of their joint discursive practices that wrote nurses as less important than other clinical staff and, despite being central to the provision of care, as paradoxically marginal to the team. Personalizing the issue also meant that the procedural and team issues become difficult to discuss. A fuller reading of this statement goes well beyond the question of clinicians' praise for the nursing staff.

What was more at stake was the need to rewrite the discursively structured professional (not personal) relationships within the team, and in the process access a far more complex, a more diffracted account of "a supportive team" than is encompassed in "being nice" or "friendly."

There is a strong association between support and affirmation. As the marginal texts demonstrated, to ask a team member about his or her actions or direction of work, and to raise questions about implications of intersections of different speakers' accounts and the adequacy of team processes, met with a certain degree of resistance, despite the fact that such processes are integral to the development of more diffracted and more effective work.

Theoretically, of course, teams are sites where questions can be asked. In practice, in the teams in the research (and, it would seem, in other teams [Solomon and Mellor 1992]), things were not so straightforward because questions that required a professional response tended instead to be heard as personal criticism. This made discussions of what constituted legitimate professional behavior and expectations difficult. One team member said:

> There's so much time-wasting involved and, and, ah to deliver the best product to the client decisions have got to be made/ decisions have got to be made aah in good time and the multi-disciplinary team (mm) approach as practised here and everywhere else—I have been involved with mainly overseas but in other places in New Zealand as well—aah, there's ah, there's very much a a sense of not wanting to tread on people's toes . and not wanting to *push* other people in the team to do their job aah, aah *well* and in good time so that even when aah, *goals* have been set that are specific for a particular therapist or the doctor or the nurses and they haven't been met there's/ there's very little aaah, aah *driving* them to say, you know, "This is an unacceptable mode of working."

AO Why do you think that is?

RESPONDENT Ah (*sigh*) . . well that's the sort of socialism kind of thing that you know/ socialism of the *worst kind* where you, you don't want to personally offend people who are/ are/ are an important part of your working environment and ah . in this particular *team* model as soon as you get personality clashes you know the whole thing becomes very very ah/ can become very unpleasant aah and so everybody sort of tippy toes around any aah/ major personality conflicts aah/ and nobody wants to make decisions that they know are going to be *controversial* within the team because there is this *feeling* that the decision has to be unanimous that there can't be a sort of *majority* decision and/aah as you've seen in some of the meetings.

And he commented later:

I find that a major problem you know/ I work with other teams *where* aah there's been *much more* um/ sort of *empowerment* of the people, the individuals in the teams to/ to say, you know, "*I'm* the case manager for this particular . person (mm) and ah/ ah *my* efficiency as case manager will be determined by the/the product that that we provide in terms of *speed* of getting the person through the system and eventually how well they do in the community," and it's a combination of the two things "and so I'm going to make *sure* that everybody . *else* in this team ah pulls their weight for my particular patient," (mm) and if it doesn't *happen* then, then you know there's a stand up row in the meetings and that can be a very *positive* thing. But *here* it's seen as ah/ ah you know, "Ooh, you know, not nice" and, and we've got a small team and we haven't got any obvious *replacements*. You know it's not as though we've got a *pool* of people that you—if the social worker aah gets you know aah their nose badly out of joint because the speech language therapist has had a go at them in the meeting then they're the only speech language therapist and social worker we've got (mm mm) and the, you can't have ah, yeah you know those two people not talking to each other and so, you know you've got to have the *right environment* to allow a bit of ah . aggro in/ in the meetings but that it's *expressed* and that everybody understands that that *expression* is/ ah *aimed* at giving a good product for the client and the provider because they will audit the performance ah, and it's *not personal* and that could work in a team environment.

Concerns about the downside of even minimally challenging other team members (and therefore risking being seen as "unsupportive") were also noted by three other speakers, all of them experienced workers. One considered that any criticism of a colleague's work would result in a damaged relationship and a future lack of cooperation. The second found asking questions about the team's actions and its role a destructive experience that left her uncertain about the point of putting herself on the line again:

A couple of months before you joined us here I went through a period where I was feeling that I was *raising* things and it was falling *completely* on deaf ears and I thought *either* I'm seeing this from a/ I've actually got rose-tinted spectacles and there's something wrong with my *vision* here or they're *all* out to get me (*laughs*) or or something and I find that I then don't deal with it because I get too sensitive and I actually feel quite tearful so I back off sort of so I'll just, I just do not bother to say anything.

And, in a different team, a worker commented on how, by associating questioning with aggression, her team's culture suppressed it:

We had *one occasion* about two years ago when, well it was one and a half years ago when one of the/ a senior person who's no longer *here* (. . .) she addressed this issue in the team context but she did it in such a way that it wasn't necessarily sophisticated but she sort of said a lot of the things like what are you saying, "Why are you saying this?; what's this got to do with anything?" as regards one client and nothing ever came of that really but it made a ***very interesting meeting*** (*laughing*), a tension-filled meeting.

A senior member of one team where there was almost no discussion in team reviews of what work members were undertaking with their clients assumed that questions he might want to ask about each team member's work focus could easily be deemed superfluous (or, perhaps worse, "unsophisticated") by his colleagues, and that the key worker, who by dint of being in that role would be expert, fully knowledgeable, and in frequent contact with the client, would obviously be aware of the relevant issues, even though these were not spelled out in meetings. These assumptions considerably constrained his behavior and undercut a significant part of the rationale for interprofessional teamwork, reducing what might be thought to be a key dimension of such work to the level of nuisance value (almost reflecting the concern about "uninformed" comments/questions raised by another speaker on this team). Further, the act of questioning could too easily be interpreted as being overbearing and implying another's incompetence. He said:

I find that {this assumption} really frustrating actually because then I *try and find other ways of getting round that and it doesn't work*. In fact/ in fact I should bite the bullet a bit more and just face, just say/ well okay I mean I, I don't mean to be *rude* about it but I, I still need to be forth-right (mm) and clear about, about the need to do that.

A further implication here is that one is vulnerable not only when being questioned but in the very act of questioning (an act during which it could be assumed that one is occupying a more powerful position). Questions may be responded to as self-evident and as unnecessary, so implying stupidity or ignorance on the part of the questioner. The implications of such comments in constructing the notion "professional" are antithetical to its more common representation as knowledgeable, in control, and con-fident. The professional body that is written in these textual segments is a body that is vulnerable, unable to defend its right to ask about work details, ready to act punitively if challenged by a colleague, and unable to hold the line between professional need for accountability and personal discomfort.

What these few texts highlighted was that a particular ethos about "support" acted to considerably constrain a key professional activity affect-ing professional accountability to the team and the team's ability to engage more fully with its members' individual and collective knowledge about a client. Such constraints could compromise client care, care that profession-als have a major responsibility to advance. The last speaker quoted above also said:

I mean we should be a *safe* environment to say, say what you *think* um in a way that isn't going to be perceived as *attacking* type of thing because that that's basically what what's happening is that people are feeling defensive, feeling they're being criticized (*softly*) that someone's having a go at them and, and responding and then you kind of get them behind these, their collective trenches (*louder*) and yeah so I mean I do think that that is a problem and in that meeting at the moment and I don't think the quality of information exchanged and the decisions made are *quite there*.[5] I think also there's a/ I mean there's *a real* frustra-tion/ at . . the lack of *turnover* and progress of some of the patients . . (. . .) . . . I mean with the systems problems that we often/ often have/ have no control over and I also have the sense that that *at times* . . . because we attempt to provide such good and comprehensive care here and have a real sense that we can do that better than anyone else because we have the expertise and the resources that other inpatient units just don't *have* that sometimes we get a little too carried away with it and become rather too enmeshed in our relationships with our patients and don't/ and see them as *belonging* to us and (*softly*) not wanting to let them go (*louder*) and oh in fact I think with that several of the patients that has happened. Their treatment has moved from being intensive . and *therapeutic* to being intensive and *intrusive* and somewhat toxic and actually P4 is a good example of that. An *exceptionally* complicated person, *very difficult* to deal with, has generated *huge* splits and I really think we should be stepping/ going stepping *right back* and and *really* looking at what we're all doing in there but that . in terms of safety I have tried/ I'm kind of stuck. Moved down that path a little just to sound out the water (*softly*) but I haven't said anything too directly because I don't think that that would be heard.

Rethinking the "Supportive" Dimension of Teamwork

While it is important not to assume that the responsibility for a lack of progress with clients who have extremely complex and entrenched histories lies entirely with staff (or is the fault of the client unwilling/unable to change), nonetheless, this speaker identified some key issues in the development of more effective and more diffracted team processes contributing to knowledge-based teamwork. His and others' commentary questioning the weight given by their teams to being "supportive" and emphasizing the need for professional accountability (even if they felt unable to demand it) highlights the organizational objective for quality teamwork as being the professional development, monitoring, and tracking of case plans in the delivery of quality and timely care to clients. Equally, this commentary collectively writes effective teamwork as a site of professional questioning and interchange, not just of affirmation of other team members. This emphasis is offered very precisely in a sentence from the above quotation, "and I really think we should be stepping/ going stepping *right back* and and *really* looking at what we're all doing in there," a comment echoed by a colleague:

> I think that at the moment that you know one of the problems has been that there are so many back/back seat drivers that we all end up talking about the scenery you know, "Oh aren't the trees nice" and . *almost* as a response to to *not having* to think about you know, "Where the hell are we actually going and where is this car off to?"

In contrast to this more pointed critique, most team members in the study defined team objectives in terms of discussing clients and developing care plans through processes of information sharing. That is, in the context of a supportive (unquestioning) environment, each professional would tell the others what he or she had been doing, comment on changes in the client's circumstances, or "contribute" in some less well-defined way to the discussion about a client. There was some emphasis, especially from the designated team leaders, on the setting of time frames. What team members generally did not discuss in the course of the individual interviews that I conducted with them was what constituted "information" and how different or competing informational accounts could be managed, issues that I take up in greater detail in the next two chapters.

What was missing from these majority accounts, however, was the points highlighted by the two quotes above that emphasize key components of effective teamwork. The difference between the mode of teamwork sketched out by these texts and the very general notions around "telling" in a supportive team context is substantial. These texts underline key components of knowledge-based teamwork. They assume that effective teamwork legitimately involves questioning about the direction and objective of members' work with a client and how such work relates to the agreed-upon wider team objective(s) for that client. In other words, effective teamwork involves a collective "standing back" and professional assessment of what each team member working with a particular client is doing, how that person's input is contributing to the overall team goal with that particular client, and what the implications of the collective team issues in working with that client are. Moving toward more diffracted (and professionally accountable) teamwork requires in the first instance understanding that the provision of some account from members as to the orientation of their work, the problems encountered and how these are being addressed, and how the team members are evaluating progress is necessary for informing the team's decision-making processes. Conceptualizing teamwork in this fashion substantially displaces the focus on the team as the site of largely unquestioning support and foregrounds the organizational and professional objective for teamwork.

"Decision making" also highlights how part of the team's responsibility is to continually and critically evaluate the information presented to it, and the need for an agreed-upon, transparent process about *how* the team formulates its plans. Without a means by which the team stands back from the day-to-day routines and minutiae of care, its evaluation of direction, team practices, and individual work may become routine, if not lacking in accountability. What rushed teams are likely to attend to is the more easily noticed—that is, what is typical and familiar. In contrast, the factors of difference and the effects of difference in structuring work and producing nuanced accounts of client need and the work to be undertaken, attending to the material outcomes of the teams' modes of representation of their clientele, and establishing individual and team goals, are easily marginalized (Opie 1997). This is despite the fact that noting and responding to such factors is crucial to change and to the production of effective teamwork.

> it's . . it it's kind of difficult because some people have been here for so long and and of course what *initially* happens is that they *do* get a very good assessment and that's, that assessment may have different disciplines in it but but they will be *all together* at the *beginning* if any decision's made about the management of them too if that's necessary and sometimes it isn't. But if it/ *that happens*—but *then* what kind of happens is you kind of get into this *routine* of of various—whoever's been allocated certain tasks . focusing on that area and and things are not coming back together again (yeah) so well because you *get used* to seeing what you're seeing with these individual patients and and you get to know *that* bit of them and you know sort of *miss* the ways in which it could change and move so I think it's actually, um, a difficult task to to keep doing that um, and to keep pulling the those disparate . bits back together.

"Standing back" carries two further implications. One of the putative strengths of an interprofessional team is that it enables the production of a range of different, discipline-informed views on a client's situation. On one plane there is a question of how the team works with and manages its internal differences, what disciplines' perspectives are privileged, and so forth. But there is also a further question about what knowledge team members have of each other's disciplinarily informed assumptions and work practices, knowledge that is valuable if members are to make connections between their work and the work of others. Is it, then, enough for one member to regard another's commentary about a client as "background" or is a more active engagement with that commentary necessary? If someone from one discipline is to make sense of another's modes of working, then something of how that work is being conducted needs to be displayed (though without the discussion of confidential material).

In one team a nurse remarked on the helpfulness of some members involving her in their work with patients. It was in this context that she learned about their discipline and what they were attempting to do with the client, and that information enabled her work potentially to intersect better with theirs and to be more informed. Without this joint involvement, such learning could come only through what was said about that work at meetings. She could not always attend team meetings because a specified number of staff had to "be on the floor" at any given time. She noted that it had taken her about eighteen to twenty-four months to more fully understand the role and contribution of one key discipline to patient care because that discipline's representative had not involved the nurse in her work and did not discuss in meetings what work she was undertaking with clients.

Comments such as these point to the inadequacy of a model of team learning about others' work that assumes some sort of osmotic learning process through "being part of the team." They underscore the necessity for proper organizational and team attention to the processes by which clients' issues are presented to and discussed by the team during its reviews, and how the development of members' knowledge about the work of different disciplines represented on the team cannot be left to chance.

In reflecting on the issues around how members, practicing in disciplines with highly complex theoretical structures, should present their work to the team, and the processes by which team members outside of such disciplines make or do not make sense of such disciplinarily structured commentary, one person noted:

> I think that/ it's a . . (*sigh*) *what concerns me* about the use of the word "inappropriate" is is . just what you *said* that it, it's a suitcase word and *in my view **all behavior*** has meaning and we actually need to *know* what the behavior *is* before we can say whether *it might still be appropriate* but *is it* comprehensible? Can it be *understood in* any context? Can we *create* between us a context which which which makes the behavior understandable?

And he said later:

> I have struggled for a long time about how to present {my discipline} um and have recently made some proposals to {a senior team member} that will take care of some of it—like, I suppose I, I should have done it a long time before but I couldn't quite see how I could productively do

that. *If people don't know* what . what the values and and beliefs *are* and
what the working systems are that you're coming from they can't *really*
make um real assessments about the—they tend to make *judgements*
about what you're saying, the value of what you're saying *based* on their
own knowledge of their own professional um position and it—you see
because we're talking about the same person because we're talking about
P9 for example it *ought to be possible/* to have . a *variety of views* of him: a
nursing view, a psychologist view, a psychiatric view and so forth and so
on which can actually *cohere.* It can come together in some coherent
way and that/ the *knowledge* of those other views helps to *expand* your
own understanding of your *own* bit but it also fills in a lot of the stuff.

These comments highlight some of the key issues necessary to the
development of interprofessional work, articulating as they do a team practice where differences between disciplines are out in the open and where
engagement and productive work with difference and difference effects
constitute a valuable dimension of the team's working discussions. Further,
the above statement also raises the question of tacit knowledge and its relationship to practice, and how that informs actions. Knowledge-based
teamwork in part requires the articulation of tacit knowledge. Therein lies
the rub. Part of the difficulty of making tacit knowledge explicit is its tacit-
ness, its unspokenness in informing professional micropractices in ways
that therefore go largely unquestioned. The complication, however, is that
the processes of professional learning involve the explicit identification
and then internalization of powerful professional values and behaviors that
powerfully assert *the* truth (not *a* truth) from each discipline's perspective
of the way the world is. Alternatively, knowledge-based work requires continued consciousness about construction of professional subjectivities
within particular discipline-related discourses and the incompleteness of
all disciplines' claims to truth in order to remain open to and engage with
other disciplines' (partial) truths and their difference effects in the production of more diffracted team practices.

Rewriting Leadership

If an interprofessional team is to become a site of more diffracted work, the
leadership role must be conceptualized differently than was demonstrated
in any of the teams in the study, where this concept remained poorly developed. There was some uncertainty among some members about whether

their team had a leader (and, if so, who?), as well as some dissatisfaction, especially at two sites, about the absence of control over the meeting's structure and over some members' behavior. These comments reinforced the general absence at these sites of organizational and team protocols and procedures necessary to achieve acceptable team behaviors and decision-making processes (Abramson 1989).

At all three sites, members described key leadership responsibilities largely in terms of an administrative focus including the following: ensuring that all clients were reviewed; establishing time frames and goals; monitoring and challenging team behaviors (lateness, talking between members, conflict management); maintaining the focus of the discussion (not letting members drift on); identifying issues to which team members needed to respond to ensure that these did not get lost as the discussion developed; and representing the team within and beyond the organization. A few members referred to the leader's role in ensuring that all members participated. As the texts of the team reviews demonstrate, however, leaders typically did not exercise many of the responsibilities outlined above with any degree of consistency, and some areas of responsibility were never attended to in the meetings I observed.

I want now to place this somewhat limited and administratively focused definition of leadership circulating within the teams against some recent alternative conceptualizing in the organizational literature about the team leader's role. Katzenbach and Smith (1993) have consistently stressed the notion of *performance.* Teams are, they argue, a means to achieving a higher level of organizational performance. They are not an end in themselves. "Organizational leaders can foster team performance best by building a strong performance ethic, rather than establishing a team-promoting environment alone" (13). The leader's focus is on team performance, and not on being a team. Teams are "*discrete units of performance, not a positive set of values*" (21). Discipline is important. A team becomes a team as a consequence of "*disciplined action.* They *shape* a common purpose, *agree* on performance goals, *define* a common working approach, *develop* high levels of complementary skills, and *hold* themselves mutually accountable for results" (14-15).

Placed in this context, the relationships among team, organization, and quality performance become explicit, thus requiring an adequate account of team leadership as one that attends to more than primarily administrative issues; neither is it sufficient to position the leader as "expert," nor, in a health care context, is it appropriate for the leadership role to be seen as the perogative of a particular discipline. The concept of leadership is shifting toward one that defines leaders as facilitators and nurturers (Senge 1990; Whiteley 1995). Within learning organizations, leadership involves challenging members' mental maps and working with the team to develop more systematic, analytic, and strategic ways of thinking. The leader's role, then, is crucially associated with the identification of different dominant mental models, discourses, the modes of representation circulating in the team, and their differences and difference effects. Leadership in an interprofessional knowledge-based team, therefore, focuses on leaders' abilities to encourage the team to think through *as a team* the professional issues with which they are confronted in a context where the "truth" does not adhere to any one discipline, where the intersection of each discipline's partial truths about the client assists with the production of informed, effective plans and actions.

Starting with the proposition that diffraction—that is, attending to difference and the effects of difference—is central to the production of knowledge-based teamwork, much of the work of this chapter focuses on three elements bearing on this mode of operation. First, I have suggested that the appropriate objective of an interprofessional team discussion is to bring into play and work with the range of discipline-informed perspectives about clients circulating in a team. As it happened, the teams in the study did in fact produce a number of different perspectives in their team meetings. The problem lay in the fact that these perspectives were largely ignored or, alternatively, that the effect of a discussion was to discount one representation and valorize another.

It could also be argued that the development of more diffracted team practices in teams located in organizations facing reduced or zero funding is too time-consuming and cannot be afforded. However, many very lengthy "discussions" of clients, as is demonstrated in subsequent chapters, did not focus on professional accountability to the team or result in a clearly understood course of action specifying the roles of the participating disciplines. My assertion is that working knowledgeably would in many instances be not more time-intensive but less so and would result in much higher degrees of accountability to the client, the team, and the organization.

Second, I have demonstrated how writing teamwork as a site of interprofessional inquiry and accountability foregrounds the significance of questioning members about the work they are doing and the relationship of that work to clients, families, and other members' objectives and the team goals; further, this representation of teamwork marginalizes accounts that privilege teams as sites of interpersonal support. This work requires the maintenance of professional relationships among team members, in part through a recognition of the incompleteness of the account of a client contained within their own discipline and the importance of other (partial) accounts if the team is to discharge its work effectively.

Third, writing teams as primarily contributing to organizational performance not only heightens the relationship between diffraction and interprofessional accountability but also involves a rewriting of the notion of leadership to underscore the leader's role in developing teams' systematic and analytical skills.

Developing more diffracted practices, then, relies on a complex intersection of envisaging and then speaking out difference within a team culture that, contrary to the dominant cultures that existed within these teams, accepts and apprehends working with difference and difference effects as critical to effective work. Equally, teams' articulation of difference/change depends on (health care) organizations' recognizing that effective teamwork requires the intersection of teams' intellectual and disciplinary capital and ensuring that training programs attend to the development of this critical dimension. In the next two chapters these issues are revisited and developed further through analyses of transcripts of the study teams' reviews and meetings and through bringing rhizome theory and narrative theory into play.

6

"We Talk About the Patients and Then We Have Coffee"

Making and Shaping Team Discussions

Mapping Knowledge-Based Team Discussions

The team meeting is the occasion where members formally meet to exchange information and knowledge about clients, and discuss and confirm ongoing plans for their care. Because much of the team literature has focused on team dynamics, there has been comparatively little attention in the past to examining how teams go about their work by analyzing transcripts of team reviews or discussions (but see Gubrium 1980). More recently, however, a number of authors have produced discussions of teamwork that draw on such evidence. For example, Roberta Sands (1993) discusses the ways in which an interdisciplinary team allocated tasks and negotiated disciplinary boundaries. Marleen McClelland and Roberta Sands (1993) have commented on the ways in which the absence of a particular discipline's representation on a team can mean that significant areas of teamwork will not be addressed. Paul Atkinson (1995) has developed a detailed account of the ways in which medical team meetings are engaged in a process of learning and knowledge transfer, and Lesley Griffiths (1997) has commented on how different work practices contribute to different modes of accomplishing teamwork, some of which may be organizationally contraindicated. None of this research, however, investigates how an effective team discussion is constituted and what its distinguishing features are.

In her article on interdisciplinary teamwork in a child assessment team developing a comprehensive assessment plan for a new client, Sands

(1993:551) described the three major components of this team's discussion as:

- Identification of the client's major problems;
- Identification of members' objectives to be achieved in their evaluations of the client; and
- The formation of a plan for achieving each objective (that is, the plan would define which discipline was responsible for each part of the assessment).

The team discussion that Sands reported on took sixty-seven minutes. Sands described it as constituted by processes that on one plane suggest focused and purposive teamwork, involving:

- A detailed case presentation (twenty minutes)
- Questions from team members (five minutes)
- Creation of problem list by the group (twenty minutes)
- Discussion and editing of problems (three minutes)
- Identification of objectives to be met in the assessment process (thirteen minutes)
- Further discussion and completion of the plan (six minutes).

In her analysis of this team discussion, though, Sands focused on only one of these tasks: the processes involved in the identification and clarification of members' tasks and objectives, in the context of a new member joining the team and the team's response to that event. The phrase *identification of objectives* suggests a relatively simple and straightforward task. Sands's analysis, however, points to a complex and somewhat fraught process, highlighting members' protective management and control of discipline-specific boundaries and the absence of much collaborative activity as members sought to assert their disciplinary autonomy and promote and protect their areas of work.[1] The fact that such difficulty was experienced in one area of collaborative work raises major questions about how, in practice, teams effectively manage or perform other dimensions of their role.

Sands did not attempt in this article to analyze all the processes of the teamwork that she had identified. Even remaining within her focus, however, she raises a number of questions. While the team involved in her research focused on determining members' individual tasks and objectives, Sands does not specifically mention how *team,* as distinct from individual members', goals were identified. Nor does she provide any indication of how knowledge other than professional knowledge entered the team discussions. Nothing in the transcript of the team's discussion that is included in the text of Sands's article addresses the family's role and relationship to the team's work, and Sands herself does not comment on this issue.

In quoting one member's highly succinct and certainly not inaccurate statement, "We talk about the patients and then we drink coffee," produced by a member of one of the teams in my research as an account to a new member of what happened in their meetings, I am signaling my intention to interrogate the constantly recurring verbs *talk* and *discuss* as sufficient descriptions of teamwork and to open for more intensive observation the (collapsed) space between "talk" (the point of production) and "coffee"(signaling the termination of that [productive] activity). My purpose, then, in this and the next two chapters is to discuss from different angles the rhetorical and purposive features of a more differentiated map of teamwork than that produced by Sands. These three chapters are intended to complement each other, addressing the same theme (the development of knowledge-based work) but working from different perspectives.

The map that informs my discussion extensively in this chapter and the next is specifically intended to enable teams to develop effective, knowledge-based team reviews of clients whose situations are complex, and to provide a basis for reviewing their teamwork processes. It is constructed from my observations of teamwork in the course of the fieldwork and from my analysis of the transcripts of team reviews. In contrast to Sands's brief phrases describing the discrete elements of the interdisciplinary team's review processes, the constituting features of the map I sketch here are described in some detail because relying on very short phrases would obscure the distinctiveness, complexity, and objective of each feature. These features, then, are:

- A focused orientation or introduction to each client which informs and to some extent therefore structures the ensuing discussion;
- The production of knowledge spirals through discussion of the focus and development of work with that client;
- Identification and recording of issues, and members' tasks and goals, in conjunction with an evolving *team* objective;

- A focused closure to the discussion, where the minutes taker checks that all issues and tasks, and the goals or objectives of both the team and each constituent discipline, which were identified in the preceding discussion, are written into the minutes and are confirmed by the team; and
- A continual engagement throughout the above process with the knowledge and perspectives of clients and families, including their inflection by ethnicity and cultural difference.

There are some significant differences between this map and Sands's description of the processes of the interdisciplinary team review that she analyzed. As with the features of that interdisciplinary team discussion, so too my map of knowledge-based teamwork has its more linear, task-oriented and problem-solving features. Teams, after all, have a highly specific task to perform. Interwoven with these task-oriented features, however, are significant process-oriented ones referring to two interrelated dimensions. One refers to how the team engages with its knowledge—specifically, how the team goes about accessing and then working with the range of knowledge about a client generated by different disciplinarily informed perspectives *and* the perspectives held by clients and/or families. It therefore writes questioning by members of each other, and commentary on input and the implications of that input, as critical to the development of diffracted knowledge and the production of purposive, effective team meetings.

The second dimension attends to the process of the discussion itself. It refers to what I am calling the "shape" of the discussion, that is, how knowledge-based discussions are not linear in their structure. Instead, they are recursive, folding back on themselves to pick up and develop significant issues from the perspectives of different disciplines, and then moving the discussion beyond discipline-specific foci; folding back also to return to issues that were raised earlier but were not at that point taken up or further developed. The visual representation of such a knowledge-based team discussion is a spiral, not a straight line. This recursive process is likely to be more apparent during the discussion of the focus and development of work with the client. It is not, however, restricted to that phase but should occur in different degrees of intensity during all phases.

The map I have developed of effective knowledge-based teamwork, then, recognizes the organizationally necessary objective of progressing the discussion: the discussion begins, issues are elaborated, the work and objectives are defined, the team's understanding of where they are at this point is confirmed/questioned/modified, the client's and family's perspectives are taken into account, tasks are allocated and recorded in the minutes, the team goal is modified if necessary, and the team moves on to discuss the next client. The process, however, is concerned also with *how* discussions develop—in other words, how the team "does" its work of talking and how it accesses and expands its collective knowledge. The delineation of the map's features constitutes one response to the question "What does an effective discussion look like?" What I am suggesting is that effective discussions of clients with complex situations require a structure that ensures that the discussion moves forward *and* allows for, indeed encourages, the interplay of information contributing to knowledge creation (the Text traverses [Barthes 1986]). While I have separated out these elements for analytic purposes, in practice they are intimately interrelated.

I have approached the discussion of the features of my map of effective teamwork in the following manner. First I discuss its theoretical aspect. The following section, "Shaping Team Discussions," focuses on Deleuze and Guattari's (1983) work on line theory and rhizomes, allowing me to theorize the "shape" of a knowledge-based discussion. The next section, "Working Knowledgeably," has four parts, with each part of the analysis drawing extensively on extracts from team reviews that I reproduce here. Each part attends to a specific feature of the map. It should be noted, however, that these parts are not presented as discrete from each other. The structure of the discussion (revisiting to some extent from a slightly different angle what has been covered *and* progressing the argument) itself picks up on the element of recursiveness that I am advancing as necessary to knowledge-based work.

The first part of this second section, "Providing the Team with a Focused Orientation or Introduction to the Client," analyzes an introduction to an elderly client with a progressive physical disability (P2) to demonstrate the value of beginning a team discussion with a clear focus on the key issues in relation to the client that the team needs to address. In the second part, "Spiraling Knowledge: Discussion and Development of the Issues," I continue the analysis of discussions of P2, focusing on how the team fails to attend to tensions between her (contradictory) reported objectives and the team's goal-setting activities, a discussion that also bears on issues of client/family inclusion in teamwork. (This feature is discussed in greater detail in chapter 8). The third part, "Strategies for Knowledge-Based Teamwork," touches upon and expands some of the issues addressed in the reviews of P2. It does so through analysis of discussions of different patients produced by the three inpatient teams and identifies discrete yet also overlapping strategies available to teams to assist in the production of knowledge-based work. These strategies, part of the second feature of the map sketched on page 141, require specific team behaviors: questioning/ elaborating/focusing, recognizing and managing difference, working toward disciplinary intersections, and theorizing the team's work. The first extract, about an elderly man (P34), demonstrates the development of a style of questioning/elaborating/focusing. The second extract, about a psychiatric patient (P9), identifies the different perspectives in the team about this patient and highlights the importance of explicit recognition of and then engagement with difference as necessary to knowledgeable teamwork. I continue to use segments of the psychiatric team's discussion of P9 to demonstrate how questioning allows for knowledge intersections between disciplines and how such work makes available knowledge that may well otherwise remain unelaborated. I foreground the value of (if not the necessity for) theorizing in order to move the team from an impasse. I indicate how, in instances such as this, theorizing could have allowed the production of a substantially different team discussion that more fully utilized members' knowledge and resulted in less polarization of members.

As its work with each client progresses, a knowledge-based team needs to develop and modify its initial objectives for that client. Development of such objectives is simultaneously a process, a strategy that assists the achievement of knowledge spirals, and a specific, discrete feature of the work of the team that is closely associated with its accountability. I use a team discussion about P37 (a middle-aged woman who had had a severe stroke) to address the issue of developing (changing) team objectives.

The final section, "Decision Making and Leadership in Knowledge-Based Teamwork," addresses decision-making processes and attends to the features of identification of the issues and a focused closure, placing them in the context of a discussion expanded from that presented in chapter 5 on leadership in knowledge-based teams. My discussion in this section draws on elements of the discussion of P9, addressing how a knowledge-based team could have approached their work differently with a client such as this.

Shaping Team Discussions

The argument informing this book is that effective interprofessional teamwork carried out in relation to clients with complex situations is knowledge-based. Developing such work is achieved through the presentation *and* intersection of the different knowledges of a client represented by the different disciplines in the team. Not only, then, does a team member present her/his account of a client but he/she takes active cognizance of how that account is open to modification, challenge, and extension from other discipline-specific perspectives and the perspectives of the client and family. This enables the team both to access and to make available to members the current relevant knowledge circulating about a client, so that the team has that knowledge and its implications to use in deciding about the direction of its work, who is to be involved, what the objectives will be and how these will intersect with and advance the team's and the client's objectives. Moreover, it is important to note that the team's understanding of these objectives may be modified as a result of each discussion.

If knowledge-based discussions are to achieve their objective, then the shape of these discussions requires some theorizing in order to foreground the importance of particular processes that inform the production of knowledge-based work. These processes include intersection, recursiveness, progression, and awareness of the margins, that is, of how comments that could easily pass unnoticed (and often do) may contribute substantially to how the team determines its work. Such discussions move in a process/shape of a complex spiral.

However, a linear structure to a discussion, and one that may well be familiar to team members because it occurs often enough in teams in health care, falls very much within the definition of multidisciplinary teamwork outlined in chapter 2. Person A speaks, followed by Persons B, C, D, and so on. Each identifies discipline-specific goals or tasks or says something briefly about his or her work with the client. There is little interaction between speakers. This type of discussion may well be sufficient in work with clients whose situations are not very complex, where things are moving forward well and the situation is such that little needs to be said on that particular occasion. It is, though, unlikely to produce effective teamwork when more intricate work is required to attend to more demanding situations.

The alternative nonlinear shape of discussions of complex work, focusing on knowledge intersections and interprofessional collaboration, is informed by Deleuze and Guattari's (1983) work on line theory and rhizomic structures, elements of which I present below. Conceptualizing the shape of a team discussion in terms of rhizomes assists in visualizing teamwork as a series of interconnecting, sinuous lines, reliant on both the production of information and the generation of questions about the professional work that is being carried out and how each member's work intersects with that of others, and with the goals of the team, the client, and the family. The processes of questioning and discussions that encourage interdisciplinary connections (including seeking connections in what may at first blush appear to be competing representations of clients and their situations) are critical to the production of knowledge-based work and the generation of knowledge spirals (Nonaka and Takeuchi 1995).

In the course of drawing the connections between Deleuze and Guattari's work and knowledge-based teamwork, I have outlined at different points in this book the type of questioning in which a knowledge-based team could engage. These questions demonstrate the conceptual (not interpersonal) work a knowledge-based team is required to undertake and illustrate such a team's orientation to its work. This mode of questioning, then, both informs the analysis I have developed of the team transcripts and demonstrates how shifting the parameters and focus of the team gaze assists in the production of knowledge-based discussions.

Rhizome Theory

Rhizomes challenge binary logic, the linearity of the tree (the dominant image in the intellectual tradition of the Western world), to engage with multiplicities and to encourage subversiveness and change. "As an underground stem," write Deleuze and Guattari (1983:10),

> a rhizome is absolutely distinct from roots and radicels. Bulbs and tubers are rhizomes. Plants with a root or a radicel can be rhizomorphic in all other respects. . . . Even some animals are rhizomorphic when they live in packs like rats. Burrows are rhizomorphic in all their functions: as habitat, means of provision, movement, evasion and rupture. In itself the rhizome has very diverse forms, from its surface extension which ramifies in all directions to its concretations into bulbs and tubers.

Rhizomes are points of connection and heterogeneity, where any point can connect with another. "This is very different from a tree or root, which fixes a point and thus an order" (11); rhizomes point to multiplicities; their lines can be cracked, but an alternative line can be followed. Maps are rhizomic.

The map is open, connectable in all its dimensions, and capable of being dismantled; it is reversible, and susceptible to constant modification. . . . Perhaps one of the most important characteristics of the rhizome is that it always has multiple entrances. . . . Contrary to a tracing, which always returns to the "same," a map has multiple entrances. A map is a matter of performance, whereas the tracing always refers to an alleged "competence."

(26)

In contrast to maps, arborescent systems "are hierarchical systems comprised of centers of significance . . . , of autonomous centers. . . . The corresponding models are such that an element receives information only from a superior unity . . . (36). In detailing the principal characteristics of a rhizome, Deleuze and Guattari note the shading of rhizomes into "root-trees" (46) and, in challenging the perpetuation of dualisms, they write of the rhizome "as a model that is ceaselessly set up and that collapses, of a process that ceaselessly extends itself, breaks off and starts again" (46). There are "plateaus" and "circles of convergence" (50) where seemingly disparate lines meet. The rhizome "is about alliance" and is "woven together with conjunctions: 'and . . . and . . . and'" (57).

In drawing this connection between rhizomes and teamwork, I am conceptualizing the disciplines within teams not as standing in a hierarchically ordered relationship to each other but as constituting multiple points of entry to issues associated with client care; the articulation of the discipline-specific knowledge as both connecting with and interrogating differently located knowledge held by a different discipline; those moments of convergence as enabling a focusing and/or development of the discussion in alternative directions; of team discussions as a fissured plane/plain where the representations of the client and the work undertaken by different disciplines within the team traverse and intersect (principles of "heterogeneity" and "connection"), not to cancel each other out or deny each other (a binary mode of doing things: this is better than that) but to engage with multiplicities: knowing this *and* this *and* this, how do we now think about this issue? If we follow this line/approach in relation to this theory, how might this structure our work? What happens if we follow a different (theoretical/practical) line/approach? How do we maintain this and this connection if this line is followed? What other lines/points of inquiry become available as a consequence of the conjunction of these knowledge lines? How does the conjunction of these lines change our relationship to particular ways of knowing?

A rhizomic discussion is not seduced by the familiar main highways crisscrossing plateaus; it will enter the bypaths, fissures, crevices as it traverses a plateau; it moves across a plane in different directions as a comment here enables a connection/challenge there or leads/circles back to an earlier point in the discussion. It is recursive *and* it moves on.

Rather than foregrounding the discipline-specific contribution to the team as the primary object of each member's "contribution," a rhizomic mapping of teamwork requires that contribution *and* equally places emphasis on attention to knowledge intersections between disciplines and to their modes of representation, as well as to the (different) knowledge of clients and families in order to develop new lines of inquiry and action. The emphasis on knowledge intersection points to the need for some elaboration of practice or principles to enable those members operating from a different knowledge base to identify points of intersection.

The work is not just about team members telling each other about clients and their situations but also about engaging and working with the different domains of knowledge represented by the team. A disagreement about a course of action to be taken can be worked on, not only on the basis of "What are we going to do with this client?" (a question that presumes a fairly immediate answer) but also on the basis of "What are the different discipline-specific and professional issues that are raised by work with this client? What do our different theoretical perspectives offer about working with these issues? If we are to follow this course of action, what may be the outcomes? What are the implications of thinking of the situation in these *and* these terms?" These questions foreground collaborative practical *and* more subtle conceptual or intellectual work. They point to lines of inquiry for a knowledge-based team to follow in order to answer the question "How does the team work with the differently located information and the knowledge that such information draws on and generates?"

In order to answer this key question, knowledge-based teamwork generates its own rules and expectations of members' behavior. Such work requires that members/teams:

- Provide a sufficient indication of the work they are undertaking to allow others to make connections to their work, to affirm what the other has observed and/or to raise questions about that work. This also includes ensuring that members have some understanding of the assumptions and practices of how each discipline defines its work;

- Respond or attend to the different knowledges and representations of the client/situation produced as a result of different disciplinary knowledge; and

- Engage with the implications of what has been said in terms of how this might reposition or reorient the work of the team, thereby allowing teams to attend to the implications of following different (theoretical/practical) lines of action in the development of team goals and decisions about the focus of members' individual work with the client/family.

This list of "team behaviors" foregrounds two major issues. First, it points to the necessity for teams not to develop, or fall back into, familiar knowledge hierarchies, in which the knowledge held by some disciplines is consistently privileged above that of others. Second, it emphasizes the organizational role in the production of knowledge-based work because such work requires members' induction and training. A knowledge-based team cannot function if there is not agreement and understanding about the process and how the process will be effected.

Working Knowledgeably

Providing the Team with a Focused Orientation or Introduction to the Client

The phrase *focused orientation* is not intended to refer to a uniform or prescriptive mode of introduction to (or reminding the team about) a client. A detailed case history and identification of problems or issues identified by the client and the worker may be appropriate when the team is beginning a discussion of a new client. However, introductions to a client are likely to take a different form as the team develops their work with that person, not least because the information presented would be contextualized by the team's evolving knowledge of the client and by team/client objective(s).

The primary objective of a focused orientation is to provide an answer to a question implicit in team reviews: "Why are we reviewing this client?" This question directs attention to various factors: the current issues to be addressed (what is/are the problem(s)?); the amount of progress (where have we got to?); and teams' and clients' objectives (what is the direction of this work and does this need revision?). The introduction, then, works recursively both to alert the team to past issues relevant to that client and to foreground the current issues of which they need to be aware and attend to in that review.

A typical, and in my reading often problematic, mode of orienting the team to issues relevant to a client, and one that occurred frequently in the disability and elderly teams, went as follows:

SLT Can we move on to P2? {reads from minutes taken the previous week} Last week we said that she had muscular dystrophy plus heart failure and she has been *depressed*. Has very limited physical functioning/ the catheter's been fixed up. The nurses cannot get her to *walk* so she's now in a wheelchair over the last four days. We have three goals. One was a home visit to assess her ADLs {activities of daily living} and OT(1) was going to do that. We've planned a family meeting on the *23rd* and I was going to follow up what physio input she was having {the team was between physios at that time}.

In this case, an extensive introduction detailing her medical and other issues was not necessary. P2 was well known to the disability team and had been admitted for a period of respite and assessment because her condition was deteriorating. This brief account notes ongoing physical problems and moves on quickly to check that tasks set the previous week had been discharged. (All the teams wrongly identified tasks as goals.)

When placed against the first dimension of my map, "providing the team with a focused orientation to the client," this account is not entirely satisfactory. It could be surmised that the failure to walk constitutes a newly emerging problem, but there is no mention of its significance for the team or for P2. Her "depression" (also a new factor?) is mentioned in passing, and the way in which it is noted offers no clues as to its intensity or what may have occasioned it, either from P2's perspective or from that of any of the team members.

The focus of this introduction is highly functional and its shape linear. It tends to foreground confirmation of individual members' task completion as the point of entry into and the focus of the discussion. While an overall team objective or goal may have been to ensure, given P2's deterioration, that she moved out of the unit into a safe setting (whether at home or in a different setting), such an objective remains implicit, and it is not clear if the team has set intermediary goals and, if so, what these are. We learn of individual members' responsibilities; there is no account of how these intersect with a larger goal. Finally, there is no allocation of significance to the different problems that are mentioned. If the depression is a "new" event, should the team address this and its implications for the focus of their work with P2 first? In fact, the doctor immediately begins to discuss aspects of P2's medical condition. She makes no explicit connection between her commentary and issues noted in the introduction, although a connection between walking problems and low blood pressure can be surmised.

> The medical review is still not (okay) [. . .] Her blood pressure was *shocking* and has slowly gone down and when she stands up it just *drops* (*very softly*) and she gets very dizzy (paper rattling) (*louder*) and we reduced her drugs {names given} (*very softly*) [and there is not much improvement]. Not very good.

A focused orientation to this particular client could have looked something like the following statement:

> OK, can we now move on to P2? Um, over the last two weeks one/ ah objective has been to reassess P2's capabilities in a number of different areas because OT thinks she needed to to look at whether she needs additional home alterations. I/ we need to get a sense of, um, just how much she can do now because it looks like she is deteriorating a bit so/ the tasks we set last week were to forward that objective/ um, OT was going to do a home visit to assess ADLs and I was going to follow up on physio input and we planned a family meeting for the 23rd to discuss these issues. But but, there are a couple of things we need to talk about first. The nurses have said that P2 now does not seem to be able to walk—in fact she's been in a wheelchair for the last four days. They have also reported that she is quite depressed. I think before we do anything else, these are the things we need to concentrate on. So, I have several questions for the team because it may be that together with P2 and her husband we need to rethink our direction. Questions: What does the depression seem to be about and how severe is it? What does P2 say about it? Why has her walking deteriorated? Is there a connection between the two? How is all this affecting P2 and her husband? How do these events affect our plan and timetable about her discharge? Who's the best person to kick off on this?

The differences between this imaginary statement and the one produced by the team are several. It is true that it is longer, but it is also considerably more focused. It places the previous week's direction and tasks against the changing circumstances of this week, and it suggests that the new circumstances may require a change or modification in the team's objectives. It seeks to open up the terrain to be traversed. It sets priorities for discussion and in so doing it foregrounds the knowledge dimension of teamwork, seeking to access members' and, equally, P2's and her husband's, understanding of and response to her changing situation. In doing so, it seeks to provide a context for the team's ongoing work and focus.

Spiraling Knowledge: Discussion and Development of the Issues

My imaginary orientation to P2, then, would have the team moving fairly quickly to talk about P2's and her husband's perceptions of what was going on as significant in guiding the team in its understanding of the issues and in structuring their work. The actual discussion, however, moved first into a medically focused and inconclusive, albeit energetic, discussion about why she was having difficulty standing and walking and then into a discussion about modifications to her house to accommodate a wheelchair, which family members were attending the proposed meeting, and what medication P2 was on. In the course of this a nurse commented,

N2 I think with P2 she's been struggling for a long *time* . . (yes) and um . . it, it's we need to really—if she's prepared to carry on struggling . . or (*softly*) not and that's what we haven't done.

NSC? She obviously deteriorated because of that struggle because (oh yes) she's very *frail* and/ you know [something about muscle loss and her being generally run down]

DR Her heart condition is not good, she's—

NSC —even if she's *prepared* to struggle (mm)/ I actually find she's got to have a lot of . . . of *help*.

N2 Yes she knows that . . she said that to me, she said "I know I'm going to need more help . *now* and I'm really [. .]" . She talked about that, about Meals on Wheels and I don't know if that's appropriate, if she fits into that category, but she . . . um, she *knows* that she's going to need more help and she obviously isn't coping with her meals and she hasn't been eating well and . . she's been run down and that so she knows that so that . if we can . . maybe get . . . more clearly defined what help *is* available and what *help* she could have but then . . to look at what's suitable accommodation as well. No point in giving her help if she's not in suitable accommodation.

There was no response to the nurse's suggestion that the team needed to work with P2 on the "struggle" question, and that issue was quickly overlaid by more practically oriented issues.

At the meeting two weeks later, the team was busy working out what it had to do to ensure that P2's house was modified in time for her discharge to accommodate the wheelchair, and a team goal was designated as "working for wheelchair independence." The introductory statement on P2 ran as follows:

SLT P2 . . . physiotherapy . report last week was she's *progressing . progressing.* Endurance was *low.* Working on increasing . walking and wheelchair independence . . *P2* now accepting the wheelchair as a backup and she's looking much better. There was going to be a home visit last *Friday* with OT1?

Typically, this statement focused on team objectives and did not address the degree of convergence between the team's objectives and those of the client. Although the strong line about progress gets disrupted and the "struggle" issue reemerges, this issue remains curiously marginalized, and the team's "goal setting" does not attend to the ambiguities in the situation to which some members have drawn attention.

OT(2) P2 seems really keen to try the walking frame. Sit to stand was going to be assessed in the *home. Increased* [drug] should be helping . . and the doctor also reported that she feels the heart failure is more under control now. Is that right?

DR She was feeling less short of breath . when we saw her on the ward round [. .]

OT(2) Right and there was a report/ um/ that her blood pressure last week was 90 over 60 and we were going to review that.

OT(1) Yeah . we did the home *visit* and . . . *yeah P2's* she's *very* unrealistic um, so we went through . sit to stand and she wanted to try walking so we did [that with her].

PHYSIO She'd been (*softly*) walking with the frame.

OT(1) Yeah but it, it was *unsuccessful* and that's where she's very disappointed so then we changed focus to wheelchair independence and the *home*. um it isn't *accessible*. you know she couldn't manage in a *wheelchair* um . yeah there needs to be some *changes*. She was quite open to the ideas at *at the time* um . and then once we got back to hospital the next . well yesterday just talking it through with her she became *very upset* . . very *dis* . *angry* and disappointed—

DR —because?

OT(1) *Well it's just* giving up *walking*. She physically *cannot do it* but mentally she's . . . well she's wanting to do it.

DR Yeah, get back to where she was.

OT(1) Yeah so/ *if* she's wheelchair dependent which to *us*/ we know that she will *have to be* um, she needs to practise the sliding board transfer in . . . how do we [.]

PHYSIO She, she needs a bit of assistance with [.] into . just perhaps seeing the general [. .] she *can't* manage . completely independently . and so that was when we first tried it . . . so I actually . I think *on the bed* it's going to be *even harder* because it's, it will just slide more . so we're going to *work* on that but . I have only actually been looking after her for four days last week and she told me that she *walked* two weeks before that . but she's never actually *walked* while I've been there . and at the end of last week not at all. She's just *not* got the hip, the pelvic control, or the strength in that right leg to actually move and I don't think it's real/ realistic to pursue that because I just don't think she's going to be able to . to cope longer and we really have *reinforced* that when we went . when we went home with her *she can't* . she can't do that. It was obviously a bit precarious what she was doing at home before she came in and she was just managing (mm) I mean she's just *lost a wee* bit of power which has meant that . it's actually an unrealistic goal for her/ so I—

NSC —so/ *if* she wasn't able to sit to stand without/ assistance? (mm) [She needed] *total* assistance—

DR —someone to hold her—

NSC —for *several weeks* before she came in . or later on.

PHYSIO Still . when she went home she thought she would be able to do it, didn't she? (mm mm) In her *mind* . in her *mind* (yeah) which was *quite* a difficult . .

SW And it's something that she's really working through, a new stage of her disability (yes) *and*. . . *up* until then she's survived *incredibly* well (mm) so I think a few weeks before . and because of the *catheter* issues—that was in her mind the reasoning why things were going *wrong* (yeah) and (mm) it's . for her it's a *huge* thing to, to even *start* to come to terms with the fact that she/ she can't just return when the catheter's "solved" (yeah, yeah), but she just (*very softly*) can't return to actually walking.

OT(2) SLT's just pointed out we need some *goals* for P2.

OT(1) Mm (*softly*) we do.

SW [.] family meeting on Monday . . .

NSC Good luck (*laugh*).

DR The dietitian *and* John (mm). Good.

OT(1) Well yeah I'll be working on *transfers*. . and so will you and *hopefully* doing the things at the *home* um, that I talked about before . .that's if . . . P2's ready for that (mm) . . because I'm sure

NSC Yes (*slight sigh*) she won't come at it easily.

RS So, how sure are you about what P2's goals are? . .

PHYSIO I, that's the difficulty. I mean at the moment she's *still* . trying to make an adjustment or trying to . work through.

SW P2's goal is to get *home* (yeah) from that point.

PHYSIO Her *goal* is to actually walk at home I would say at the moment.

DR "I haven't given up wanting to work, *walk*," she says/ (no) she says on the ward round and I said, "Yes that's fair enough but at the *moment* you can be safe in a wheelchair"/ and that she accepts (*overlapping*)

PHYSIO [.] walking thing

RS No no no but—

PHYSIO —and I think that her goals/ are/ *still* . *that*.

RS Sure *but that's a worry.*

PHYSIO Every time she starts therapy she's disappointed because she's not doing (yeah) . she's *not aiming* for what she wants and *I think her goals are different to ours* (my emphasis).

RS Yeah . and that's what worries me, that we're going to end up *aiming* for a compromise goal which she isn't going to accept.

OT(1) Yeah/ that's what it *feels* like.

RS And that, that *our* that if we write down *our* goals here, ah, we're going to be missing the point.

NSC She wants very much to get *home* (mm) and then . and be independent at home. I think she *begins* to see that . it's better to be home in a chair than not at home at all—

DR —she said that?

NSC Because you know, yes we had a bit of chat yesterday about *and she* ended up saying/ she talked about the bench—that might be a good idea and that yes and and *so on* and . yeah, it's not good enough but it's better than . *being stuck somewhere.*

OT(1) She hates the wheelchair . . it . *represents* . *dependence.*

NSC Yes it does. In fact she said she wouldn't go shopping in it. She didn't think she would but a lot of people start out like that when they first get chairs don't they so . . (*softly*) just keep working on it I think.

RS That's/ so we're happy to . accept that we've got slightly different goals at the moment . but we're going to *hopefully* (*next speaker overlaps here*) we are going to unify our goals?

OT(1) Well I don't know. I don't know what else we do . because if she wants to walk and (mm) and we can't *support* her in that (no) and—

RS —no just along there . she doesn't . she isn't going to come . back and say . , "If I can't walk at home I'd rather be in a rest home"?

DR No.

OT(1) She's not saying that.

DR She said at the meeting that she wants to go *home* and "if it's going to be in a wheelchair I'll do it in a wheelchair." She already said that.

NSC Her dread about coming in here and having that meeting is that we're all going to sit down and say, "No, you have to be in a rest home."

RS No no no . it's . just . just so long as we are able (*overlapping*)

WARD DR [. .]

SLT OT(1), you mentioned a third goal to do with the *house.* Is that just . needing some clarity (mm) on . what . like her needs *are*? . . .

OT(1) And then/ is there a meeting next week . on that with . the daughters?

There is no doubt that the team has the client's welfare at heart; equally, the discussion's process very substantially marginalizes her resistance to admitting her increasing dependence, a factor that, it could be argued, should be foregrounded in the team's immediate plans. My reading of the transcript highlights P2's ambiguity about her situation. The majority of the team instead goes for certainty, that she really does "accept" being in a wheelchair and, having affirmed that in the face of conflicting evidence, some (but not all) focus on defining their tasks. It is not clear from the transcript, for example, whether the social worker is or intends to become involved or how she might define her role and its relationship to the very functional team objective, which appears to concentrate on a safe discharge home.

I suggest that this process occurs in part because the team has substantially defined the primary objective of its discussions as "progressing the client." Progress is best achieved by focusing on actions to be taken by specific team members on the client's behalf, and actions have the effect of attesting to and confirming the validity of the team's objectives for the client. It is not, however, as though competing knowledge about P2's situation is absent. The suggestions that there may be tension between the evolving focus of the team's work and P2's different (and possibly multiple and contradictory) positions on this are voiced early on, and recur regularly, with the nurse, social worker, and physio attesting to her difficulty about accepting a wheelchair and with RS's various attempts to draw the team's attention to their persistent marginalization of P2. What is striking, though, is that these comments fail to derail the team from determining the focus of its work (as happened when comments about the disparity between P2's and the team's goals in the first meeting were raised). The more diffracted knowledge is advanced but is ignored. Most members powerfully position themselves and their objectives as center, as knowing (beneficently) what is best for the client.

The shape of the different discussions about P2 over several weeks was primarily linear. Members ignored the fissures (here the competing and disrupting knowledge and questions that would destabilize their self-evident focus) that could have challenged their purposes, but that if attended to, could have moved the team into more tricky, terrain; such paths could have begun to produce a different "map" of the work to be undertaken. It is not as if the work on which the team focused was unnecessary. What their work lacked was a key contextual feature about how this related to P2; and (to continue my metaphor) having foregrounded that key "topographical" feature, how this could have structured the nature and timing of various members' ongoing work. The team addressed the necessary practical dimensions of their work while overlooking its more complex emotional dimensions.

Had the team attended to the complicating knowledge (the "difference patterns" and their effects) held by some of its members, thereby introducing the rhizomic structure "and . . . and . . . and," it could be that their objective would have shifted from a purely practical focus on wheelchair independence and discharge to include the psychological issues for P2. The value of doing so would have been an increased focus on P2 and her concerns and a more explicit linking of the different disciplinary inputs. The focus of the discussion could have moved from members' individual tasks to attending to how their different tasks could relate to and advance a (revised) team objective and to the timing and ordering of those tasks. This did not happen.

There is, of course, some tension here. Things may not be perfectly in step. Organizationally, health teams are under continual pressure to move patients out within tight time frames. A member of this team said they could not wait to undertake the necessary work in house adaptations while P2 came to terms with her increasing dependence. Such a position assumes, however, that any counseling would be lengthy and could not focus on the complexity and pain of making decisions that the client wants to resist making, yet on another plane knows cannot be avoided. Moreover, had members identified P2's distress as a key factor in their work, the team could have decided that its intermediate objective(s) could be better achieved by a slight modification to the pace of some of its other work.

Strategies for Knowledge-Based Teamwork

Deleuze and Guattari (1983) write of rhizomes as allowing connections and permitting multiple entrances, of maps as "susceptible to constant modification." Within the framework that I am advancing, the objective of interprofessional work is to allow cross-disciplinary connections to be made that, in their turn, allow modifications and changes of direction to occur and be made explicit. From this perspective, much of the effectiveness of a team discussion relates to how a discussion develops, how knowledge intersections are made, how the effect of attending to such intersections allows and encourages the creation of new knowledge about the client and, consequently, how modifications to plans/objectives are achieved. There are issues of pacing and of quality of knowledge presentation. If the discussion moves too quickly toward closure or if the information available lacks sufficient detail (or is not made available at all), then it becomes more difficult to make substantive connections. Equally, knowledge work involves moving away from dominant lines to explore alternative routes and perspectives. Moreover, working connectedly requires that the team hold different strands of the discussion together and be aware of the possibility of collapses into repetition or the familiar as a result of possible knowledge intersections being lost or overlooked. At such moments strategic questions, refocusing the team on issues and directions or on comments that draw attention to information or knowledge about the client that have been overlooked, are likely to be valuable.

I have used extracts from transcripts of two teams' reviews of clients to address these issues. In the first extract, I analyze segments of text from one discussion in which there was no divergence between the representations of the client produced by the team and, while there were a number of factors to address, the case was not particularly complex. Nonetheless, aspects of the review process demonstrate features important to the production of knowledge-based work. In the second extract, I reproduce textual segments from two discussions of a significantly more complex case, in which the shape of the discussion was substantially linear. In these reviews, members produced competing and unresolved representations of the client, and it was difficult to see what strategies they had as a team, apart from waiting the situation out, to achieve a commonly agreed-on end.

Questioning/Elaborating/Focusing: Discussion of P34   The patient reviewed in the following team discussions was an elderly and somewhat demented man with a hip fracture who had been admitted to hospital. The elderly team's discussion indicates that the immediate issues confronting the team were how much he was going to improve, what degree of ongoing care he would require, and what role (if any) his wife was going to be able to play in his care.

SN5 P34/ another (*overlapping discussion*) another . . that's/ having trouble with rehab um he's a 74-year-old fractured left hip with um/ [. .] and he's/ an old CVA/ um/ as far as the nursing goes he/ has a urodome at night but is continent during the day . um . he's . very hard to/ he sort of makes *grunting* noises (mm) when he transfers and you think it's *pain* but he was showering this morning and he was making the same sort of noises (*laughing*) so I don't know whether it's from pain or concentration or what but

OT How much assistance are you giving him in the shower?

SN5 Quite a *lot* (mm) yes a *lot*/ he/ he can wash his face and under his arms but that's about all (mm) oh and his chest.

PHYSIO He wasn't making those noises last week.

SN5 No.

PHYSIO Not at all.

SN5 No he has had a fall and he's been thoroughly checked out by/ Mr. Brown and he doesn't think there's another fracture but then he's got this terrible . habit of *rotating*/ he gets in the bed and we went down the other night and he was all curled up and on the/ right side you know . *despite* the/ pillow being/ in between his legs and everything and he's got a very short term memory/ there's a *lot* of/ um memory deficits there and he/ *badly* neglects his right side/ he's not able to read and I said to his wife/ I put his glasses on and he actually drank a cup of tea alright without this tilting it and spilling it and I said to her, you know, "I think I've got it he needs to wear his glasses when he's drinking" and she said, "oh no he was like that at home"/ so

OT Have you seen that right side neglect? Because that's certainly out {evident} in my assessment.

SN5 Yes/ definitely.

OT Today/ yeah very much.

SN5 Yes/ but I I really/ I was wondering about have you seen him, SLT?

SLT No.

SN5 I was wondering if the next phase we try to [. . . .]

SLT Better see him then.

SN5 Yeah I think/ it might a good idea. Do you want to talk now, OT?

OT Right. I did a couple of assessments with him yesterday and one was ah um/ a memory assessment and he scored/ 75 out of 100 indicating/ quite um severe dementia I mean not to [. . .] and also I did the/ perceptual assessment and once again um/ he has major deficits in all of his perceptuals and in fact he couldn't do *anything*/ the whole perceptual assessment [. . .] (*several speakers overlap*) and it was right and left sides um/ visual/ things were out/ color and the shapes sizes/ spatial concepts he'd no/ no (*softly*) idea/ major deficits there/ perhaps yeah yeah so um/ yeah I think he's got a lot of problems actually/ I don't know how she's going to cope/ at home with him um/ the thing is that/

they've got all um/ OT3 did a home visit/ because he was over in Ward 2 and what with that/ his access and his access is quite bad/ to the house and they've got a *very very* steep ramp like um/ it's like it has to be modified so if he was going to go home they'd have to (*voice becomes progressively softer*) make a lot of modifications into his house/ even to get him/ get him inside so

SN5 He's another one that's cot sided at night he's been (mm) getting out of bed and/ confusion nocturnally and so/ I don't think he'd ever manage at home.

OT No.

DR Well before the stroke he was okay at home wasn't he? (mm)

HS (*softly*) Well it depends what you mean by "okay." (*louder*) I think his wife covers for him quite a lot (yes) she does just about everything for him (mm) I mean/ apart from him drying the dishes and I don't know how well he did that that's *all* he did (mm) around around the home.

CN Like physically he's not as good now probably as he was—

HS —no—

CN —before so/ you know that's

HS (*softly*) Obviously not no.

CN Might make it more difficult for her too.

DR Right.

HS At least he was mobile then.

CN Yes.

HS He was/ fairly independent with his mobility/ but she was having increasing problems with his incontinence and all that sort of stuff as well (. . .) you know I get the impression that he's not (*softly*) really/ a candidate for going home unless/ there's no *because his wife's* actually quite sort of/ she's

OT Got angina/ she's not very well herself is she?

HS Yes.

SN5 She's a lot shorter than him too.

HS Yeah

SN5 and she's very/ quite *nervy.*

HS Yeah (mm) but on the other hand I think she'd be/ she'd I don't know what/ last time she was in when he came in with the/ TIA she was quite adamant that he was going to go home with her/ despite (mm) the fact that/ you know he was almost totally dependent on her and things weren't getting any better/ I don't know whether she's changed her/ views on that.

SN5 (*overlapping last three words*) I think she might have changed now yes because with that groaning every time you go to transfer him.

HS (*softly*) Yeah.

SN5 She *worries* you know but I don't think it's actual *pain* I think it's just—

HS —no.

SN5 It's pain (mm) mixed in/ but he does it other times when there's no need for pain.

The discussion up to this point is structured around two related questions: How much is this man likely to improve? What plans for his future care may be appropriate? The introductory nursing report begins what becomes a cumulative and reinforcing narrative of P34's deterioration. The discussion moves out over a number of complementary planes, amassing evidence from a number of different perspectives, a process assisted on several occasions by members asking others to comment on their understanding of the situation. A certain amount of detail is important if different knowledges are to intersect. The nurse does not end her commentary on P34's showering capabilities by noting only that she gives "quite a *lot*" of help; she augments this by noting the limited number of parts of his body P34 can wash by himself. Several lines of inquiry and information develop early on: P34's limited ability to perform self-cares; his somewhat strange and new grunting behavior, which at the very least is disconcerting; his increasing and severe memory deficits; the extensiveness of the alterations that will be needed should he go home (so there is a question of timing of discharge and perhaps a question about whether the cost would be justified, given his limitations and the team's severe doubt about his ability to survive at home); his nocturnal confusion; and his deterioration since his previous admission. The question of his health is approached from a number of different directions, and the reality of his being discharged home in light of the team's uncertainties about his wife's expectations and her general state of health and ability to manage him is raised by the house surgeon's unpacking of the doctor's "he was okay at home wasn't he?"

A discussion needs both to canvas the different accounts of its members and to move on and avoid becoming repetitive. Following a short but nonetheless detailed report from the physio about changes in P34's gait (again confirmation of his deterioration), CN moves to relate these (in this case converging) lines through her identification of a key issue: the team may have concerns about P34's wife's ability to cope, but it is unclear if any member has explicitly discussed these issues with her.

CN um SW3, have, have you/ had a chat to his wife at all?

SW3 I I met her um yesterday.

CN Did she say anything yesterday? Sorry I wasn't at the meeting yesterday afternoon.

SW3 Well Physio's seen her at home too so um/ I I'll talk with her. I'll catch her when she comes to visit.

The social worker's lack of contact means that this line of inquiry terminates at this point, and the Physio, whose turn it is to take minutes, asks for individual "goals."

PHYSIO I need to get some *goals* from everyone.

CN Oh right.

PHYSIO (to nurse) From you/ that's if you can.

SN5 um . . . . um for P34/ um . . we'll have to stop him/ try and stop him rotating won't we? . . we can tell him a dozen times but it doesn't seem to penetrate/ I mean it sounds *terrible* but I mean you have to be honest don't you um . . and to be/ more independent with simple things I mean even eating his *meal* he's—

CN —Oh he's supposed to be getting on.

SN5 He's getting a bit better he's not putting the um/ pineapple with the you know the/ mince (*laugh*) um but but you wonder how what his/ you wonder what his sight's like too/ I put his glasses on but whether they are any use is—

OT —but his sight's way off because he had (yes) the assessments we just (yes) couldn't get over how much he could see (mm)

SN5 So you have to butter his toast you know (mm) help/ initiate everything really.

OT And he he actually can't if you put something down there like a pen on a table he can't actually see that he thinks it's somewhere else.

SN5 Yes. Yes.

CN Is that his vision or or is that through his [stroke]?

OT Well I'm not sure if it's through the stroke or (mm) if (*softly*) it's his vision mm.

PHYSIO So what are your goals?

OT Well . . I don't know . . . um/ oh just to see where some assessments [.]

(*whispering and pages of diary being turned*)

The story lines have been articulated, but the team has not moved away from its concrete accounts. In fact, the request for "goals" would appear to have reinforced the practical focus of its work. Without a (conceptual) point, a "circle of convergence" or beginning the articulation of a team goal to bring those diverse lines together ("how do we think about all we have just described?"), the team flounders and reverts to its repetition of disabilities. CN's two interventions below (a question about how the team views P34's future and a statement about the central importance of his wife in that future) provide a stimulus, a refocusing of the discussion. These interventions are highly purposive in that they highlight issues that specific members of the team should know about or about which they need to inform themselves (and the team). The discussion continued as follows:

CN *Realistically* what can we expect to um . . reach with this man?

HS Not a lot.

CN Yeah.

SN5 Yeah.

CN So I'm just/ so/ some of you talking with his wife will be sort of quite relevant for/ where we're going really.

HS We need to talk to [her].

SW3 Well we had a meeting yesterday.

HS Oh yes.

SW3 Yeah initially/ initial meeting . . . didn't really pick up on that at *all* actually in that meeting.

PHYSIO She spoke to me quite a lot beforehand when I phoned her and/ you know indicating that I/ whether am I going to cope?

DR Did she say that?

PHYSIO I/ *not directly*/ no but the implication was there.

SW3 She has/ angina and I know she's finding it difficult to cope at home on her own but that's all I know that's only at a very superficial level.

PHYSIO In fact her questions during the meeting were/ you know how long is this hospital stay going to be (yes) (mm) and when is he coming home . .

CN So maybe/ SW3 if you could let us know?

SW3 (*very quietly*) Yeah right.

CN What/ where we/ because um/ does she usually/ does she usually come in for a visit?

SW3 Oh 2 o'clock every day.

CN 2 o'clock yeah oh okay.

DR Yeah like I mean if she's/ really um adamant about taking um him going home then of course maybe we need to/ try and optimise his physical state but ah (*very softly*) you know

SW3 We really—

PHYSIO —his x-rays—have you received them?

? I haven't seen them.

SN5 They haven't come back I don't think yet.

PHYSIO Because I'm not prepared to continue mobilising him at all—

SN5 —no I wouldn't either—

PHYSIO —until those x-rays are out just to check just—from the sort of pain he's indicating.

The value of CN's more directive line, "So I'm just/ so/ some of you talking with his wife will be sort of quite relevant for/ where we are going really" was that it elicited some significant, albeit tentative, information about P34's wife's uncertainty about what she wanted. It resulted in a further indirect instruction to the social worker in a comment highlighting the team's dependence on family and the significance of the gap in their knowledge ("So maybe, SW if you could let us know") as P34's wife's role in the future care of her husband will closely affect the team's plans.

What these segments demonstrate is a progressing and also recursive discussion, where members respond to and develop or qualify each other's commentary. At points where the discussion is breaking down it is refocused by strategic questions, and significant gaps in the team's knowledge about P34's wife's hopes and intentions are noted and steps taken (twice) to try to ensure that this knowledge would be made available to the team in the next meeting.

What this team did not do, however (nor were there any examples of this in any of the transcripts), was to move its work onto a slightly more conceptual plane to bring together different discipline-specific tasks through the identification of a team objective. For example, if the major objective was still "discharge home," then a team task relating to addressing P34's and his wife's capabilities in relation to a discharge home could have focused on an immediate objective; moreover, this objective could have reflected CN's question about where as a team they are going to get to with P34 and ensured that other possible outcomes could be entertained. Defining, for example, the immediate team objective as "assessing the reality of home care" could have then made the uncertainty inherent in the situation explicit and allowed individual members to identify their tasks in relation to it, with the OT, physio, and nurses, say, following up on issues related to P34's ability to perform daily tasks (self-care and so on) and the social worker discussing with P34's wife her hopes for and her ambivalence about his discharge home. Describing the social worker's role like this would have rather more clearly articulated her role than just " 'seeing' the wife," and this more elaborated objective would have made apparent to other team members some of the elements of her work.

Recognizing and Managing Differences: Discussion of P9   The team discussions in relation to this and the next two strategies that are reproduced here are taken from several reviews of a psychiatric patient. Rather than illustrating, as did the previous example, the development of converging lines through affirmation or qualification of each other's observations and assessments of the situation, the discussions about P9 highlighted significant differences between members' representations of this client.

The reviews of P9 are different from P34's in two ways. First, many of the statements about this man were typically sparse, lacking in more fine-grained detail, their smooth, undifferentiated surfaces offering few points of (interprofessional) connection. Second, there was overtly hostile disagreement, reflecting very different ways of representing the client and beliefs about the ways in which P9 should be managed. The critical issue is not the disagreement per se. Disagreements between members would be, one might think, the stuff of interprofessional teamwork. They are a necessary consequence of following the different lines of inquiry that arise from disciplines' different conceptual models of the world and different foci in the provision of care. They are critical to effective cross-disciplinary teamwork. In this discussion, however, the different narratives of the client's behavior, each producing very different discursive accounts of the client and, indeed, of those producing these accounts, became the point beyond which the team could not progress. The fact of difference was crippling rather than generative, despite efforts by the counselor to encourage the team to work more subtly through attention to the professional and theoretical issues involved in the client's care.

P9 was a large man in his late middle age, with a complex delusional system. He had no family in Aoteaora/New Zealand. He had been on the psychiatric inpatient unit for some time. He had for many months refused to cooperate in a number of ways with all staff and was refusing medication to control his increasing delusional system. The team was divided about forcing him to take medication, in part because that medication was contraindicated because of his other health problems, including his weight.

The team had reached something of an impasse with P9. It was not clear from the reviews presented during the time I was at the site which members of the clinical team, apart from some of the nursing staff attempting to control aspects of his difficult behavior, were actively engaged in working with him, what their objectives were, and how these connected to team objectives. The complicated issues confronting the team centered around whether the team or the patient was in control; what areas of P9's life the team could legitimately exert control over, including whether they could impose medication; the point at which control became punitive; the difficulty of not responding negatively to the challenges P9 posed and, on a metalevel, what it meant to cast the work in terms of "control." The nursing staff were concerned that ignoring P9's behavior would result in other patients' behavior deteriorating, leading to serious management problems on the inpatient unit. The orientation of their concerns reflected their location within the care system and their twenty-four-hour responsibility for this client.

Unlike many of the introductory statements about the clients with whom this service was working, the first that I recorded about P9 identified a range of problems: his refusal to cooperate in unit activities, his rejection of his management plan, his intensifying mental illness, his very poor general state of health and his deliberate refusal to help himself, his turning on their head attempts to involve him in the inpatient programs, and the increasing anger of other patients toward him. These problems, with their variations and points of intensification and expansion, continued to be noted throughout six reviews I recorded about him. The shortest discussion about P9 was eight minutes, the longest twenty, with the others lasting between nine and twelve minutes. As one member observed in the second (taped) discussion and following the polarization of team members around the implications of a nurse's comments, P9 was not an easy case for the team to work with.

Following a rather acrimonious discussion around what and how the team should respond to P9, the following exchange occurred:

COUNSELLOR I say/ we do need to/ we need to remember that the word *punishment* has been *used* two or three times this morning talking about *this guy* and and and I think it it's a very *dangerous/* process I think that it reflects the kind of pressure that he succeeds in putting on us.

UM I don't think it is punishment Counsellor and I think that's probably an inappropriate word to use. We don't *see* it like that *at all* as I reiterated in the last clinical (sure) meeting we ended up getting in an argument and the fact is/ this *man/* we are concerned about his physical state we are concerned about his mental state . . *we have to* at some point decide that he needs to *conform* with the rest of the patients/ with/ regular routines/ and that's what we've implemented he/ this is a *man* who's been freewheeling around here for *months* because/ *staff* have been reluctant to challenge or confront him over very *very basic things* that we would challenge anybody else in the unit because we *are/ concerned* that he could drop dead (mm) and we've decided that we need to take some control over that. Punishment is not/ is not the right use of the word.

COUNSELLOR Oh I I'm absolutely certain that that is *so/* it's just *interesting* that the word/ *pops up.*

UM Well it just describes very quickly.

COUNSELLOR Well it describes very accurately I think what the the kind of feeling that that he engenders here/ amongst us /and I think *that's* a measure of the psychological problem ah and I think it's going to be a delicate and difficult one to deal with. I'm not saying we shouldn't deal with it /at all/ I'm just saying that we're walking/ a *tightrope* with this *guy/* in ways that are similar to the ways ah/ that are very different but they have some similarity to a tightrope that we have to work/ walk with some/ *extraordinarily disturbed and very psychotic* patients. This is a/ a different version of the same kind of thing.

What these quite detailed and frequently emphatic statements demonstrate is very different foci about client treatment and, drawing on very different discipline-based knowledge, physical location, and focus, very different assumptions about the work of the team, how that work might be conceptualized and what the roles of individual team members are. The focus of the nursing staff, in contact twenty-four hours a day with this difficult patient, is on issues of practical management and on the danger of "contamination" of others by this patient. From this perspective, it could be argued, the work of the team was to support (that nebulous word) nursing staff in what was without any doubt a difficult and demanding task in their management (control) of the patient, a task complicated/contradicted by the (legislatively mandated) desire to protect patient rights. However, although it was acknowledged—as, for example, by the unit manager in the above extract—that the nurses had specific responsibilities, the *fact* that staffs' different location in the system in itself generated different accounts of the problem and the work to be done was never acknowledged.

In contrast to the emphasis of the unit manager's statement, the counselor, occupying quite different occupational, locational, and discursive spaces from the nurses, produced a meta-analysis of the discussion, locating the work of the team in the context of complex, psychotherapeutic dynamics and noting how, because of (professional and organizational) pressure to move this man on and his flagrant resistance to their efforts, the team's behavior could come to mirror/repeat that of their client. *And* he suggested a way in which the team could proceed—a move toward theorizing/conceptualizing, and away (momentarily) from the preoccupation with controlling/disciplining. Within knowledge-based, rhizomically structured teamwork, the task for the team is not to fall into binaries but to develop points of convergence across seeming oppositions, to engage with the problems that such interprofessional work creates. The binary in this instance was in part between "disciplining the client" and analysis of team transference, each reflecting very different, but never acknowledged, knowledge locations. The next speaker (a nurse) drew the team back into more familiar terrain: "Okay I think that once PR2 clears it {the right to impose a diet} and talks to the district inspector {the lawyer responsible for protecting P9's legal rights} and if that's all okay we can put it/ together and it's like a behavioral program and will (*softly*) overcome some of this."

As the discussion progressed, it became extremely clear that the team had covered this territory before and was not easily able to progress the discussion in what was, as noted earlier, a very complex case. Given that all teams are likely to encounter such cases, the critical issue is the strategies available to move beyond well-worn lines, to shift, realign the discussion and open up intersecting alternatives. Despite the real problems the team had in substantially developing a plan of action, there were points in these discussions when the strategies I have identified as necessary to the production of knowledge-based teamwork were demonstrated, albeit not worked with more systematically.

Working Toward Disciplinary Intersections   Questions that encourage only (in this context) the development of a linear discussion ("What work have you done; what work have you done?") do not work to allow the team to progress their discussion as they restrict speculation and clarification of professional conceptual maps; they too easily place work in parallel lines ("I have done this; I have done this; I have done this"). Although such questions are not entirely redundant in a team context, there is a danger that, rather than encouraging connections, they encourage repetition. An alternative process, important in the development of knowledge-based work, goes beyond reporting on work done to include positive engagement with and questioning of each other's work. This approach would include explicit recognition of how different members' roles with a patient produce quite different, but nonetheless legitimate, agendas and those agendas would be placed alongside each other to reinforce the breadth of the team task and to shape work and allocate priorities and tasks. The following extract is indicative of a quite lengthy but focused interdisciplinary exchange of the type necessary to establish the parameters of what work might be able to be effected.

In this exchange, a psychiatric registrar asks about the possibilities of psychological input for P9. I have boldfaced what I see as the key questions or statements. In contrast to CN's questions and statements to the team about their work with P34, these questions are very focused and the questioner is persistent.

PR2 Has P9 been seen by psychologists?

SP2 Yeah I I've seen him on a number of occasions and documented um/ the history of his delusional disorder.

PR2 mm yeah

SP2 Looked at the idea of doing some cognitive work with that

PR2 yeah

SP2 And he's just not accessible at the moment.

PR2 No.

SP2 I mean he's too/ unwell.

PR2 **Too unwell**

SP2 Well he's too deluded. There's no/ there's no way to get access to him

PR2 yeah

SP2 *at all/* and it's sort of one factor I found that he's just

PR2 mm

SP2 so highly rationalised and defended that um/ there isn't the subsidiaries this time I'm not going to go for the main one

PR2 mm

SP2 and I mean I can't even squeeze in there.

PR2 **But I mean does that/ that's the only other avenue really to get into his/ his system isn't it?**

SP2 I'll try it again. We need to keep approaching him really though he/ says/ contradictory things about the time I spent with him I mean

PR2 mm

SP2 I could start up again/ maybe look at trying to help with/ hopefully with SSW1 (*CP3 laughs*) and try and do it/ organise him to do/ not with me/ but I'll do that as well try and organise.

SSW1 Is that [. . .] his delusional system *incorporates* all the workers here and how you know [. . .]

SP2 I don't see him/ being able to *change/* or um/ yeah (delusional) yeah delusional while he's unmedicated.

PR2 **So what's the general prognosis for/ cognitive work in a person with a delusional system?**

SP2 Well most people I've worked with um I've broken through that [.] with the patient (mm) with those that have been on medication. I mean it's just/ that the ground is so *changeable* that/ and you end up getting incorporated so there's no sort of *wholly* [. .] you know (mm) it's just free flow and it just *expands* all the time (mm) that's what I think is happening here.

PR2 So it is expanding/and it's/ continuing to expand?

SP2 Mmm . . so at the moment um/ there's no chance of—

PR2 —I I just wanted to to see what had and hadn't been done because

SP2 yeah

PR2 because we we could maybe go with the second opinion to see what else/ what else we could do for him we might well just give him the [.] tablets.

SP2 Okay

SSW1 The rest of it I spoke to his family whether they want [.] tomorrow [. . . . .]

PR2 But his system isn't [.] from the outside and it's now/ developing inside.

SP2 But as soon as he/ I mean it would seem to *me* as soon as he familiarizes himself quite well within an environment then/ that's when the delusional system starts feeding back again into that and often that's why he's *changed* because I mean he actually feels extremely uncomfortable with the whole delusional system/ it's not what he *likes*/ um that I mean that is just sort of constantly from what he's like you know his *transient* um lifestyle [.] and in this environment he's stuck.

PR2 yes

SP2 And in fact you know his transience has really been quite helpful for him (yeah) and it's reduced the ability for it to expand you know just keep going.

This particular discussion on P9 concluded here, and the team began a discussion of another patient. One of the aspects of this extract is that, unlike so many of the team's other discussions, it offered some detailed information about the patient's condition and how that affected what work could be undertaken; the detail also enabled the registrar to advance his questioning, and the interchange provided the team with some valuable knowledge of P9's psychological state and of the constraints facing the psychologist in working with him. This information had not been expressed before in the meetings at which I had been present and, having been brought to the team's notice, could have assisted in delineating future possibilities for work or for highlighting the difficulties or impossibilities of particular courses of action. Although the team did not determine by the end of this discussion how it was going to progress its work with this client, this interchange made available more specific information about the possibilities of work with P9.

Theorizing the Team's Work   A further strategy available to a team working on a complex case is its use of theoretical knowledge. All work is theoretically informed. All theories offer modes of conceptualizing the world and describing behavior. They structure how "facts" are represented and produce different discursive bodies. How the team positions itself discursively will result in its focusing on one mode of work rather than another and will assist the team in thinking through the rationale and value of working in a particular way or ways. Part of the function of knowledge-based teamwork is to make these dimensions more explicit. In its discussions about different possible interventions with P9, the team could have engaged with two theoretical questions: "How do we conceptualize his behavior?" and "How does this relate to the approach we take, and how does that approach structure our work?" These are complex questions; asking them encourages the team to rupture or break the narrative structure in which many team discussions are cast and attend to the conceptual, analytic possibilities of their work.

The discussion from which the transcript is drawn indicated the existence of two seemingly competing but associated representations of the client and of his behavior. One, proposed twice by the counselor, represented the client as adolescent:

COUNSELLOR I think it's the *clearest possible* I came in and read/ through his *file* I think this *behavior* is so *clearly regressive* that ah/ anyone who's ever raised an adolescent/ ah/ will will will recognize the/ the *whole* pattern of of his behavior and his reactions. *What is not clear to me* is the/ I've never/ *I don't know* what the *role/* and what the relationship was with his *father* um/ and whether in fact he's um/ more difficult (*sigh*) ah when he's when he's in this rebellious ah adolescent, "I won't do anything and you can't make *me move* and it's not in my contract," I mean it's that's a wonderful/ nitty/ picking of the little legalistic *points* that's absolutely/ um/ just so reminiscent that/ you know

The counselor went on at this point to talk about his lack of detailed knowledge of P9's early family dynamics, although he outlined his impressions of how P9's family managed authority and control issues, knowledge that could help the team structure their approach if they were to adopt the "adolescent" view in their work with P9. His theorizing of the behavioral issues confronting the team as those of an adolescent was, however, not taken up. In the discussion the following week he returned to this observation after the team's reengagement with the issue of forcing P9 to limit his eating. On this occasion, his suggestion about a possible course of action for the team got lost in a parallel nursing narrative of the real difficulties of managing the deteriorating inpatient relationships, inpatient routines, and resourcing.

COUNSELLOR I think he's *chosen/* I mean he's chosen this he he sounds *more and more and more* like the adolescent in the family (mm) you know/ who this is the *only . only way the only avenue he's got to to ah dig his toes in and I think one of the problems about the food* is that/ the punishment doesn't *fall on him* it's falling on the rest of the family who is to be—

UM —that's why the patients are getting so shitty with him.

COUNSELLOR That's right so I think that one of the things to do is to look at some different way of dealing with the issue/ if he's dragging his feet and taking hours and hours and hours to to *eat* it's *unreasonable* for the rest of the family to have to sit there so ah/ we we ought to be able to devise some way of/ if he's going to take all morning to eat that that's *possible .* and the others can get on with what they want to *do.*

UM Well what happens is that he takes his time about eating/ by the time everyone's actually finished he's then heading for his *second* helping (yeah) in in the morning (yeah) because when I was out there {on the ward} the other day I watched him quite carefully and then what happened was/ P3 got so pissed off with him *she* ended up doing the dishes/ which was his job/ and there's *slamming* and banging in the kitchen like most people would do when they think they're doing somebody else's job (mm) because they're too lazy (mm) and so it's actually um/ isolating him even further from the patient group in fact the patients/ have very little to do with him now they're just *so* angry with him they confront him in the community meeting and of course nothing/ nothing happens.

PR2 Well he's got to be able—

COUNSELLOR (*overlapping*) —well he certainly shouldn't be able to eat and eat and eat and then *not* do the dishes if it's his turn to do the dishes if he's doing them at 12 o'clock just before lunch I don't think that matters/ ah ah it's unreasonable to—

UM —it does from a resourcing point of view for *us.*

DM The problem is that that area gets locked off until it's time as the cutlery is counted.

Theorizing P9 as adolescent could have meant that the team started to think about their treatment plan: how it could be informed and shaped by the relevant extensive theoretical and therapeutic literatures and, taking into account the issues raised by the nurses, how the plan could be activated. What happened instead was that a more simplistic, absolute representation of P9 was advanced. In this representation, P9 was described as "a slob" and "a pig," as someone with whom some of the nursing staff were "at war." Although in less therapeutic discourses these terms could well stand in for "adolescent," they nonetheless carry strong repressive, punitive, and moral overtones. They marginalize the person so described; they define as moral turpitude what in the alternative discourse of delayed adolescence is represented as a normal (albeit here delayed) developmental phase *with the possibility of moving on;* they justify more punitive behavior. They close off alternatives, inscribing the patient as gross, if not to some extent alien. As this discussion was constituted, the team had two seemingly radically different representations available to it. Neither was taken up with a view to thinking about possible connections or how they might affect the team's approach. (In a later section on team decision making and leadership I return to this review in order to discuss how a knowledge-based team discussion could have produced a somewhat different focus with the possibility of a different outcome.)

Work with P9 also raised significant ethical considerations. As soon as there was a suggestion of imposing a diet, the team became polarized over the issue of control, presented here as a management issue, devoid of any of its more theorized implications.

CNS1 Well we're actually recording a baseline of everything he eats and to have a look at it it's quite *amazing* the amount of food like not just what he eats here but what when he goes to the canteen he's *always got* three to four big bars of chocolate and they go fairly quickly you know.

CP3 Just run through what what are you proposing again, CNS1.

CNS1 Well what what I wanted to know is *can we control* you know ah the amount he eats I mean you know oh I just wanted to get some feedback from you guys if we said to him, "Well look you know *this* is a reasonable amount of *food* and this is what you're allowed to *eat,*" apart from/ ah what he buys himself you know/ I mean

CP3 yeah/ I mean there are—

CNS1 —can we do that? Can we say, right you can *have*/ a maximum of four weetbix/ three bits of toast/ whatever?

CP3 I think you're going to run into two problems with that the issue the issue [.]

CNS1 That's that's why I want some clarification.

COUNSELLOR The other point is is the risk of/ any confronts on passive aggressive behaviors and they are entrenched with him um/ certainly it would be seem at least reasonable to audit/ the *time* anyone is allowed to eat in/ the set times breakfast lunch dinner and that seems like a pretty reasonable *start*.

N2 And *then* we are actually challenging, him we're challenging him many times and um one time he came in and thumped on the door/ of the MDT and wanted to see the manager and any time when we *challenge* him/ you know he wants to see the *manager*/ you know he doesn't want to talk to *any* of us (well) and it it's *his right* he says to do what he wants to *do*.

CP3 Yeah well clearly clearly *that that isn't* um . . have you spoken/ PR2 have you spoken to the district inspector yet?

PR2 No I haven't/ no.

CP3 Be best to catch up with him as well and (mm) and and talk to him—

SP1 —because he's involved in anything—

CP3 —because in *two* ways generally he's there's some some related to to P9's/ complaints but also so so we can talk with with him about what his views about that are/ those kind of issues/ because it's a form of compulsory treatment really I guess and/ (*softly*) and um/ I don't quite know where that's going to take us.

CNS1 Well you/ in my mind is we're not actually doing him a favor (mm) by allowing him to eat 8 chocolate bars over the weekend you know.

COUNSELLOR Well yes but we're also not doing someone a *favor* who/ who refuses *medication* and yet we *say* that we'll do something about their *food* but we won't *force* you to take the medication.

CNS1 Well I/ *I I agree with you Counsellor.* I believe that/ this person should be medicated and I have been saying that for a while but I'm try/ just trying to work on this *issue* first (sure) you know.

Possibly because the ethical and legal issues of forcing medication and controlling food intake loomed so large, no one asked what the team collectively knew or did not know about working with the issue of obesity (complicated by a very tight delusional system). Instead, the focus was on the legal and practical implications of enforcing diets and the fact that without a weight loss the use of the medication some team members considered P9 should have was contraindicated. One member remarked that he had been reading around the issue of forcing medication, but this knowledge was not brought into the team to inform its discussions.

Developing Team Objectives: Discussion of P37   Because defining team objectives is interwoven with the process of team reviews, I have written about this dimension of teamwork to some extent in the analyses I have presented so far. It is, however, a significant feature of the map of effective teamwork and requires some specific discussion in its own right.

The transcripts of the team discussions, such as those about P9, typically indicated a lack of clarity among members about the *issues* raised by a client's circumstances and their implications. The introductions to each client provided very sketchy outlines of *problems.* Problems and issues may be, but are not necessarily, identical. At the end of the introduction to clients, members typically started responding in several ways. First, they addressed specific problems (as was demonstrated in the discussion with P2), often in terms of the work they had undertaken or were planning to undertake. Second, they related these current problems to previous events in the clients' histories, hence contributing to the ongoing construction of team narratives about the client. Third, they discussed immediate past events, external to the client but affecting the client. The discussions felt very crowded. There were few instances when the teams paused to take stock of where they had got to or had come from.

Part of the work of this chapter (and continued in the next) is to argue both for the value of the development of team narratives about clients *and* for the need for more theorizing and conceptual work. This work includes defining team objectives. The intention of such work is to move the focus of attention from problems to issues and to understand how thinking about issues more conceptually can assist the team in accomplishing its task. How does such a process work?

Especially when teams get stuck, it is very easy for discussions to become repetitious, to be endlessly recycled so that each revolution results in diminishing clarity of vision about focus of immediate work and objectives. On the one hand, problems are the stuff of teamwork. On the other, there is a point at which, in order to most effectively use their collective knowledge in complex cases, a shift from narrative to conceptual mode becomes necessary. Such work assists in creating (unexpected) connections between disciplines and providing different ways of thinking about clients and their circumstances. Defining a team objective in relation to identified issues (not just problems) may well reposition (some of) the work that needs to be undertaken and provide a useful shared team focus for determining ongoing work.

In the next extract, the elderly inpatient team was discussing their work with a middle-aged woman (P37), who had had an extremely severe stroke. She had come onto the ward for an assessment of whether she was capable of living in sheltered accommodation, so that she could leave the rest home, where she was very unhappy. She had multiple problems, including double incontinence, extremely limited speech, and difficulty in transferring learning (for example, she had relearned to turn a tap on and off. She could do this in the OT training room but could not reproduce that learning in the inpatient bathrooms). The following discussion occurred after she had been an inpatient for two weeks.

PHYSIO *She's sort of* slightly better with the duvet than with blankets and sheets and that but, with the continence problem at night it's a bit of a problem providing duvets then . . and it hasn't been ideal. She *is getting into bed* independently and out of bed and

SW (*softly*) mm she does.

DR And feeding ah?

CN Yes she can feed herself. She's okay with that now.

DR Mm

SLT She can't do things like, you know, peel bananas or anything—

CN —no—

SLT —like that but everything

DR If something is put in front of her?

SLT Yeah if it's set up for her she can manage (right). She can eat one way or another.

CN And she manages quite well with that actually. Like she asked me for a cloth to put on the front of her so that she doesn't spill, like she's aware of sort of *it's really very sad* actually.

DR Mm

CN Because/ you know she *is* sort of quite unhappy where she *is* but

DR Mm

CN And she realises that she really kind of isn't there um—

SLT —when did she do that when she did ask you for that cloth when did she actually?

CN Um it was towards the end of last week.

SLT Mm okay because what I've been working on is getting her to *initiate* communication instead of sitting there *waiting* till somebody *asks* her do you want a drink or, do you want something you know.

CN Oh well yes. Yes.

SLT She has been trying?

CN (*overlapping*) *Oh yes.* Yesterday at lunchtime she got up and got herself to the table before I asked her. Usually, we say um, "Come on, P37, you know, lunch is here"/ but yesterday when she saw that um that it was, you know, like we were getting everybody organised, but before I got to her she was up and moving. I said, "Oh" you know (yeah). So she did initiate that.

SLT So that's what I've been working on and also just initiating some conversation and just giving her some . giving her a topic and having her tell me *anything she wants* about that topic. And that's improved a lot because at the beginning she just couldn't and now she's able—

DR —so the question is—

CN (*overlapping*) —and when her, when her mum was here yesterday, I went and said to her, "Mrs. M, how *are you*," and um, she said something back to me and P37 said, "Oh, um, she forgets things," like she kind of contributed that without me asking her so she is starting to improve—

SLT (*overlapping*) —starting to improve.

DR Yeah. So the question is do we feel that she will require further treatment of inpatient rehabilitation . or are we . too early to . . .?

In briefly (recursively) rehearsing the presence or absence of strategies for promoting knowledge work, I note that this text offers a valuable example of interprofessional work through the articulation of closely informed disciplinary gazes. A key moment in this extract is in CN's, "Like she asked me for a cloth to put on the front of her so that she doesn't spill," a more detailed statement than might be absolutely necessary in terms of reporting strictly on progress. This more elaborate statement enables SLT to question CN further and connect her observations with the work she (SLT) had been doing with P37; her comments were generative of further commentary on observed, positive changes, which, if maintained and developed, could point to the possibility of P37's being able to leave the rest home.

What members did not do, however, was to conceptualize the associations between their work through the production of team objectives. The work as it was represented in the discussion appeared to be moving in parallel: the nurses were continuing to observe activities of daily living (ADLs), SLT was working with speech, the OTs were working on P37's ability to transfer learning. The potential opportunity for connecting disciplines' seemingly disparate work and simultaneously focusing the *team*'s work by defining a team objective did not occur. In this situation, the team could have described its work in relation to an important conceptual and practical notion: "ability to initiate." Being able to initiate actions (and follow them through) was a crucial element in P37's safe discharge to a sheltered setting. It could be argued that the team's failure to define an intermediate team objective such as this contributed to the subsequent complications in its work with this client.

The initial team objective had been to work toward P37's moving into sheltered accommodation, an objective to which one team member in particular was deeply committed. However, part of teamwork involves the *explicit* articulation of *team* criteria (that is, criteria on which there is majority agreement) against which to evaluate the feasibility of initial objectives. When in a later meeting a nurse produced evidence highlighting P37's probable inability to live in sheltered accommodation, the committed team member implied fairly explicitly that the nurse (and those agreeing with her) were letting the side down by not being properly committed to the objective of relocating P37 in alternative accommodation (thereby personalizing a team and professional issue). What was highlighted by such processes was the lack of any clearly articulated team agreement or understanding about the (tentative or exploratory) nature of an initial objective and how team objectives have to be continually reevaluated in light of new evidence and evolving circumstances.

Decision Making and Leadership in Knowledge-Based Teamwork

Teams do not always make explicit decisions. In the reviews at which I was present there were no occasions when the team leader either explicitly confirmed a line of action that was implicit in the direction of the discussion ("Okay, given what we have been saying, we are in agreement, then, that X will happen") or, when there was a dispute around possible courses of action (as with the diet imposition), sought team agreement or rejection of the proposed plan, asked for elaboration of reasons for this or that plan, or rehearsed the different positions that the team had discussed and the actions it had taken to date in relation to that issue. There is clearly a balance to be achieved between overstructuring and understructuring discussions, and although my emphasis is on the fluid and contingent nature of teamwork, some formal decision-making processes are nevertheless necessary if all members of the team are to be clear about what course of action the team is proposing and take some degree of collective responsibility for the team's work. Some structuring of discussions is also vital when there is disagreement, in order to attend to that disagreement explicitly and seek to resolve it. Structure also assists in focusing the work of individual members toward team objectives, and the fact that the team can later point to its collective decision may assist in containing any subsequent acrimony over responsibility for specific courses of action.

Recalling one member's words about how the team should have available to it a range of team accounts/narratives about P9 ("it *ought to be possible/* to have . a *variety of views* of him: a *nursing view,* a psychologist view, a psychiatric view and so forth and so on which can actually *cohere.* It can come together in some coherent way and that/ the *knowledge* of those other views helps to *expand* your own understanding of your *own* bit but it also fills in a lot of the stuff"), I want to outline a possible alternative structure of a knowledge-based discussion about this client. It is important to note that I am not suggesting that structuring the discussion in the manner proposed will enable teams to identify solutions/answers to their problems easily. Rather, it is intended to clarify the range of issues, reflecting different members' locations in the care system, and possible responses to those issues with which the team needs explicitly to engage. *How* they engage with these will be determined by the local context.

Confronted with such a situation, there are two obvious strategies available to the team. One, which was what happened in relation to the competing representations of P9 (adolescent/pig), is that the team can split and argue over the morality of one mode of representation. A second is that the team can take both accounts seriously and look at where they connect, what issues they raise, and so on. My point here is emphatically not to support the use of pejorative language. It is, though, to affirm that the account of P9 as a "pig" could have told other team members something about the nature of that person's experience with P9 and about the daily difficulties confronting nursing staff—in particular because of their organizational role with this client—which made different demands on them than those made on the clinicians. By attacking the speaker and distancing themselves from the language used, however, the team shut off any discussion of these issues. This response complicated any systematic identification of the connections between "adolescent" and "pig," the issues to be addressed, the constraints in adopting various courses of action, the team's responses to date, and the possibility of establishing an agreed-upon course of action.

By taking note of the team's range of discipline-specific views or narratives of P9, a leader of a knowledge-based team could have written down (say, on a white board) a prioritized list of problems and the issues they raised for the team to discuss. Such a procedure ensures that each speaker knows that his or her position and issues are being heard by the team. Further, in this context the leader has the dual responsibility of ensuring that all narratives are heard and of moving the team into a more conceptual mode. "How do we think about what we have heard? What have we not accounted for? What are the issues here?"

Had the team structured their discussion along such lines and written the representations down, instead of treating the two as contradictory and highlighting one as primarily morally ambiguous, it would have assisted in the development of interdisciplinary links. Questions that could have been asked in relation to such work include: "What are the implications of both ways of thinking about P9 in relation to structuring the team's and members' work?" "What are the practical constraints (the resourcing and practical issues relating to his management on the unit)?" "What further knowledge is required to augment a possible course of action, who will provide it, and in what time frame?" "Are these different approaches contradictory or are there points of connection?" "How do we as a team respond to the practical difficulties confronting the nurses in their seeking to better manage this client?"

Part of the role of a leader of a knowledge-based team is to continually push at the discussion's boundaries. "We've established the problems—what issues do these raise?" "Are these all the issues?" "How then do we think about these issues?" "What frameworks are available to us?" "What are the implications of following down this or that path?" "What else do we need to know?" "Are we agreed here that we proceed in this (these) direction(s)?" "If you don't agree, what alternative possibilities do you propose, and on the basis of what knowledge or information?" "What is the majority decision here?" "What is the team objective(s); who is going to be involved with this client over the next period; what work will you undertake that will advance that (those) objective(s)?"

A team may not come to a final decision about its actions in one meeting. It may require further information before that is possible. What I am illustrating is how knowledge-based work calls for a narrative structure that merges with issues, objectives, and task identification in a process that allows for knowledge spirals and structured decision making. Moreover, part of an effective decision-making process is that the team undertake a process of focused closure for each discussion, where the plan, by whom and how it is to be advanced, and so on, are confirmed, enabling all members to be fully cognizant of that plan and their role in it.

Thinking the Leadership Role

Fleshing out the above points also makes it possible to identify more clearly dimensions of leadership in knowledge-based work. This role includes:

- Encouraging the speaking of discipline-specific knowledge;
- Assisting in identifying different representations of clients generated by the team;
- Assisting in the team process of identification of issues generated by teams' discussions, including more marginalized ones;
- Raising questions about the direction and focus of the discussion;
- Asking for the introduction into the team's work of relevant theoretical perspectives from different disciplines to inform that work, and encouraging the team to engage with the different implications of those perspectives;
- Attending, in the context of task allocation, to how those issues shape the next phase of the team's work;
- Ensuring that (changing) team goals are responsive to and incorporate members' individual tasks and objectives; and
- Ensuring that there is (majority) team agreement to a developing plan.[2]

While I have suggested that these responsibilities rest particularly with the team leader, they do not exclusively do so, since the production of knowledge-based work requires that all members participate in the analytic processes I have outlined here.

Two final points need to be made. One relates to how the map I have drawn relates to different cultural and geographical locations. My objective has been to develop a map enabling teams to more effectively structure their reviews in the context of an assumption that organizations are more effectively served by knowledge-based teams that are able to produce more fully informed care decisions and plans in which professionals, clients, and families participate. Such a map is not intended prescriptively. It is open to modification as local circumstances require. For example, as the transcripts of team meetings indicated, the length of discussions and complexity of the issues relating to individual clients varied considerably. A discussion about one client might last three minutes one week and twenty or more the next because of changes in that person's condition or situation. If there were few issues in relation to a specific client, it could be expected that the dominant features of team discussions would be the introduction, identification of tasks, and closure. More complex situations would dictate longer discussions, so that teams could review and assess the efficacy and direction of their work in some detail. In such situations, they would be more likely to work across all dimensions of the map, the constituent features of which have been the focus of the discussion in this chapter, and to progress their discussions by employing some of the identified strategies.

The second point attends to another process issue. My desire in this chapter has been to unpack that deceptively simple account of teamwork "We talk about the client" to demonstrate the complex process by which effective teamwork involves members' engagement with diffracted knowledge to arrive at more subtle understandings through a formal but flexible process relying on producing structured information; attention to the process of the discussion; consciousness of how developing discussions differently positions or occludes knowledge advanced by different disciplines and by clients and families; conceptual work; and articulation of detail to enable connections. The objective of such discussions is the development of a practically and conceptually informed case plan that has been confirmed by team members. The plan itself is necessarily contingent, since its continued appropriateness must be tested against changes or stasis in clients' and/or families' circumstances and explored through ongoing processes of information and knowledge convergence and divergence that can contribute to reevaluations of client, family, and team objectives.

7

Teams as Author
Narrative and Knowledge Creation in Case Discussions

Narrative is the most common method for ordering and refocusing experience (White 1981). In describing narrative as inseparable from human experience, Peter Brooks wrote: "Our lives are ceaselessly intertwined with narrative, with the stories that we tell, all of which are reworked in that story of our own lives. . . . We are immersed in narrative" (quoted in McCloskey 1990:7). Within their professional worlds human service workers attend to the narratives of others and create/author their own as part of their everyday work (Pithouse 1987). In this domain, representing a client narratively allows service workers to present and redefine issues, to speculate or entertain possibilities, and to reposition their work and their representations of clients as their narratives develop. Narrative is not necessarily or only a facilitative means of forming and communicating knowledge, however; its universal currency and assumed "naturalness" may well suppress its problematic dimensions (H. Miller 1995). Furthermore, expectations about narrative based on traditional, "well-formed" narratives may prevent recognition of the existence and role of narrative in discussions (as in those of interprofessional teams) that demonstrate many features now recognized as characteristic of postmodern narratives.

To ground and develop my narrative of health professionals' narrations, I have drawn on Hunter's (1991) and Atkinson's (1994, 1995) sociological accounts addressing an underdeveloped area of inquiry within medical sociology: medical narratives developed and exchanged between doctors during ward rounds, in case conferences, and in informal work settings. My interest in professional talk and its role in knowledge production touches upon but is different from Hunter's and Atkinson's. My focus is on an equally neglected area of health work, the textual productions of inter-professional health care teams. My attention to the teams' narratives and their relationship to knowledge creation moves beyond issues of discipli-nary transmission of medical knowledge to focus on how interprofessional teams are positioned between and work across disciplinary knowledges, and on the organizational conditions that facilitate such work. As with those medical teams involved in Hunter's and Atkinson's research, so also were the teams in my research engaged in extensive processes of narration; in contrast to Atkinson and Hunter, I have located my work in current narrative theory, a position that has much to offer, given the discursive nature of the verbal and written texts that these teams authored/produced.

The first section of this chapter, "Narratives of Medical Narrations," presents my reading of key issues in Hunter's and Atkinson's work. The second section, "The Narrative Productions of Health Teams," presents my analysis of team narratives about two clients developed by two teams over several weeks. The final section, "Knowledge Creation in Teamwork," moves on to a discussion of knowledge creation and the organizational conditions necessary to facilitate such work.

Narratives of Medical Narrations

One reading of Atkinson's (1994, 1995) and Hunter's (1991) work is that it underscores the functionality of medical narrative. Both writers present narration as a critical factor in the process of evaluating and weighing an often extensive range of (competing) complex medical evidence when decisions about client management are being made, and in the organiza-tion and transmission of medical knowledge.

Although both of these two writers' analyses are concerned with the function and the organizational shaping of narrative, Hunter's emphasis is on *interpretation,* while Atkinson's (here working from an ethnomethod-ological approach) is on the complex, skilled, and situated *work* associated with the production of medical narratives, an area of work that he notes is ethnographically insufficiently mapped and delineated. In her account, Hunter identifies parsimony as a distinctive feature of medical narrating, arguing its importance in sense-making (sifting out the unnecessary or extraneous detail) and suggesting that achieving the ability to produce (appropriately) parsimonious narratives is a critical part of professional development. In commenting on the processes of transformation of patients' narratives into medical narratives, she argues that this process of reworking reflects the different narrator positioning of patients and doctors—the patient's story being told from a position of being subject to a medical condition, the doctor's story being told from a position external to that condition but including an obligation to resolve or attend to that state because of the possession of relevant expert knowledge. The resultant highly purposive medical account, Hunter maintains, develops in relation to strict criteria of inclusion and exclusion. Its structure represents psychological as well as professional needs. "The achievement of the regular, patterned, self-effacing plot of medical narrative is to control insofar as possible the subjectivity of its observer-narrator and the variables of its telling" (62); further "the narrative organization of the case is shaped by the physician's quest for an understanding of the patient's illness. . . . The plot not only reveals to its audience the meaning of the puzzling events it recounts but is also the narrative of discovery of that meaning" (65–66). The defect of such narratives is that the "tradition works well in difficult or puzzling cases . . . but it is insufficient for long-term patient care. . . . Chronic illness and dying tend to be 'uninteresting' to many physicians" (xxi). While highly medically functional, these narratives are nonetheless problematic because of the marginalization or absence of patients' life-worlds. Hunter suggests that the development of "enriched" (166) narratives incorporating patients' subjectivity may become more necessary, particularly in the areas of chronic and aged care.

Hunter's work, then, is grounded in a long-standing preoccupation in medical sociology and anthropology (see, for example, Good 1994)[1] about the lack of attention given in medicine to the life-world of the patient. Her foregrounding of the interpretive dimension of narrative, however, opens the possibility of a postmodern reading. Her concern with interpretation and her identification of parsimony, inclusion, and suppression as shaping factors in the composition of medical narratives questions the concept of narrative as "reporting" or revealing the world as it really is and challenges the assumption of a high degree of correspondence or mirroring between the event and any narration of that event (H. Miller 1995). What is produced is always a representation of the event. Current theories of representation emphasize that a representation of a person, event, or situation can never be complete because it is a function of the perceiver's position or location in time, space, culture, and discourse. Moreover, narratives are linguistic events. Narrators speak not from a neutral or objective position but from within language that is embedded in power relations, shapes thought and perception, and provides models for the composition of appropriate narratives[2] (Clifford and Marcus 1986; Foucault 1988a; Nicholson 1990; Smith 1990; Trinh Minh-Ha 1992).

In his valuable but somewhat celebratory analysis of medical narratives, Atkinson (1995) seeks to foreground that which in an earlier text he has described as sociologically "backstage" (1994:118): the complex professionally acquired skills involved in selection, differentiation, and evaluation of evidence from different sources in medical settings, and the rhetorical structures underpinning the resultant narratives. In particular, he posits that twentieth-century medicine produces a multiply sited body (Atkinson 1995:89), a body produced/appropriated by a range of disciplines, each with different methods of measurement requiring particular knowledge for their interpretation. This body, then, is a

> series of representations. These representations are themselves dispersed in time and space within the complex organization of the clinic. They are inspected, interpreted and reported by different cadres of specialized personnel. . . . One should think of the modern clinic as producing a disembodied body . . . a body . . . divorced from the body of the patient. The body may therefore be read at different sites. . . . It [the patient's body] is, however, one among many possible versions of the body that may be assembled in the modern clinic. The patient thus may have a multiple existence within the clinic. . . . the various fragmentary aspects of the patient and his or her body are brought together under the auspices of *the case*.   *(Atkinson 1995:89).*

Atkinson argues that describing and theorizing the production of this complex, disembodied body, however, requires more attention than has hitherto been given to the analysis of a number of key, core activities "in the accomplishment of medical work" (37) taking place in settings from which the patient is absent, and it is to this task that Atkinson turns his attention. His analysis focuses on the processes by which intricate and multifaceted medical knowledge is articulated in everyday practices through the development of "plausible accounts" (Atkinson 1995:90), whose rhetorical structure is responsive to the organizational context and confers credibility onto the narrator. Plausibility, he suggests, is accomplished through attention to relevance, through the employment of a number of rhetorical features (such as "hedging" and the use of "shields"

[126]), and through the production of a "good account." The distinguishing features of a "plausible" account are that it

- Has sufficient detail to allow the audience to follow the chronological development of the illness,
- Is "sufficiently *eventful*" (Atkinson 1994:119) to enable the audience to reconstruct the most significant findings and follow the management of the case.
- Provides evidence of clinical reasoning and decision making,
- Provides an adequate grasp of detail, so providing evidence that the clinician has understood the case.

Such accounts provide the evidence that the clinician has grasped the case and that the selection of detail is related to others' "need to know" (Atkinson 1995:97). This model is not without its parsimonious dimensions. He also argues that many clinical medical presentations follow Labov's evaluative model of narrative events, having the following dimensions: abstract; orientation (locating in time and place); complication (what happened); evaluation (how speaker views the events and conveys the point of narrative); result (resolution); and optional coda (closing summary) (103).

There is some tension, however, on which Atkinson remarks, between the formality of Labov's model and his (Atkinson's) comment on the incompleteness of many medical narratives—these are often provisional and open to revision and negotiation, and they disrupt the Aristotelian unities of actor, duration, and setting that underpin Labov's model. Since the theoretical and textual implications of such disruptions are significant, it is worth quoting White (1981:23) at some length on the problems with traditional narrative forms. He wrote:

> I have sought to suggest that this value attached to narrativity in the representation of real events arises out of a desire to have real events display the coherence, integrity, fullness, and closure of an image of life that is and can only be imaginary. The notion that sequences of real events possess the formal attributes of the stories we tell about imaginary events could only have its origin in wishes, daydreams, reveries. Does the world really present itself to perception in the form of well-made stories, with central subjects, proper beginnings, middles, and ends, and a coherence that permits us to see "the end" in every beginning? Or does

it present itself more in the forms that the annals and chronicle suggest, either as mere sequence without beginning or end or as sequences of beginnings that only terminate and never conclude? And does the world, even the social world, ever really come to us as already narrativized, already "speaking itself" from beyond the horizon of our capacity to make scientific sense of it? Or is the fiction of such a world, a world capable of speaking itself and of displaying itself as a form of a story, necessary for the establishment of that moral authority without which the notion for a specifically social reality would be unthinkable? . . . Can we ever narrativize *without* moralizing?

The significance of this quotation is twofold: first, expectations of what constitutes "narrative" need to be flexible (Nash 1990) and may not accord with formalist aesthetics of narrative; second, narrative cannot be separated out from issues of representation and power, albeit that that power may be productive and not necessarily repressive or prohibitory (Foucault 1980, 1988a). As Miller (1995) has noted, narrative contains a policing function; it is embedded in dominant discourses. Equally, one of the cultural functions of narrative is to critique the dominant representational practices sustaining the existing social order. This paradoxical positioning places narrative in an interrogatory role. Narratives themselves, through their capacity to represent/re-present difference, become vehicles for change (although that "change" cannot necessarily be read as progressive or linear). Highlighting the possibility of challenge to the existing social order, they demonstrate its tenuousness and its potential for renegotiation (Mumby 1993).

The Narrative Productions of Health Teams

Atkinson (1995) remarks on the constitution of the medical field by competing specialisms with different frames of reference. Nonetheless, that field is constituted by a range of commonly held assumptions relating to the nature of scientific evidence as informing interpretation and decision making and by a shared knowledge base. The medical teams involved in Atkinson's research could be described as operating within a master narrative (Lyotard 1984).

In contrast, interprofessional teams bring together professionals whose training calls on highly diverse assumptions and very different knowledge bases, in a context where each discipline accords others differential status. Such teams, then, are grounded in heterogeneity, where each discipline provides the means to compose a fully plausible account or, in other words, to tell the "whole" story of the client; in practice, only fragments of that fuller knowledge can be and are presented in team meetings, yet it is from working with these heterogeneous fragments that the team is required to develop a plan. The intersection of disciplinary knowledge or knowledge systems, a requirement in an interprofessional context, also complicates the application of "parsimony" in any evaluation of the efficacy of team discussions, since the definition of an "extraneous" detail is a disciplinary, not a self-evident, issue. In an interprofessional team, members need to talk through their different perceptions of the client and their situation as part of a necessary process of displaying how each discipline shapes knowledge and determines action. Rather than regarding redundancy as an irrelevancy, the team can regard it as necessary to this mode of teamwork. The interprofessional teams in this study were not concerned with the internal transmission and learning of disciplinary knowledge but (ideally) with the intersection of *different* knowledges in order to develop an appropriate care and management plan for and with (many) long-term clients or patients. Instead of typically foregrounding a detailed chronology of the illness/condition and its management, they focused on their work in relation to the demands of long-term care, quality-of-life issues, and the provision of holistic care.

Relevance can become a contested issue in an interprofessional context. Interviews with members pointed to an absence of shared agreement about what was significant information and the *purpose* of the team's discussions in light of the team's responsibility to achieve positive outcomes for clients. One of the consequences of chronic illness or long-term care is that a client's body may become very vulnerable to an unnecessary exposure to the team gaze. Extensive discussion of elimination processes and toileting problems is arguably unnecessary in such teams. The discussion may also move too easily to an evaluation of clients' moral worth or that of their families. Situations in which staff members used the meetings to develop detailed and frequently unchallenged negative narratives about clients highlighted the problematic nature of representations of clients developed in teamwork and teams' lack of reflexivity (Opie 1997). In this context, accessing the concept "relevance" acquires not just a functional but also an ethical dimension: protection against violation of privacy through unnecessary or ethically questionable exposure.

This suggests that defining teamwork primarily in terms of contributions of information (as did most members and their organizations) is a somewhat simplistic account of a more complex process. One social worker, recognizing that her contribution of some of the information about clients that she gained in the course of her work with them might result in the formulation of representations of the clients with which she was unsympathetic, remained substantially silent about her work with clients. Because the team had no structure that enabled it to discuss how it carried out its work, it was therefore unable to discuss how different information contributed to different representations of clients and how these different representations affected the orientation of the team's work. The social worker's silences were misinterpreted by some other members, who believed she should be contributing more (but did not say so).

Team Reviews as Narrative

Interprofessional team reviews are distinguished from accounts of clients spoken within the context of meetings held by a single discipline by their heterogeneous sources in different disciplinary perspectives and the fragmented representations of knowledge that result from the flow of conversation among the various members of the team. My purpose is to show that, in this situation, the most common mode of representing knowledge adopted by team members is narrative. Because the texts that result from this shared discursive activity are not "authored" by any one member of the team and yet are the sum of all the team members' attempts to provide an adequate and purposeful account of the situation of the client, I describe them as *team narratives* and elaborate on the significance of this term.

The examples of team narratives presented here are typical of the way each of these teams went about its work. Their reviews of clients were not characterized, to refer back to White's (1981:1) problematizing of narrative form, by well-formed accounts, a single speaker, a "central subject," or "proper beginnings, middles, and ends." They were not coherent. As I noted in chapter 3, members interrupted each other, their voices trailed off, some spoke inaudibly. Different agendas were inserted into the conversation, issues were not developed. Many of the discussions were provisional and inconclusive. Their outcome was dependent not just on the teams' work but on a series of factors beyond the teams' control: the ability and speed of the individual body to heal; the speed of the return of tests and conclusiveness of results; the agreement of other organizations to proposals; the availability of alternative placements; the extent to which these teams' work with their clients may be compromised by other organizations' problematic input into different areas of work with the family. The teams could not "conclude" their narratives about clients too quickly—the pacing was dictated by the events that would unfold in the fullness of time. There were no strong beginnings and endings, no easily claimed coherences, there were possibilities for the team to develop its work in various directions other than that with the client (What of the work potentially to be done with parents or spouses? To which "client" should the team turn its gaze?). These stories, as White (1981:23) would have it, were "sequences of beginnings that only terminate and never conclude."

The team discussions are the product of a distinctive situation—the reviewing of clients' progress by members of interprofessional teams—and they result in the production of distinctive texts. These texts are in the first instance oral productions, generated through a mini-narrative process and achieving more permanent, (i.e., written) status because of the presence of a researcher. As written texts, they become available for classification, description, and analysis. They were not, however, solely oral texts. For example, the reviews carried out by the disability inpatient team were minuted, and the minutes were then used to start the team discussion the following week. The four reviews I taped of this team's opening commentary on P15 ran as follows:

Review 1

OT(1) P15/ his back has improved, it's stopped seeping, there's good progress. Query the prospect of going home in a wheel chair. . . .

Review 2

OT(1) Okay/ *P15* . . last week his *back* had been seeping um/ possibilities to overcome this were *discussed* and we decided it was to be *looked at* on the ward round/ on Thursday.

Review 3

OT(2) Okay is that all for P11?. P15 . that [.] tincture started seems to be/ *improving* and that's to the/ area on his buttocks that is *seeping*. . . the supra pubic/ *is mucky* . . and Ward Dr. is going to follow that up. The area on his ankle's almost *healed* and his *mood* seems a bit depressed/ and he can cause . trouble in the dining room at night although there's um/ a *positive* to that he's also cheerful and can cheer up all the others this way.

Review 4

NSC P15: continue to mobilise slowly/ very small blood blister/ on *great* toe from his stocking. Discussion/ re mood/ ah/ wheelchair reviewed by OT and physio. Comfort/ cushion unsatis/factory . and the psych registrar was going to see him.

Although the disability team's introductions to each client were very short, they demonstrated an interprofessional authorial process. Each introduction, which focused largely on different tasks that were to be discharged with particular reference to medical, nursing, and paramedical concerns, was used to focus the team on its direction and immediate treatment goals (hence attending to issues of accountability) and constituted a partial summary of members' input the previous week. The responsibility for minute-taking was shared by all disciplines except medical. Minute-taking was taken for granted, however, and not understood as invoking an authorial role involving processes of selection, like foregrounding, suppression, or exclusion of aspects of the team's discussion, nor, as a result of these features, as weighing subsequent input and so orienting the team's gaze and structuring its work. As is apparent from the transcripts, significant dimensions of the team's discussion either were recorded in a way that did not well reflect the discussion or were omitted. The following exchange occurred at the end of the first taped review:

SW How does Prozac seem to have been affecting him?

NSC He was a bit grumpy when he first came in didn't he because he's only been on Prozac for about—

DR —he's always been ah *really good* about once he's come here but the fact that he told me he wanted to be staying in bed/ that *did* drop that mood *down* quite a bit.

NSC He's been *really down* at home/ no/ he's been *really down*. Not like P15 and um/ so that when you suggested to put him on the Prozac and he seems to be/ he *seems* to be feeling much better.

SN He's enjoying stirring P5 along and making suggestions/ left right and centre and that's/ perking people along.

SW But is that because he's here or because of the Prozac? She says that's helping him. I don't *know*..

DR Yes it will be the environment.

NSC If he really wants to go home there's no doubt about it. He's not/ you know .. so

SW He doesn't think enough happens up in that end room. He thinks he's been stuck away up in the end room. We put him there so we—

SN —we haul him out twice a day and dust him off/ (*some chuckles*) take him down to the dining room and TV room.

(. . .)

SLT Any more for P15?

Review 2

OT(1) Okay/ *P15* . . last time his *back* had been seeping um/ possibilities to overcome this were *discussed* and we decided it was to be *looked at* on the ward round/ on Thursday.

There was no procedure to enable the team to attend to the adequacy or fullness of the notes' representation of the team's work or discussions, or a place where the role of the notes and their appropriate structure could be discussed.

The psychiatric inpatient team's review of each client was initiated by a nursing report read by the client's nurse for the day. The taped introductory commentary on P1 went as follows:

Review 1

N3 P1 (*big sigh*) management no change in presentation. P1's had three documented periods of [aggression] where he's been [aggressive towards another patient during a] game of pool. Made a gesture of his hands across his throat and down there/ down his stomach [. .]; carries out present [.]. Interactions of self [. .] Social and family: Continues to be visited by guardians. Aunt contacted the unit Sunday night . the following day said she'd like [.] to be checked out. P1 has a red throat. He wants [. .] why does he compensate so much for [. .] guardians [. .]

Review 2

N1 (*reading another's handwritten notes with difficulty*) P1/ (*sigh*) P1: his/ current issues are/ are continue investigating his eventual/ transfer to the brain injury unit. His physical: no concerns . ah mental state nil change in/ presentation. Some frustration if kept inside during the bad weather/ occas/ occasionally/ flush/ flashes of brilliant humour . aaah . . and was virtually involved in a fight between other *clients* . Did not react violently/ violently and quickly forgot. His management: continue plan/ update ah/ became a little hostile after guardians'/

visit. Blaming same on being in this nuthouse. Soon calmed down. Guardians want to know if P1's/ friend/ Julie can be *present* when P1 visits their house on his next home leave. Social and family: regular visits by guardians. Aaah/ no leave during this period. Ah/ update *after* weekend visit, visitor left behind some books on trailbikes and some on/ fish/ *hunting*. . Aah is it appropriate that (*sigh*) P1 has hunting books in his room/ possession/ query that.

Review 3

N3 . . . okay we'll move on to P1. Ah, his current issues: case conference on the 25th of this month at 9 o'clock in the morning/ ah complex needs assessments to be arranged/ through ACC, day leave next Sunday. Ah, his physical: no no concerns there. Mental state: no change in mental state. Settled week/ with only one documented period of irritability due to P1 not/ being able to go out in the courtyard/ upon his request . . ah commented on seeing service sign and saying "Anyone would think I attacked someone." Also he requested scissors to cut his toenails and on being told there were none available at the time/ stated/ "You should you shouldn't oh you couldn't stab anyone with these." P1/ and P12 appear to enjoy each other's/ company and appear to interact well. His management: no change in his management. Attending groups/ visit by guardians Saturday, visit by uncle on Wednesday. There has been a a request by ah/ his aunt this morning over the phone. She's requesting ah/ if P1 could have/ oh to go to the gym during a/ weekly program on smoking . . ah that's from Dr/ forget his name (*overlap*) um

Review 4

N1 P1 aah/ competence *needs* assessment/ has has been *arranged* . *Aah*/ query family meeting. SSW1, has this been arranged? It says here CNS2 that you will attend a full family 22 July and/ whatever. *Physical:* seen by house surgeon re scarring about left arm/ aah (*sigh*)/ about statistics from/ query statistics related to [ ] ah orthopaedic review at Outpatients. [ ] also *sent* . Guardians are aware of the same, a review of the same. Mental state: no change in mental state or on presentation. *Became* frustrated during letter writing groups swearing and throwing arms in the air but was easily distracted from this/ after being directed to something of *interest* i.e. his book on car mechanics. Management: nil change in management continues with present regime as per plan.

Social and family: visited by guardians/ Wednesday to *Saturday* . He had home leave on Sunday with two on one escort escorting nurses. Report/ not a successful home leave with some concern documented over guardians mostly uncle/ constantly asking P1 if he would remember/ or if he *could* remember various things. For example showed P1 photos of the past. P1 became mildly agitated and annoyed and stating loudly on *several* occasions, "I can't remember a fuckin' thing. My memory's failed." Aah/ this is an issue for the MD team. (*2-3 people comment simultaneously and briefly.*) Do the guardians need to be addressed *re* this? And his requests are a *very long* walk/ to get some food (*someone laughs*) to have leave to go shopping and/ buy a—oh this is from his guardians—have leave to go shopping to buy a birthday present for his aunt . . . mm.

Review 5

N2 Okay mm hm ah P1 ah he's finished his case conference on the 25th of the 7th and his family meeting on the 22nd of the 7th um . . . okay mental state there's been no change in mental state on presentation ah one incident this week where/ P1 misinterpreted a conversation and challenged a nurse this morning [.] Usual agitation, and irritability evident at times unless actually directed redirected. Generally occupies um time alone either playing playing pool or watching TV [tuning it to topics in which interested] ie motorbikes, fighting and hunting etc. Ah continues to acknowledge um/ from [.] and um/ yesterday when we tried to get his/ [blood]/ levels [. .] / as the diagnostics lady was about to put the syringe in his arm, the needle in his arm he just/ went/ his anxiety just gradually increased. He got all agitated running around the room and swinging his arms a bit um/ so if those levels need to be taken again—well they will need to be be taken—and we will have to/ look at some way of managing that either . . through an overall group approach or maybe possible sedation.

Each report was a written summary of what the key worker had defined, in reviewing the week's nursing notes, as the main issues bearing on P1 over the past week. Some of the team members who were not nurses were dissatisfied with this mode of introduction because it was so explicitly discipline-focused and appeared to contradict the intended interprofessional mode of conduct of the team. The psychiatric team's introductions were more complex and extensive than those of the disability team, although the comments about P1 were brief in relation to some introductions of other clients. Each summary was presented under headings: current issues, physical, mental, management, social and family, and patient's requests. Three of the summaries about P1 explicitly requested team discussion on particular issues or identified the need for the development of management strategies. Overall, however, the summaries offered little in terms of team or organizational accountability, and the specific requests for discussion or agreement were not always attended to.

These summaries, the starting point of the weekly reviews, can be described as "narratives" because they represent in a conventional, shared mode some team members' knowledge about and experience of clients in order for that knowledge to become available to other members. They possess the primary narrative components of events, actors, and time (future, past, and present); they include inference and speculation; they are expository. Together with the discussions that they generate, they contribute to the developing "story line" about each client, which can be thought of as composed by the team as a corporate author. Making their shared and unique knowledge explicit in this evolving story about the client is a fundamentally important means by which team members affirm, question, and refocus that knowledge, and by which they can make manifest the team dimension of their individual work. In defining such accounts as narratives, the conventional association of narrative with literary or fictional accounts of events and people, and with complex stories of loss, violence, courage, determination, intransigence, marital breakdown, and family problems, played out against an organizational backdrop, has to be put to one side. Rather, the crucial factor is that the health professionals who have produced these texts in an interprofessional team setting have habitually used the distinctive features of narrative representation to organize and communicate their knowledge, including selection (and exclusion) of factual material and interpretation of that material. A brief account, beginning "We had a lovely meeting," contains the basic narrative elements of place, time, actors, and point of view.

CP3 (*overlapping*) oh right. Well, we had a/ *lovely meeting with his* family yesterday afternoon/ didn't we SP?

SP1 Yep.

CP3 It was nice meeting for the first one.

SSW1 Yeah it was nice.

CP3 SSW1 was a coward also [. . .] (*laughter*)

ssw1 (*overlapping*) I don't think [ ] (*laughing*) yeah just

cp3 I mean . . they seem to me like a lot of guardians with kids with head injuries might be/ slightly better advocates than most but at the same time there's anger and/ and rage at the system etc etc . . The other thing is though/ this referral to the unit. Well, I don't think we should be holding our breath and actually expecting it to work.

This account is as much an act of interpretation and representation, however abbreviated, as is the counselor's much more elaborate narrative of an earlier meeting:

> Well I'll report on the I'll report the meeting . . soon/ perhaps I should do that now. Um/ it was an interesting meeting. It took over an hour. Ah/ there were two people from the ah brain injury unit, ah the ah clinical manager/ and um/ and the uncle ah/ and ah/ what took a *long* time was that the/ aah/ the uncle/ as the principal spokesperson ah/ went over the the *whole* history of the of the process/ and um/ and in some ways it was *useful/ not so much to* ah/ to get the ah/ the reiteration of the theme/ but really to ah/ to establish the *starting* point/ um/ which *I/ I* in fact wasn't wasn't aware of that/ their um/ what happened/ with *P1* is that he was ah/ in a coma and remained so for some time and ah/ the first sign of movement was a/ was a slight movement of his um/ I think left *arm* and the guardians have persevered. Um/ um/ just a complete absence of of ah/ medical or any other kind of staff in the whole story but/ there's *certainly no doubt in my mind* that whatever they have *done* they have been very persistent and/ they have *refused* right from the outset to accept some/ um/ limitations which they say/ have been stated very flatly and very baldly. One was that P1 would not walk *again* and ah/ that he wouldn't be able to be as active as he is and/ so forth and so on and so forth. *In some ways* the impression/ at the end of ah/this *quite* long drawn out meeting was that ah/ ah they were tremendous advocates for a *severely* ah brain injured person and ah/ you would want them/ on your *side* if ah/ something like that *happened* um/ *however* the/ what's *going* to happen is that/ the um/ the *ACC* will be requested *by* ah/ the Brain Injury Unit to/ to set up a formal assessment/ um/ *of P1* ah/ *complete assessment* um/ um/ of his ah/ to establish a kind of *baseline* ah/ clear baseline where he's at. That includes um/ occupational therapy/ physiotherapy. This will *all* be done by people who come in to do that to do the assessments and ah/ on the *basis of that* they'll ah continue to negotiate with ah ACC as to

his/ um/ *suitability* for the *unit* um/ which they hope will be established next month. They were going on later that *day* to/ talk to ACC and it seems to me that in/ the *current* political climate there's a fair chance that they'll succeed in in getting the funding to establish. Ah, they have a/ they *have* an *option* on a building somewhere in the central city area aah which ah/ they're able to retain ah for about a month or *five weeks/* ah/ so that's the kind of operating *so we'll know relatively soon* whether this is going to happen or not. They've got quite a *large/ staff* or a potential staff and they've actually or they must have a certain amount of confidence in it coming through because they've already started the process of/ *staff training.* Ah/ the unit/ they have a/ they have a *secure* ward within a 100 bed private hospital and *this* campus will be/ located in in a separate/ *place* . It won't be as *secure* as as this/ ah unit *here* . It will have um/ a *much* more *discreet* ah perimeter fence than we have around here and um/ the/ the unit itself will be locked but the individual rooms will not be locked/ um and they *intend to* base them/ to *move out* a lot into the community aah/ ah doing a *whole range* of activities. So *um* . . .

The language or team discourse that is used by the speakers is also significant, insofar as it closely parallels that of ordinary conversation, where speakers typically engage in narrative and quasi-narrative forms. Each contributing account to the developing narrative about a client is produced in substantially unself-conscious language, that is, the language used is descriptive, not "analytic," in that it does not particularly overtly engage with concepts or seek to integrate, examine minutely, or critique either the individual narrative or the team narrative about a specific client. Each team narrative is contributed to at different times by various team members, who have different experiences and perspectives of the client. These narrators at different points complement and contradict each other's narratives, creating competing representations of the client (or, in the psychiatric team's narrative about P1, of informal caregivers).

To note the largely unanalytical mode of the teams' discourse is in no sense to suggest that the narratives lack purpose. They are not spoken by a random collection of individuals or a group of professionals chatting about clients over a drink, but by a group with a specific organizational task to develop and modify care plans and monitor clients' progress in the light of two organizational objectives: achieving an improvement in the clients' quality of life through attention to those areas of their condition that can be modified or adjusted and working toward their eventual discharge.

I do not intend to suggest that the discussion should from the outset be conducted in a more "analytic" or conceptual mode, nor to privilege narrative above concept. Each mode of discussion generates and is dependent on the other. The processes of selection, organization, and interpretation that are consistently at work in the composition of these texts convert the experiences of individual team members into knowledge that can be shared. The significance of a team narrative is that it allows a mapping of multiple interpretive possibilities, enables unpredictable connections to be made, and generates alternative frameworks. More explicit conceptualization occurs when team members introduce discipline-based knowledge to interpret further or to critique the adequacy of the differing narrative representations of the client's situation. The effect of such discursive shifts is not to permanently anchor a particular interpretation but, because of the ways in which teams' narratives are shaped by the work to be undertaken, to facilitate through that (temporary) stasis in the production of narratives the generation of other narrative possibilities and modes of conceptualization. The metaphor is rhizomic rather than arborescent (Deleuze and Guattari 1983); there is no single perspective that will offer a full account, and each individual account may well raise several different possibilities that could be pursued.[3]

The model team narrative draws on individual members' narratives but does not necessarily mirror them; it is built up during a series of discussions and is shaped by the team's need for purposeful action; and it can always be adapted in response to changing circumstances. The team narrative may contain, with varying degrees of explicitness, reference to several interrelated but distinct professional modes of narrative formation—administrative, medical, nursing, psychological, social, and organizational—which are embellished and played out in the ensuing discussions. The rehearsal of a detailed chronology of the client's condition, while assisting in the identification of team issues, questions, and plans about engaging with a client in some situations, may not be necessary in all cases where the team has longer-term ongoing contact with that client. However, the development of a team narrative may well make explicit the different representations of its clients and of the team's role vis-à-vis the clients, which may be circulating within a team. Open identification of such differences (which is not without therapeutic implications for the client/family) in the process of generating the team narrative shows that a significant aspect of teamwork is the recognition of interpretative differences between team members and developing processes that allow the team to explore the implications of following particular narrative and conceptual paths in order to arrive at a workable plan of action.

The Team Narratives

I want to exemplify my argument by reference to team reviews of two clients. The first, P15, had become a quadriplegic following a sporting accident about two years earlier. He was an inpatient in the disability service initially for two weeks as a respite care patient (a program designed to give informal caregivers a break and to allow the team to reassess clients' care levels and changing needs). Part of the issue for the disability team was finding a different "type" of bed (respite beds were available for only two weeks) to prolong his stay in the hospital in order to further stabilize his condition. Shortly after his admission, another young woman who had been a continuing-care patient on the ward for some years died. Her death particularly affected the other continuing-care clients on the ward.

The psychiatric inpatient team was responsible for the care of the second client, P1. He had been on the unit for more than two years, following a car crash in which he sustained severe head injuries and both of his parents were killed. After his discharge from the hospital, he had seriously assaulted a woman and then had been committed to care. With his parents' death, his uncle and aunt had become his guardians.

Within the course of these reviews, the teams developed a series of parallel mini-narratives and more extensive narratives around medical, administrative, psychological, and organizational themes. While at first blush the team discussions seemed to move in what could be regarded as a relatively random fashion across these themes, the way the discussions were structured can also be read as pointing to the interrelatedness of events and issues that confront the client and the team in the course of its range of work with that client. Neither team imposed a strict order of speaking. Although there were no overt rules defining particular areas as the prerogative of particular disciplines, nonetheless, in the disability team nonmedical staff rarely commented on medical issues (such issues were less dominant in the psychiatric team). Each narrative, though, had the potential, if not the actuality, of a heterogeneity of voices/disciplines contributing to its development.

Nor did these narratives follow a pattern of linear development. Thus, one initial confident narrative of improvement ("his back has improved") was replaced by a more cautious one, constituted by a commentary that moved across different, although substantially medical, aspects of P15's care and his healing processes. This narrative contained moments of uncertainty, or challenge ("What are we going to do?"), hypotheses that were affirmed or rejected, and questions and statements built on observation and past knowledge of the client. Although the disability team's particular medical narrative finally achieved (for the time being) a successful closure, the psychiatric team's considerable confidence at the beginning of the reviews presented here—that P1 was going to be transferred to another unit—was not sustainable as they began to grapple with the consequences of ACC's funding priorities. As a result, the team had to return to their earlier narrative about their own organizational roles and responsibilities.

Review 5

CP3 The other thing is though/ this referral to the unit. Well, I don't think we should be holding our breath and actually expecting it to work because I I've had a very long conversation with the ACC case worker and I I'm I'm suddenly completely confused as to to *what* the process is/ needs to happen for him to get to the unit. *It seems to me* like ACC are going to drag their feet/ over it unless we can get many many of the legal issues/ very *clearly* sorted out first/ and it would/ so it seems that I need to talk to the Director about that/ *now* and get that sorted out. As far as him having a further *assessment*—I was under the impression that the unit *wanted* an assessment.

COUNSELLOR That's true/ and they not only want it/ they need it.

CP3 And then ACC were/ were then going to *arrange* and pay for that?

COUNSELLOR Well/ it's that's just the second step in the process. The first step is the/ ACC *head office*

CP3 Yes

COUNSELLOR has to agree to funding the/ the ah the unit. *Until* that happens the rest of it/ you know the/ actual assess the assessment and so forth are extremely hypothetical and the local caseworker *probably* doesn't know.

CP3 No she doesn't.

COUNSELLOR Yeah.

CP3 She/ she in fact said that herself that it it was/ it was happening at a higher level (*softly*) than her.

COUNSELLOR Yeah.

SP And my understanding from the past, SSW1, is that ACC has said this is a mental health issue (*softly*) and they weren't going to do anything.

SSW1 Yeah it's a very complicated issue um

CP3 (*overlapping with SSW1*) Well it's *made* very complicated.

SSW1 But the problem is with us [. . . . . .] is now, is the facility there and that's the problem/ so so we have to work through the highest level.

CP3 Well good on them!

SSW1 We we wouldn't know a lot about that.

CP3 They've got another problem/ that that in fact the uncle talked about sort/ ah/ sort of peripherally and that is that *ACC won't* put money *into it* unless they're going to get a result (*he speaks over someone else*) so it's um/ *unless* this this—

SSW1 [—this is what I am saying]

CP3 —is the thing we're looking at. *Unless this guy/* can *be rehabilitated/* and is going to *improve/* they *won't fund it* despite the fact that . . they could improve his quality of life *hugely* and maintain him at his current level which to all of us is a pretty acceptable outcome. They wouldn't they wouldn't accept/ they won't *buy* that/ from what/ this woman was saying yesterday.

Both sets of reviews have examples of abrupt transitions between narratives, where narrative possibilities are left unexplored and where issues that could have significant bearing on the development of work remain marginalized. For example, as the counselor concludes his summary of a meeting with P1's guardians, he raises a highly significant issue—the guardians' response to P1's attack on the woman. No one responds to the issue, and the team moves on to the review of the next patient.

COUNSELLOR *the meeting finished* with um/ with a degree of *warmth* ah about the um/ um the Unit's care/ ah for P1 and ah/ ah the view that this wasn't really/ the/ kind of appropriate place for him to be um/ and um/ ah/ *some* where buried in the middle of that is somewhat/ somewhat *worrying* um/ the indication that/ P1 *didn't really* attack anyone (*2 people talk simultaneously*) and that this woman somehow attacked herself.

SP Are you up/ with P1, CP3?

CP3 Yeah yeah he was here before I left yeah . . .

UM Okay next.

If part of the function of narrative is to assist in a reworking of significances and a (re)assessment of direction, then an example such as this points to the seeming difficulty of disrupting and reorienting the team's gaze through an unreflective narrative process alone. The difficulty of critical information's entering the team's consciousness is demonstrated again in relation to the highly pertinent possibility of P1's recovery of his memory, which goes unremarked because the team is pursuing an alternative narrative about how to control the uncle's behavior.

COUNSELLOR As you as you probably all know his uncle has this idea that if he continues to stimulate P1's memory/ his memory will develop some form of *collateral* system that will/ regenerate his memory, you know, short and long term memory. (Well maybe it's—) It tends to *annoy* him.

SP If they can access part of the memory and stimulate activity/ like he may remember things he's done in the past *like in doing them now.* It is quite likely I think that that will happen because I don't think that he/ [that the] amnesia goes *all the way back.* It's quite substantial it's—

COUNSELLOR —[.] mm

SP Could be/ if we stimulated *activities* around the brain you know/ has to be.

N1 The question is is he going to do it? It frustrates him because he can't answer the questions his uncle asks him all the time and—

COUNSELLOR —but you're not going to stop his uncle from doing it because he's basing it clearly on the/ on the way in which he was able to/ in which he was responsible for P1's *physical* recovery by the the fact that he's saying/ he's saying so/ you're not/ you're not *ever* going to shift that out of his—

DM —you know if it *agitates* and irritates *P1* then it raises some concerns for the nursing staff [.] if you know/ I think we *do* need to discuss it with them.

Equally, the discussion about the disability team's consistency in its work with P15 is left hanging.

NSC We're going/ he hasn't been out for *two years* for any length of time/ this guy—*for goodness sake* let's give him that *extra* bit of time, let's get him home in a *chair,* let's get his wife *organised* um/ there's issues of care attendants, there's the issues of the *family* stuff um/ and at least if he can go home and/ um/ the other thing is that his legs swell *very badly* when he's up for any length of time so you know there's all sorts of issues with him/ that he's a nightmare/ he's like a time bomb out there waiting to go/ so let's get him . .

SW Mm, but can we be consistent about what we tell/ what we tell him about that because . . . all the "when am I going home?" bit goes around *everybody* and . . if he/ if he starts to/ *hear* different/ different stories (mm) he will/ play everyone off.

NSC How can we tell him?

SW No/ well either we—that's what I'm saying. If, if we don't know let's all be consistent about *not* saying.

OT(2) Anything?

SW Anything *definite* (mm) because he'll hang on to that and he'll be *really* disappointed.

DR Oh he's very crafty/ he just goes on and on and gets you/ down.

SW That's exactly what I mean.

DR And/ he he does that but then again [.] also for the fact that you've got to go by *day by day* . You can't/ [.] can't say what it will be *end of the week* or even next week and he accepts that.

SLT So we've got some clarity on what he/ what level he even needs to reach before he goes home/ so if we give that clarity to him (mm) so he's got an understanding he needs to boom boom boom (mm) to be *whatever* and then he—

DR —we couldn't just

SLT [. . . .]

DR [. .] just can't be *sure* how he's going to progress (right)

RS I think you've got to let him know though/ how you are going to do the assessment process about

SLT How do you mean?

RS He's got to have some sort of/ little *goal* ah/ no *landmarks* (mm) and even if we said, "Well we/ ah we would like to see you/ what you're like up in the chair/ increasing periods of time/ and we'll assess it in two weeks (mm) but/ but in saying that it depends on how things are going as to/ as to *how* we should look towards going home." But you *can't* leave it open ended otherwise he'll just go/ he'll get *more* depressed . . if everybody holds off and says, "Oh/ we can't talk to you about that" (mm) /and that's sort of secret ah then/ then he will just sit there and go "Aaah"/ or crawl back into his shell and [just stay asleep]/ I mean you've got to give him *some sort* of look for the future/ even if it's just to say there will be an assessment in a certain period oh well/ if two weeks is appropriate we'll go in two weeks.

SLT All right we'll go with that.

OT(2) Is two weeks appropriate?

RS Oh yeah/ or shorter or *longer* or

SN Assessment in two weeks doesn't mean to say he's *going home.* It's going to be looked at.

RS Yeah.

SW Is there a bed for him? I mean is that okay . . . because he's aware of the bed situation too.

OT(2) Because his intermittent care bed/ finishes today.

SW Mmm

SLT Does he not need more *clarity* than *that*? I mean . . do we have a clear understanding of what/ what he needs to get to that point? If we do/ why not share that with him?

RS Yeah/ yeah would have thought so/ but that's what we're talking about.

NSC He is actually/ up in the chair for most of the day. (*end of discussion*)

Review 4

NSC P15: continue to mobilise slowly/ very small blood blister/ on *great* toe from his stocking. Discussion/ re mood/ ah/ wheelchair reviewed by OT and physio. Comfort/ cushion unsatis/factory . and the psych registrar was going to see him.

CNS (*softly*) I keep forgetting her name. (*more loudly*) What is it?

There is no clear evidence from the transcript that the disability team as a whole has subscribed to RS's provisional plan for action. The team scribe fails to identify either the principle or the plan as significant "events" in the team minutes, as is evident from the minutes read at the outset of P15's fourth review. The question of how the team responds to P15's psychological needs is converted into a decision that the marginal and absent psychiatric registrar is to "see" P15. There is, however, no team discussion about the rationale for her involvement or by whom or how she is to be briefed, or of which of the different narratives about P15 circulating in the team she has been apprised.

Representing Clients

In the remainder of this section I want to attend to a related but different issue, that of the competing, indeed polarized, representations generated within the disability team about P15 and about P1's guardians within the psychiatric team. That teams do generate different representations of clients is in itself not surprising, as representations are informed by members' positioning within a team and by their discipline. For example, each discipline's role brings the team into contact with clients in a different manner from that of other disciplines; further, each discipline offers different explanatory models of human behavior and foregrounds different issues as significant in relation to the work to be done. What is then important is how members elicit, identify, and then work with these differences articulated through narrative to achieve a point of provisional closure (a team plan), which then generates further narratives to inform the development and modification of that plan.

The following extracts are taken from the second, third, and fourth taped reviews about P15.

SN (*softly*) Yes I know. (*more loudly*) Anyway P15's mood. I was going to talk/ *sometimes he's quite depressed* and/ he sort of gets when he gets down to the dining room he gets shit stirs and caused quite a problem one *night*. . . because he likes to spark everybody/ but then he started picking on P7 and P7 got quite angry and quite upset about it/ and now and somebody said to/ to him, "Now you knew you were/ what you're doing. *Why didn't you* stop? You've just got to can it/ control it." Um (*softly*) and he was quite angry himself (*louder*) but then I discovered that *his wife* had been in to see him on Friday night for two minutes and pushed off to New Plymouth for the weekend and didn't tell him/ she was going to New Plymouth for the weekend . .

NSC There's *no change*. There are *huge marital* problems.

SN They're still/ yeah.

NSC *All* of them insoluble/ and um

DR But then it's not fair to take it out on the other residents here.

SN No it's not/ it's not fair to take it out and he *knows* that/ but he said he felt he couldn't help himself.

DR (*overlapping last words*) In that case he's got to be/ I mean he's to to— does somebody take him back to his room?

SN I've done that/ I've taken him from the dining room when he starts picking/ I say, "Out/ get him out."

DR I can see this on the ward round *too*/ he's just *waiting* to pick on the surgeon or somebody (yes)/ and he just *loved* that. You see he just wants us to be/ doing that arrangement for the/ the TV so that somebody else could see that. The poor house surgeon running around trying to adjust that TV in the corner and then he's getting everybody running around *as usual* but it is okay to be just the once off/ that's fine/ but not with other residents who can't handle that you know/ that's really not/ help themselves.

SN Unfortunately it was P10 . . threw the *angry*/ and got told off until we discovered that P15 was the/ culprit.

NSC As usual.

SN But/ but on the/ on the *positive side* P15's started really interesting um/ talk with/ everybody last week/ and he got them talking about what they would like when they *die,* what music they would like at their funeral which (*raises pitch of voice*) I actually thought was *really* helpful (*drops pitch*)/ for/ for/ for them to start actually thinking about it and and actually it was a/ it was a fun conversation but they/ P6 was saying, "*Oh I'd like this*" and "I'd like that" and somebody else was saying, "Well I'd like this." (mm)/ but it was/ it was an interesting conversation.

DR Yes. Oh that's all right. It's just like *P15* isn't it/ to have thought of that.

NSC Well it's like him because he's starting to be quite suicidal at *home* . . um/ *really* for/ the the first time *I've seen him* as bad as/ as that um . . and that . . was why he went on the Prozac/ he's never really /*needed* an anti-depressant and things are *very bad* at home (mm) and he's/ he's made a *huge* effort/ to try and/ resolve some of the marital stuff and/ and and move on a bit . . and he's got/ gets frustrated all the way along/ this is—

DR —and here was this young man/ who was a league player and the activity was his/ soulmate and then suddenly he's/ stuck down/ lying in the back room.

NSC (*to SW*) Have you talked to him about this while he's in?

SW Um . . *no, I'm a shrink* (*laugh*) but I/ I just like to say that/ you know for one night when he's actually/ pushing people over the *edge*/ overall/ I think he's had *enormous* benefit for others—

SN —oh he does he does—

SW —the residents here/ and he *definitely* has kept/ people going and/ in a really *positive* ways and I think we need to make sure that just because one night he's over (yes) he's over the *top* (that/ that's fine) we don't actually sort of say *that*—

SN —and then on the other side he initiated this conversation (mm) which allowed people to/ sort of start *saying* and thinking about (*softly*) oh yeah well . .

NSC You're *quite right.*

SN Yeah

SW And he brings a lot of humour into the place too.

SN Yeah.

NSC But you are quite right/ it is tied to his wife suddenly going off and that. What he/ what she does at home—leaves him *alone* with the care attendant/ and he's alone all night/ and he can't stop her and she won't say where she's going/ she's got (*softly but with emphasis*) *enormous* frustrations and problems herself actually (*louder*) (mm mm) and I try to grab her every so often but it's like/ it's like holding on to a moon / I just. . . .

Review 3

OT(2) Okay is that all for P5? . P15 . that [tarin] tincture started seems to be/ *improving* and that's to the/ area on his buttocks that is *seeping* . . . the supra pubic/ *is mucky* . . and Ward Dr. is going to follow that up. The area on his ankle's almost *healed* and his *mood* seems a bit depressed/ and he can cause . trouble in the dining room at night although there's um/ a *positive* to that he's also cheerful and can cheer up all the others this way.

Review 4

SW mm, but can we be consistent about what we tell/ what we tell him about that because . . . all the "when am I going home?" bit goes around *everybody* and . . if he/ if he starts to/ *hear* different/ different stories (mm) he will/ play everyone off.

NSC How can we tell him?

SW No/ well either we—that's what I'm saying. If, if we don't know let's all be consistent about *not* saying.

OT(2) Anything?

SW Anything *definite* (mm) because he'll hang on to that and he'll be *really* disappointed.

DR Oh he's very crafty/ he just goes on and on and gets you/ down.

SW That's exactly what I mean.

The representations of P15 led to two polarized narratives within the team, each drawing on competing models of human nature. One, generated by the ward doctor (and one to which she and others returned subsequently in their description of P15 as "crafty") was of P15 as highly manipulative, aggressive, lacking in insight and emotional control, as deserving to be treated as a child and an organizational nuisance to boot. (It is, too, P15's relationship to the organization that is recorded/repeated in the minutes of the next meeting).

The competing representation is first articulated by the nurse. It is then picked up and emphasized by the social worker and the community nurse (who moves the narration of P15's problems beyond the organizational confines). This representation is of a man who is caring and concerned about his fellow ward mates, who is resourceful, and who has made considerable, although unsuccessful, efforts to resolve his personal problems. This narrative about P15's behavior finishes extremely abruptly with a return to the (more controllable?) medical problems, which continue to dominate the remainder of the team's discussions. At no point does the team formally "note" the existence of these differing narratives or begin to discuss how such accounts may differently structure aspects of the team's work.

The second discussion to which I wish to attend more fully is the psychiatric team's complex and lengthy narrative surfacing throughout the reviews I recorded about P1's guardians, their relationship to the team and their contribution to P1's care.

Review 2

COUNSELLOR Well I'll report on the I'll report the meeting . . soon/ perhaps I should do that now. Um/ it was an interesting meeting. It took over an hour. Ah/ there were two people from the ah brain injury unit, ah the ah clinical manager/ and um/ and the uncle ah/ and ah/ what took

a *long* time was that the/ aah/ the uncle/ as the principal spokesperson
ah/ went over the the *whole* history of the of the process /and um/ and
in some ways it was *useful/ not so much to* ah/ to get the ah/ the reitera-
tion of the theme/ but really to ah/ to establish the *starting* point/ um/
which *I/ I* in fact wasn't wasn't aware of that/ their um/ what happened/
with *P1* is that he was ah/ in a coma and remained so for some time
and ah/ the first sign of movement was a/ was a slight movement of his
um/ I think left *arm* and the guardians have persevered. Um/ um/ just
a complete absence of of ah/ medical or any other kind of staff in the
whole story but/ there's *certainly no doubt in my mind* that whatever
they have *done* they have been very persistent and/ they have *refused*
right from the outset to accept some/ um/ limitations which they say/
have been stated very flatly and very baldly. One was that P1 would
not walk *again* and ah/ that he wouldn't be able to be as active as he is
and/ so forth and so on and so forth. *In some ways* the impression/ at
the end of ah this *quite* long drawn out meeting was that ah/ ah they
were tremendous advocates for a *severely* ah brain injured person and
ah/ you would want them/ on your *side* if ah/ something like that *happened* um/ *however* the/ what's *going* to happen is that/ the um/ the
ACC {Accident Compensation Corporation} will be requested *by* ah/
the Brain Injury Unit to/ to set up a formal assessment/ um/ *of P1* ah/
complete assessment um/ um/ of his ah/ to establish a kind of *baseline*
ah/ clear baseline where he's at. That includes um/ occupational thera-
py/ physiotherapy. This will *all* be done by people who come in to do
that to do the assessments and ah/ on the *basis of that* they'll ah continue to negotiate with ah ACC as to his/ um/ *suitability* for the *unit* um/
which they hope will be established next month. They were going on
later that *day* to/ talk to ACC and it seems to me that in/ the *current*
political climate there's a fair chance that they'll succeed in in getting
the funding to establish. Ah, they have a/ they *have* an *option* on a
building somewhere in the central city area aah which ah/ they're able
to retain ah for about a month or *five weeks/* ah/ so that's the kind of
operating *so we'll know relatively soon* whether this is going to happen or
not. They've got quite a *large/ staff* or a potential staff and they've actually or they must have a certain amount of confidence in it coming
through because they've already started the process of/ *staff training.*
Ah/ the unit/ they have a/ they have a *secure* ward within a 100 bed private hospital and *this* campus will be/ located in in a separate/ *place* . It
won't be as *secure* as as this/ ah unit *here* . It will have um/ a *much* more

discreet ah perimeter fence than we have around here and um/ the/ the unit itself will be locked but the individual rooms will not be locked/ um and they *intend to* base them/ to *move out* a lot into the community aah/ ah doing a *whole range* of activities. So *um* . . .

SP1 In there/ do they take special patients?

COUNSELLOR And they/ they may—

SP1 (*very softly*) —Or will they take special patients?

COUNSELLOR They they *say* that they *will* but they *are reliant on*/ us doing *our* bit with the *Ministry* ah/ while *they* do their bit with ACC and in a more *general sense* ah with the/ with the Ministry /but they're *relying* on/ um/ *us* to make the/ *overtures* because we know the people we know the processes/ ah which they *don't*. So they're certainly looking at taking ah special patients yes.

UM We've probably actually/ need to flag that with ah/ {*Legal Services*} (yes) to see what their *opinion* is about that because of his *short/term/* because of his being a special patient.

SP1 Presumably he could stay a special patient (*softly*) though. It's a hospital we're talking about.

UM Legal Services might have to get it to the director though.

SP1 Oh okay . . . okay.

UM mm hm . . (okay) maybe we should probably check out (*softly*) that with Mary and I mean he doesn't/ P1 doesn't require medium security *he requires 24 hour* supervision.

COUNSELLOR That's what will be supplied *in this ah/* in this unit. It will be *quite intensively staffed /* and it will have a/ a/ *quite a high level um* of ah/ patient activity . *so um I I assured/* the um/ the *guardians* that ah we would ah that if the opportunity *arose* ah/ for P1 to ah to transfer to that unit that we'd be *very supportive* of that and ah/ they'd ah

SP1 We'd be *very supportive* I guess (*general laugh*) we'd even pay for the escort to get him there.

COUNSELLOR Yeah ah/ I mean that *that's* that seemed to/ I/ you know in the context of what's happened they say they *say* that they've had/ a lot of difficulty with people being/ *initially/* from a um/ a *medical* survival and *mobility* point of view *extraordinarily gloomy* um/ prospects and that um/ if they hadn't adopted a kind of 24 hour guardian role um that/ that P1 would be much less active and he/ the uncle ah/ described the situation where/ a physiotherapist um in a kind of a/ *gymnasium* ah situation had said that it wasn't that it was neither possible for P1 to walk/ or ah/ practicable or even *permissible*/ for ah P1 to *scale the wall* and wherewith the uncle/ umm took up the challenge and encouraged him to scale the wall (*softly*) and so forth so I mean that's/

UM I mean while they/ *maintain that ah* without them he wouldn't be where he is today/ a Rehab Unit actually did the majority of his rehabilitation (mm/ of course/ mm) so you know then they *need to feel like they are the/ the pivotal*

COUNSELLOR (*softly*) That's right yeah/ that's right. (*more loudly*) um and you know/ *wherever* he goes that's going to be/ that's going to be the/ the dynamic that the carers/ have to put up with and—

UM —well—

COUNSELLOR —and *really* it's a/ it's it's *nicely* placed in the context of how they described both P1 *and* the family process *pre* the accident and it's really just a continuation (*softly*) of that.

UM Well hopefully the new unit will take him and we won't have to worry about it too much.

Later in this review

COUNSELLOR *the meeting finished* with um/ with a degree of *warmth* ah about the um/ um the Unit's care/ ah for P1 and ah/ ah the view that this wasn't really/ the/ kind of appropriate place for him to be um/ and um/ ah/ *some* where buried in the middle of that is somewhat/ somewhat *worrying* um/ the indication that/ P1 *didn't really* attack anyone (*2 people talk simultaneously*) and that this woman somehow attacked herself.

SP1 Are you up/ with P1, CP3?

CP3 Yeah yeah he was here before I left yeah . . .

Review 3

COUNSELLOR Has he ever said that *before*? "Anyone would think that I've attacked someone?"

SP1 Yeah he's said it.

N3 Oh he's said it a few times.

CP3 He said the same thing to me.

UM He does a lot of [.] (*speakers overlap briefly*)

COUNSELLOR What what do you say when he *says* that?

UM "Yes well you did."

COUNSELLOR Yeah/ I think that's (*overlapping*) just that it's really important *to say that* even with all of the/ the difficulties of retention and all the rest of it.

UM And then five seconds later he doesn't know that he's said anything.

COUNSELLOR (*overlapping*) Sure but even so/ I think—

SSW1 —well *it is* far better/ far better actually ah to [. .] sometime.

COUNSELLOR That/ I mean that it it's interesting in the context because of the/ in the meeting with his guardians *the other week* ah/ his *uncle* very clearly raised doubts about whether *he in fact* attacked *anyone*. I mean that's the/ that's the kind of stuff that—

SSW1 (*overlapping*) well that—

UM —it's historical.

COUNSELLOR "He hasn't assaulted anyone. It's really open to question." He doesn't *quite say* that she assaulted *herself* but that's what he's saying and it's really quite interesting that that—

UM —that's the kind of/ thing they've maintained for/

SW mm

COUNSELLOR Sure.

UM Is he um . [on a 2 to 1 ratio]? {This is with reference to the number of staff he must have attending him if he moves outside of the locked unit.}

Review 4

CNS2 We have to find out too about um/ if/ all the patients have a um/ personal *folder*. P1 *hasn't got one* and in in the information personal folder in ah/ in um keeping up with um section papers and ah management plans and um/ patients' rights information that that sort of thing. I'm just wondering what the MDT think about P1 having that information and it's like um while his section papers that do have information um/ of what he was charged with etc um/ whether that would help or *hinder* him/ or whether that information could be perhaps passed on to the guardians instead . . .

N1 I think in a way it's almost *cruel* for him to come across information like that all the time because every time he sees it it's something new to him.

DM Yes.

CNS2 It's information that

N1 (*softly*) Because [he says I can't have done something like that].

CNS2 You know just/ yeah yeah.

N1 So you know and and he continuously asks—

? —it might be easier

N1 (*raises tone of voice*) He has days when he asks, "Why am I here?" you know (*drops tone*) and half an hour later he will say, "Why am I here?"

? mmm/ that happens.

N1 His latest *theory* is that somebody else has done something that he's being blamed for so

COUNSELLOR Well I mean that's the point of view that his uncle in particular takes so if it's constant/ he'll be being *reinforced* from there.

N1 That's so? (*raises tone*) I haven't heard his uncle (*drops tone*) say anything *like that* [.].

UM I mean the whole idea of the personal files for the clients was to/ give them some input into what happens to them here and why they're here and things like that. I don't know that he would benefit from that for (no) the reason that you were talking about.

COUNSELLOR He doesn't/ he just does not know.

UM Possibly the *guardians* might benefit from having his personal file.

Review 5

CP3 (*overlapping*) oh right. Well, we had a/ *lovely meeting with his* family yesterday afternoon/ didn't we SP2?

SP2 Yep.

CP3 It was nice meeting for the first one.

SSW1 Yeah it was nice.

CP3 SSW1 was a coward also [. . .] (*laughter*)

SSW1 (*overlapping*) I don't think [. .] (*laughing*) yeah just

CP3 I mean . . they seem to me like a lot of guardians with kids with head injuries might be/ slightly better advocates than most but at the same time there's anger and/ and rage at the system etc. etc. The other thing is though/ this referral to the unit. Well, I don't think we should be holding our breath and actually expecting it to work because I I've had a very long conversation with the ACC case worker and I I'm I'm suddenly completely confused as to to *what* the what process is/ needs to happen for him to get to the unit. *It seems to me* like ACC are going to drag their feet/over it unless we can get many many of the legal issues/ very *clearly* sorted out first/ and it would/ so it seems that I need to talk to the Director about that/ *now* and get that sorted out. As far as him having a further *assessment*—I was under the impression that the unit *wanted* an assessment.

COUNSELLOR That's true/ and they not only want it/ they need it.

(*Later*)

UM Is there anything else relevant that came up at that meeting? I mean the medical issues? [You guys raise those issues with them, talk about that]

SSW1 Well the ah—

UM (*overlapping*) —until the cows come home.

SSW1 Well [.] x-ray information there and we are—

UM —no moans groans complaints?

SSW1 [. .]

UM (*overlapping*) compliments

SSW1 No no no. They were fairly nice people I mean.

CP3 (*overlapping*) Actually quite a few compliments.

SSW1 Very nice they're very nice.

CP3 (*overlapping*) and no real complaints.

SSW1 No no there wasn't any.

SP2 No.

UM That's good.

SSW1 [. .]

UM (*very softly*) Oh good had heaps today (*chuckles*)

CP3 And they're getting in a big lawyer to look at P1's case he's got—

SP2 —and to what end/ it's not clear. I mean they sort/ they're a little bit confused when they talk about issues. I sometimes get a bit lost about what their point is but/ ah I think that is to follow up the idea that the/ *person* P1 attacked had so much {drugs} in her system when she was assaulted. *I don't know how they would assess that* given the depth of her wounds, she must have lost a lot of *blood* you know

(Later in this review)

COUNSELLOR there's a certain amount of difficulty in [relation to the assault] about what you were saying ah/ since it's his uncle's friend who taught him all that.

SSW1 What!

COUNSELLOR Well his uncle's friend is the one taught him all the hunting skills.

SSW1 I knew that.

COUNSELLOR And/ it's very difficult I think to approach *that* ah directly or even indirectly with the with his uncle.

SSW1 What [. . .]

COUNSELLOR I know that/ I'm saying it's very difficult in terms of of what to do about this gesture that he made when he was out/ ah the other day it's all part of a/ mm it's part of a process that's infinitely bound up with his relationship with his uncle and his uncle's friend.

SSW1 And he should know that. He should be well aware of this but it's important to [. .] clarify the issues] the dangerousness.

SP2 And I think that that's something we're *actually going to have* to address with him.

SSW1 That's right.

SP2 And I think we need to think very carefully about how we are going to do that.

SSW1 Exactly.

SP2 mm

SSW1 Well I come [. . .]

PR2 Sure

UM Okay . . .

(end of discussion)

From the way in which the counselor constructed his initial story of the meeting, from some comments made to me by team members outside of the meeting, and from comments through the reviews it would appear that the dominant team narrative about P1's guardians is thematized by difficulty, obstruction, and a failure to appreciate others' input into P1's care. In order to open this narrative of "difficult relatives" (a common

enough narrative in human services) to scrutiny and revision, the counselor engages on several occasions in some complex work, the process of
which reflects his disciplinary orientation, in his delineation of the relevant
"facts," his placing of these in different and increasingly intricate relationships to each other as more become available, and his seeking to avoid
moral strictures. Further, I would argue that the detailed way in which he
goes about his narration can be read as demonstrating a method of narrative construction in which interpretation and closure are suspended for as
long as possible in order to encourage the team to identify the problematic
issues and to collectively bring these to a provisional point to allow the
team to identify a course of action.

Although P1 has been on the ward for some time, so it could be
assumed that most of the team are familiar with his history, the counselor
notes his own unfamiliarity with the details of the story (so these could be
unfamiliar also to others), particularly the guardians' story of their centrality to P1's rehabilitation. His full and informative account is significant in
a number of ways. He makes a lengthy statement in the context of meetings where members typically comment briefly. He speaks slowly and with
deliberation. He takes up team time. His emphases are important—the
tiny movement of the *arm* as that to which the guardians responded and
which gave them hope, the assertion of rehabilitation staff about the
impossibility of P1's recovery and the guardians' refusal to accept their ver-
dict, their huge significance as advocates, and the counselor's crucial identification of the issue of their positioning—to the team they may be nui-
sances, but someone in P1's situation is critically reliant on such determination and intransigence.

His narrative, then, offers the guardians a degree of credibility that it
would appear the team has not afforded them to date. And the story is not
that simple.

UM I mean while they/ *maintain that ah* without them he wouldn't be
where he is today/ a Rehab Unit actually did the majority of his rehabilitation (mm/ of course/ mm) so you know then they *need to feel like
they are the/ the pivotal*

COUNSELLOR (*softly*) That's right yeah/ that's right (*more loudly*) um and
you know/ *wherever* he goes that's going to be/ that's going to be the/
the dynamic that the carers/ have to put up with and—

UM —Well—

COUNSELLOR —and *really* it's a/ it's it's *nicely* placed in the context of how they described both P1 *and* the family process *pre* the accident and it's really just a continuation (*softly*) of that.

His account, then, is immediately problematized by the manager, who then, and later, produces a more rigid narrative about the guardians, which highlights their psychopathology. In contrast, the counselor's response is to define the dynamics of the situation as a "fact of life," as a given that (formal) carers will need to understand and manage; and then he himself introduces a further complexity in a statement that highlights his positive contact with the guardians *and* a further problematic that bears significantly on the team's work—the guardians' apparently puzzling denial of P1's role in the attack. But the way in which he does this is important. He persistently foregrounds issues of interpretation of the event rather than the moral character of individuals, in part through his use of the word "interesting."

COUNSELLOR *the meeting finished* with um/ with a degree of *warmth* ah about the um/ um the Unit's care/ ah for P1 and ah/ ah the view that this wasn't really/ the/ kind of appropriate place for him to be um/ and um/ ah/ *some* where buried in the middle of that is somewhat/ somewhat *worrying* um/ the indication that/ P1 *didn't really* attack anyone (*2 people comment simultaneously*) and that this woman somehow attacked herself.

While it could be argued that the success of this particular narrative strategy in getting the team to attend to its competing perspectives is open to question,[4] what the discussions foreground as a significant issue in teamwork is the difficulty of easily privileging or giving greater weight to an account produced by a particular discipline. It is not possible to summarily dismiss as "wrong" the competing representations produced by team members of the client and guardians, and the different narratives to which each representation gives rise. Each one has evidence to support it. The issue facing the team is how they engage with these different representations and the narratives that they inform, the implications of adopting or working within one or another narrative framework, and the relationship of that engagement with knowledge work and creation.

Teamwork assumes that the group thinks of itself not just as a group of individuals coming from different disciplines but as individuals actively bringing those disciplines to the development of work with clients. It assumes that members have not only the language and ability to develop mini-narratives about clients but also the conceptual and linguistic skills to respond to the concept "interesting" and to develop and analyze their own narratives and those of others. It therefore bespeaks a familiarity with one's own tacit disciplinary knowledge and a willingness to make such knowledge overt. It also suggests an ability to work with the different implications of this or that representation and narrative focus as part of the process of the team's achieving provisional closure and an orientation for the next focus for its work, a focus that in turn will develop other narratives and different provisional closures.

Conceptualizing interprofessional teamwork as knowledge-based focuses on the generation of different narratives, and thereby in a dynamic process allows for their articulation of possibilities and their (temporary) meetings at nodal points. In emphasizing the range of possible interpretations a team can make, it foregrounds the postmodern concepts of provisionality, incompleteness, and undecidability. But, because these teams are operating in the "real" world and not a fictional world, they need to be able to develop a plan of action. This foregrounds the twin issues of working across different knowledge domains and the organizational structures that facilitate such work. It is with these aspects that I wish to conclude this chapter.

Knowledge Creation in Teamwork

The following account draws heavily on Nonaka and Takeuchi's (1995) work on organizations and knowledge creation. At the risk of producing an oversimplistic account, I wish to emphasize several points of their complex analysis:

1. It is no longer sufficient to foreground knowledge as a significant organizational resource. Instead, the organization needs to engage, through the development of processes and structure, in knowledge creation. This involves regarding knowledge as other than formal and easily transmitted. The reworking of diverse knowledges requires the (difficult) articulation of tacit knowledge (on both its craft and its cognitive dimensions); the questioning of one's own knowledge; the presence of productive, because unsettling, ambiguity; the presence of redundancy, which

enables the identification of shared ground and of difference; and the arrival at a different mode of sense-making.

2. *Knowledge* is not synonymous with *information.* Rather it is "the function of a particular stance, perspective, or intention. . . . knowledge, unlike information, is about *action.* It is always knowledge 'to some end.' And . . . knowledge, like information, is about *meaning.* It is context-specific and relational" (58). Information is the material enabling the creation of knowledge; knowledge enables the development of the new position, the achievement of a dynamic truth. Moreover, this positioning of knowledge as active corresponds to Miller's comments on narrative: "A story is a way of doing things with words. It makes something happen in the real world" (H. Miller 1995:69).

3. Knowledge is the interaction between explicit or formal knowledge and tacit knowledge, defining tacit knowledge in Polyani's terms as "indwelling" (60). This interaction depends on several processes—those of:

- *Socialization,* i.e., the sharing of experiences informing tacit knowledge,
- *Externalization,* i.e., the articulation of tacit knowledge into explicit knowledge, a process involving dialogue and "a sequential use of metaphor, analogy, and model" (66),
- *The development of combinations,* i.e., the combining of different modes of explicit knowledge,
- *Internalization,* i.e., the translation of newly acquired explicit knowledge into tacit knowledge bases to inform work (Nonaka and Takeuchi 1995:61–72).

In light of this discussion, part of the significance of the transcripts of the team reviews is the absence of the processes outlined above in the teams' discussions. In relation to P1's guardians, for instance, if discussing the question of P1's involvement in the assault with his guardians was necessary, then the team's processes of reflection, dialogue, and identification of tacit and explicit knowledge could have led it to formulate a series of questions about the ways in which different disciplines would approach the issue; their cognitive, behavioral, and developmental models and assumptions that underpin each approach; the strengths and limitations of each; and who should undertake this work and when. Following these lines of questioning could result in a shift from the hitherto dominant narrative of "difficult relatives" to different (and more interesting because more ambiguous) narratives, contributing to different modes of engagement.

It is axiomatic that such a development cannot occur without a facilitative organizational environment. To borrow Winnicott's phrase in relation to models of parenting, teams require "good enough" organizations for them to achieve their potential to voice and then work conceptually with the different narratives circulating within the team. A critical first step is a transition from conceptualizing teamwork within human service organizations as primarily about the development and management of the interpersonal relations of team members, to conceptualizing teamwork as engaged in knowledge work. Nonaka and Takeuchi (1995) have set out the organizational conditions that promote a "knowledge spiral" (70) as:

- *Organizational intention,* i.e., the organization needs to develop a strategy to "acquire, create, accumulate" (74) and use knowledge, thereby conceptualizing what kind of knowledge it requires and how this knowledge can best be utilized. This, then, involves problematizing the notion of teamwork, rather than regarding it as something to be taken for granted, and addressing team processes and organizational structures that could facilitate the development of knowledge-based work.

- *The presence of autonomy,* which enables the development of new knowledge and permits individuals to work creatively.

- *The presence of fluctuation and creative chaos,* terms that refer to modes of dialogue and discussion that allow for the questioning of one's own premises and the premises of others and encourage disciplinary overlap in order for team members to push the boundaries of their own knowledge, recognizing that the ensuing "creative chaos" can increase organizational tensions. In contrast, in information-processing modes, the problem is defined within pre-established boundaries. Doing this "ignores the importance of defining the problem to be solved. To attain such a definition, problems must be constructed from the knowledge available at a certain time and context" (79).

- *The utilization of redundancy,* i.e., the "existence of information that goes beyond the immediate operational requirements of organizational members" and assists in "intentional overlapping" (80). "Sharing redundant information promotes the sharing of tacit knowledge, because individuals can sense what others are trying to articulate."

Redundancy encourages concept development and "enables individuals to invade each other's functional boundaries and offer advice or provide new information from different perspectives" (81).

- *The presence of requisite variety,* i.e., the organization's or team's "internal diversity must match the variety and complexity of the environment in order to deal with the challenges posed by the environment" (82).

Teamwork and the generation of team narratives, then, are about "making things happen" in a complex world. Teamwork occurs in an environment productive of different narratives because of the heterogeneity of representations available to the team; representations of situations and issues by the clients and their significant others; reporting of those representations by team members; and the team members' various representations of clients and issues informed by the different disciplines within the team. The team narrative is the result of a recursive and interactive process that enables the team to explore the possibilities and constraints made available to the team through its different constituent knowledge bases (hence drawing on and working with its tacit and explicit knowledges) in order to develop a plan that allows the team to *move on* but that is also regarded as provisional, as open to change as clients' situations change. The outcome of interprofessional teamwork cannot, therefore, be a single, authoritative narrative or "case" defined largely by knowledge deriving from one discipline.

8

"Nobody's Asked Me for My View"

Clients' Empowerment in Interprofessional Teamwork

The active involvement of clients, family, and significant others in decisions about clients' health care implies a realignment of power relations away from the more established model of care, which defined patients as passive and grateful for services received (Gilleard and Higgs 1998). In Aotearoa/New Zealand and elsewhere (Lewis and Glennerster 1996) such changes reflect an increasing focus on a "consumer" ethos located within politically dense discourses of holistic care, professional and organizational accountability to consumers/clients, client choice, and the empowerment of clients and families in the processes of care (Shipley and Upton 1992; Ministry of Health 1994), efficiency, and the responsibility of the individual subject in decision making (Petersen and Lupton 1996).

Given the historical marginalizing of older "consumers," those with a physical disability, and their families in health and welfare systems (Biggs 1989; Gilleard and Higgs 1998; Oliver 1990; Opie 1995; Priestly 1995), it could be argued that meetings held between them and members of interprofessional health teams to discuss concerns, progress, treatment goals, and discharge planning constitute a significant mode of empowerment, a shift from professionally dominated decision making toward active client/consumer and family involvement in this domain. Indeed, Saltz (1992) has suggested that the inclusion of clients and families in the work of health teams represents one mode of evaluating team effectiveness, and McClain and Bury (1998), in writing about the care of children with chronic health problems, also affirm the importance and value of health professionals' active inclusion of family in their information-sharing and decision-making processes.

Such significant realignments in power relations, however, do not come without their complicating discursive implications. Noting (as have Petersen and Lupton 1996), that the "underlying motif of a consumerist ideology in health care derives from a New Right belief in the economic virtue of shifting responsibility from the state towards the individual and family," Chris Gilleard and Paul Higgs (1998:234) have foregrounded the ambiguity and the tension between the intention of empowerment and the increased modes of self-surveillance that are an outcome of such intentions.[1] Nonetheless, they have suggested that despite the politically double-edged siting of empowerment, its entry into health discourses could contribute to more client-focused health care practices. They argue that, given the fragmentation of lifestyles, "the 'pretence' of a voice can set up structures that are forced to take account of individuality however much they circumscribe it" (247).

Developing a service that empowers clients and their families requires significant changes in organizational and professional practices. Although much of the analysis that I present here focuses on professional practices because the client/family experience of the organization is mediated through contact with health professionals, this interrelationship of organizational endorsement of changing professional practices and any implications of those changes must not be overlooked.

The development of client/family-centered practices discursively writes the professional body no longer as dominating and monologic but as less certain, as more interactive, and as seeking participation. The concept of empowerment, however, also implies the presence of more-authoritative and questioning behavior from clients and families than has been encouraged in the past. In so doing, it also works to produce different bodies—those that are active, knowledgeable, participatory, and assertive, untroubled by factors such as frailty, ill health, dementia, other modes of impairment, lack of knowledge on which to base a decision, or an inability to interpret or difficulty in interpreting complex information. Foregrounding these factors considerably complicates the whole notion of empowerment. They point to the need for a process that organizationally and professionally is recognized as complex, requires carefully constructed interaction between team, client, and family, and balances the need for efficiency and time management against effective consultation.

The first section of the chapter, "Conceptualizing Empowerment," discusses the concept of empowerment, as contextualized by two articles (McLean 1995; Young 1994), each drawing on the work of Michel

Foucault. The second section, "Empowering Practices?," first identifies constraints for the teams in the study in attending to some more macro-level dimensions of empowerment; second, it presents analyses of two family meetings, one held with a frail and moderately demented older woman and the second with a younger woman who had a degenerative condition. The third section, "Developing Empowering Practices," discusses teams' development of more-empowering practices and the organizational role in such developments; such commentary equally needs to be read in light of its own complex discursive productions discussed above.

Conceptualizing Empowerment

The Oxford Dictionary of Current English defines *empowerment* as "giving authority to." This phrase has dual implications: the reallocation of authority between (unequal) agents (note "giving")[2] and the notion of "taking seriously," that is, of being seen to be *authoritative* about situations or events. Empowerment is a concept embedded simultaneously in the structural and the psychological: structural in that it refers to a change in power relations within the social so that an individual's or group's authority (that ability to make statements about, to be taken seriously, and to control resources) shifts; psychological, in that it refers to independence, to an ability to control one's situation deriving from a recognized ability to speak authoritatively. Athena McLean (1995), writing on empowerment, discusses Thomas Szaz's and especially Foucault's writings on power. Szaz, she suggests, defined power as a negative and coercive force. Within this framework, empowerment is positioned as an oppositional force focused on the elimination of oppression and enabling those in the process of becoming empowered to assert rights of self-determination and responsible action.

Her discussion of Foucault picks up his emphasis on the productive nature of power and highlights the significance of attending to difference between actors within empowering practices because actors' different positioning in the social domain produces different issues and different perspectives with which those actors need to engage. In the health care context, *empowerment* refers to political processes that affect individuals and organizations directing attention to processes that involve individuals in decisions about their health options, as well as opportunities to influence and be engaged in service planning. *Empowerment*, McLean notes, refers to a goal, a process, or both; equally, it may also refer to a process within an individual, an organization, or a larger social structure enabling individuals (in her text, mental health clients) to achieve (more) control over the material conditions of their lives.

> "Empowerment" defines the personal and political processes by which . . . consumers gain validation and restore their sense of dignity and self-worth. Through these processes, consumers come to recognize and begin to exercise control over the material circumstances of their lives. How they exercise control will depend on how . . . they determine *for themselves* how to handle their problems and how to improve their situation through meaningful engagement at several levels. At the individual level, this involves working to improve their self-concept or personal circumstances; at the group level, advocating for programs to respond to community needs; at the societal level, acting to transform social conditions through laws and policies that challenge discriminatory practices and economic structures that reproduce disabling material conditions. *Praxis* at each level serves as an oppositional force that empowers through shifting multiple power relations.   *(McLean 1995:1059)*

While I would argue that this text sustains a modernist division between the individual and the social world, thereby failing to grasp a key dimension of the theory in which she has located her work, McLean nonetheless draws attention to the multiple and dynamic intersection of planes through the operating organization and institutional micropractices in the empowering of mental health clients. In contrast, Young (1994) places significantly greater emphasis on the structural dimensions of empowerment if change is to be achieved (although not denying the interrelationship of empowerment of individuals and social transformation). Critiquing the extensive social science literature on empowerment as overfocused on the attainment of individual autonomy and marginalizing the necessity for changes in material oppressive social conditions, Iris Young defines *empowerment* as "the development of a sense of collective influence over the social conditions of one's life" (48) and foregrounds the desirability of social transformation to be achieved through collective political action by disempowered groups. Young is suspicious of too easy definitions of therapeutic, individually based encounters as empowering because of the historical association of such services with individual adjustment to oppressive conditions, an adjustment achieved through what she describes as "confessional" and therefore "monologic" talk (50). She contrasts such modes of interaction with empowering, "*dialogic*" (my italics) talk aimed at consciousness raising and collective action (50), where a change in power relations is intended. Such a change, of course, requires substantial shifts in professionals' conceptualization of their role and changes in organizational practices. Together Young's and McLean's essays foreground empowerment as embedded in complex but changing relations of power where the interrelationship of individuals, organizations and the practices they generate, and dominant social structures (rather than the privileging of one of these elements) needs to be fully acknowledged, as does the different positioning of individuals (clients/professionals) within and outside of the organization and the implications of such different positioning. Furthermore, the development of empowering practices requires recognition of their complex discursive consequences, particularly as they relate to the construction of subjectivities.

Empowering Professional Practices

The issues of the discursively produced subject and attention to the different positioning of subjects within health practices are critical in informing the development of more diffracted and empowering professional practices in health care. In writing against the dominance of "expert" discourses and by repositioning the "expert" and layperson through the valorizing of lay or alternative knowledge, Chapman's (1994) and Smale and Tuson's (1993) concerns are to legitimate that differently structured and located knowledge and to bring it into play, a process that inevitably challenges the adequacy of professional knowledge and dislodges it from center stage; this in itself contributes to that complex reworking of power and changes in discursive practices through a challenge to health professionals' colonizing practices.

The inevitable presence of power relations in transactions between professionals and clients and the interconnectedness of the psychological and structural are reflected in Alan Chapman's (1994:113–114) account of professionally empowering behavior as involving:

1. The need to respect individuals' decision-making abilities and to recognize their capacity to make those decisions;

2. The need for workers to surrender their need for control and link in with support networks in a cooperative and collaborative manner;

3. Identification of the power imbalances in relationships;

4. Awareness that the client may reject the help offered;

5. The need for workers to "secure and use the resources that will promote or foster a sense of control and promote individual ability"; and

6. The adoption of a person-valuing approach.

These principles also inform Gerald Smale and Graham Tuson's (1993) identification of three models of empowerment and assessment within (social work) practice in the United Kingdom. They have called these models "questioning," "procedural," and "exchange" models. The first two position the worker as expert, in control of the interview, his or her behavior predominantly that of asking questions and seeking information intended to meet the worker's and/or the organization's objectives. These models assume transparency of language (that one can ask straightforward questions and receive straightforward replies, unproblematic in their interpretation and untrammeled by considerations of gender, ethnicity, or cultural and organizational allegiances). They reflect Young's concept of "monologic" talk. In contrast, the key dimensions of the "exchange model" (which bear closely on achieving empowering practices in family meetings), focus on information exchange *between* professionals and others, and on the creation of a mutuality of understanding grounded in assumptions about the complexity of communication. Workers operating within this model seek to facilitate clients' attempts to articulate and determine issues and avoid taking control of the process. The focus is on "dialogic" talk (Young 1994:50).

Empowering Practices?

Empowerment in Relation to Services and Planning

On the structural plane in the health care field, *empowerment* refers to lay actors' having a voice in planning and in choice of services and providers. It may also refer to professionals, policymakers, and so on making information available to educate lay actors, and to the work of advocates. The "ladder of empowerment" presented by Hoyes et al. outlines different levels of involvement in decision making (here about service provision).

HIGH Users have authority to take decisions
  ▲   Users have authority to take selected decisions
  │   Users' views are sought before decisions are finalized
  │   Users may take initiative to influence decisions
  ▼   Decisions are publicized and explained before implementation
LOW   Information is given about decisions made

(quoted in Nocon and Qureshi 1996:50)

In outlining a range of ways in which users may be "consulted," this ladder highlights the extent to which behaviors that an organization could define as empowering in fact hold users at the margins of decision making. Means and Lart (1994), in their discussion of empowerment strategies of "voice," have usefully highlighted the complexities of more-meaningful processes of organizational consultation. If clients and their families are to have a meaningful "voice" in issues of service delivery, then the consulting organization must:

1. Address the representativeness of the range of organizations approached;

2. Recognize that creating a network is time-consuming;

3. Recognize that if people are consulted at public meetings, then clear mechanisms for taking on board messages from the discussion need to be in place;

4. Recognize that document distribution requires that such documents are readable and sufficiently informative to enable people to be clear about what is being proposed; and

5. Recognize that groups need to be given time to consult with their membership.

Gilleard and Higgs (1998:242), however, in their article on the positioning of older people—especially the "old old" and those with significant age-related disabilities—in the empowerment rhetoric of older people, identify additional problems embedded in the notion of consultation.

> Giving a voice to those not normally known for voicing their concerns
> is part of the rhetoric of modern society and its systems of governance.
> In place of public action, we have public consultation. Concerns are

addressed but no guarantees are given of any action. The recent Carer's (Recognition and Services) Act (DOH 1995) exemplifies this point. Carers are "recognised," there [sic] needs acknowledged, their voices heard. Nothing more substantive is required. . . . Everybody's position is taken into consideration and at no additional cost. It appears as if the text is all: inclusive, democratic and empowering and, at the same time, empty of practical significance.

They go on to note that while "active third agers" may well be able to shop around for services, thereby exercising "choice" (part of the empowerment deal), other older people are not. Contrasting "active, agentic third agers" (242) with many other older people, they wrote:

> The vast majority of consumers deep in their old age remain the subjects of others' language, their desires submerged beneath their accumulated disabilities while their needs are constructed by others (whether through professional or voluntary "advocates" or simply arrived at through the actuarial logic of assessment) (242).

How, then, did the service teams work to empower their clientele in the context of a structural approach to empowerment? That none of the services in which these teams worked had provision for relevant client organizations to be involved in issues of service provision or evaluation is not surprising given the difficulties of implementing such policies by health authorities elsewhere (Lewis and Glennerster 1996; Nocon and Qureshi 1996). Although each hospital conducted frequent client-satisfaction surveys, such modes of participation have been critiqued as unsatisfactory (Nocon and Qureshi 1996). A service manager in this study spoke of their clientele being "surveyed out" and noted that the results of such surveys had to be treated with caution. Further, as Pollit (1988) has noted, these types of survey too often deal with signs and parking issues and do not enable an informed, ongoing discussion on more-substantive issues between user organizations and health providers.

Members in the teams involved in the research regarded their advocacy work on behalf of their clients as important, especially given the structural inequalities that many faced as a result of their disabilities. Over the years, staff at all sites had made a number of submissions in response to policy documents circulated by government and their Regional Health Authority (RHA)[3] and had also been frequently engaged in arguing for additional resourcing for individual clients; equally, there were expressions of cynicism and despair about the effectiveness of so doing. One person, his emphases underscoring his feelings about the situation, commented on the frequently identified absence of a less secure unit for the psychiatric patients in the secure unit to subsequently move on to, and on the service's efforts over years to get this absence remedied, said:

> *that* particular that that *issue* is perfectly illustrated by the . illogicality if not the professionally inept or unethical process of setting up a secure unit which has *no* follow up or follow on or step down programs available to it. It is, it's the *same* mentality which builds prisons and provides *nothing* to follow on that that's, ah, that's an *abiding* difficulty which causes the the *deepest* personal and professional distress.

Changing health policies also constrained what advocacy work might be undertaken. Although advocacy on behalf of and with marginalized groups has long been understood as part of empowering social work practice, this dimension of practice has been fast disappearing under the increasingly regulatory health environment in Aotearoa/New Zealand.[4] The teams did, however, engage in advocacy with other service organizations on behalf of individual clients. For example, staff at a sheltered workshop reported that they could no longer manage P25 (whose family meeting is discussed below) because of her "difficult," "manipulative," and "uncooperative" behavior. By doing an extensive assessment of her physical and medical functioning, the disability team was able to identify and attend to some of her health-related problems that contributed to the issues that the workshop staff saw as evidence of her lack of moral fiber, define these instead as health-related, and in the process continue the education of the workshop staff on issues related to this particular client's physical disability.

Empowerment of Clients and Families in Family Meetings

Team members, especially members of the inpatient disability and elderly teams, described the objectives of meetings held between themselves and clients and their families as providing them with information about the illness and the clients' overall progress, as an opportunity for them to air concerns, and as a site of joint decision making about discharge plans.

Nonetheless, there was no unanimity among members about the success of or necessity for such meetings, which were, especially in the discharge meetings, largely structured around professionals' feeding back information to the family. This format positioned the team as "expert," casting team members in the role of "telling" the client/family about what had been happening in the different therapies, rather than engaging also with their and/or their families' understanding of the issues that they jointly were facing as a result of their illnesses or their perceptions of issues arising from the therapies. There were no team forums where different members' perspectives about the value of the meetings or the quality of their process could be voiced. Although some spoke very positively about how families and clients valued the meetings and were empowered by them, other team members considered that some families found the process threatening and/or inhibiting and unresponsive to cultural differences. Others, under pressure of work and less convinced of the value of the meetings, commented on their nuisance value, saying that there were too many and they were too time-consuming. The teams responded to work pressures by allocating twenty to thirty minutes to each meeting (although some meetings took longer). While that length of time was sufficient when a client's situation was straightforward, the relatively small amount of time that was allowed complicated the likelihood of achieving that more-detailed process of exchange indicative of more-empowering modes of practice with clients and families whose situations were more complex (Smale and Tuson 1993).

The absence of agreed team guidelines governing aspects of the meetings was problematic. Agendas defining the meetings' objectives and discussion points were not circulated in advance to families, who tended to be asked "cold" if there were issues they wished to discuss. (In point of fact, there were no agendas, either written or constructed verbally in the meetings.) One woman told me when I approached her about my taping and observing the meeting that she and her husband were to have with the team that she was very anxious about it and was assuming the team's intention was to give her "bad news." A routine practice for the team had substantially different ramifications for her. The psychiatric team appeared to take a slightly more planned approach than the teams at other sites insofar as, at the one meeting I observed, they clarified team issues to be addressed and ensured that team members attending the meeting were familiar with and in agreement about the client's current situation before inviting the client and family to join them.

The value of such brief clarificatory meetings before meeting with the family was highlighted in the context of P37's family meeting with the elderly team, in which no such discussion had taken place. Because there was no opportunity to discuss recent developments in her patient's health with her colleagues, a nurse's major concerns about the viability of the team's proposed objective for P37 was raised in the meeting. This resulted in the team's having a protracted argument in front of the client and family about issues that should not have been aired in this forum. Despite the fact that several team members believed that the team had not acted professionally in this instance, there was no occasion, as in other teams when the team did not manage the meeting well, for discussing how such problems occurred and how they could in future be differently handled. What this event and others similar to it highlighted is the need for teams to have established processes to ensure that they review their input into family meetings that for one reason or another turn out to be problematic.

Only minimal documentation of the meetings and recording of decisions was kept at two sites. One of these teams had only very recently started to record minutes of the meetings, but the extremely truncated minutes that were produced listed only the tasks the professionals were to undertake and excluded any reference to the presence of the client or family. They also excluded clients' or family members' input to the meeting and the nature and level of care that families were offering the client, a dimension that is a significant part of an empowering relationship (Smale and Tuson 1993). Such practices had the effect of placing the professionals and their concerns at center stage and clients and families on the margins. The minutes were placed in the nursing notes and were not circulated to the client or the family.

Because the whole issue of empowering practices was much more complex, given the legal status of the psychiatric team's clientele, the team ensured that the patients had a folder in their possession containing information relating to their committal to care and copies of reviews, progress reports, and so on. In some cases workers, with the patient's agreement, wrote monthly reports on his or her progress to the family. These were signed off by the patient, who also received a copy for the folder. However, the community team (although substantially the same professionals as the inpatient team) did not forward minutes of family meetings to clients or families.

The format for the meetings run by the disability and elderly teams (where most of this data subset was taped) was that team members reported back one by one to families and clients on the progress in the clients' therapies. At the end of each team member's summary of his or her work, clients and families were generally asked if they had any comments or questions about what had been said, a practice that, while seeking to include the clients and families, nonetheless positioned them as respondents, not as initiators of commentary. My reading of the following text, with the physiotherapist's emphases on movements with which the client continued to have difficulty, on her achievements, and on the focus of the therapy, is that the therapist is seeking to encourage the client. In this case, however, as was typical of the family meeting transcripts, the visual pattern is of substantial professional input and correspondingly minimal input from family and clients, a pattern that places the professional as more in control of the situation and discourages the development of the more dialogic talk discussed earlier.

PHYSIO Right I'd also been seeing you, P37, as an outpatient, and we'd more or less decided that in fact physio was not doing all *that* much to help any more, that you need to concentrate on the occupational therapy. But during your time here I've picked up one or two things that I think we've needed to work on a bit. One thing was to try and get another splint made like that one that can be washable and the sewing room are looking at that at the moment. Um, during the course of going *across* to go to the sewing room we picked up things like stairs that don't have a *rail*

P37 mm

PHYSIO and that's been something that we've been working at quite hard um and even kerbs you find quite difficult to go *down* don't you?

P37 (*very softly*) mmm

PHYSIO Just one little step down but in actual fact you're going up and down my flight of stairs *beautifully* as long as the rail is there and you've just got to get your (*softly*) confidence back (*louder*) but in most things that we do, if you pick it up straight away as an automatic sort of reaction you manage to do it really well. If you struggle to do it initially and I try and *correct* you, it makes it worse doesn't it? And yet you sort of find it more difficult when I'm trying to tell you how to do it, so if you work out for *yourself* how to do something it seems to be a lot easier. So, I still feel that physio probably doesn't have a *large* sort of input to play in that a lot of *my* work tends to be working on specific little areas *breaking down* an activity into its components and working on the component. If we do that for you it makes it more difficult so, I think the, the whole emphasis is *still* on the occupational therapy but I'm really happy to, you know, pick up areas from the OT that we perhaps need to work on strengthening or something. Your walking is looking good/ um, the stairs this morning were fantastic, and Friday they weren't good at all (*softly*) so the/ I think that was possibly because I started to correct on Friday and that threw you off kilter. Today, I said just do it and you did it really well . . so, yes, not a whole lot from physio except perhaps to keep working a little bit on stretching your *hand* and seeing if we can't find something that's more satisfactory than the splints that you've got at the moment.

CN Is there anything you'd like to ask (the Physio) about?

P37 (*very softly*) No.

During this account, P37 nodded and leaned forward, she and the physio retained eye contact, and family members nodded. I am not assuming that P37 and her family got nothing from the exchange. But the lengthy account was complex and at points unfocused, especially in light of an intention to provide feedback not just to the family but to P37, who as a consequence of her major stroke had significant cognitive and physical problems. The nature of P37's difficulties suggests that a much briefer, more structured report, rather than a loosely constructed one, highlighting issues that the physio thought were important, could have been more helpful, and that some written notes for P37 and her family about what each therapist had been able to achieve and was intending to continue working on could also have been valuable. What was also noticeable was that neither P37 nor her family were asked about their concerns or how they and she thought she was progressing, although P37, because of the nature of her disabilities, would likely have had difficulty in managing a response. These procedures and processes, then, positioned the client and family as subordinate, marginal, and passive in contrast to the active and knowledgeable team members, and as recipients of information about different therapeutic processes but not as significant sources of knowledge and information to be exchanged with the team.

What follows is an analysis of two meetings. The meeting held by the elderly team with P10 and her niece emphasizes these differences in positioning between client and team. While this meeting was particularly graphic in its illustration of a disempowering process, similar processes occurred in nearly all the family meetings I attended. P10's family meeting is, however, unrepresentative of the meetings I attended in that it contains *no* occasion when the team set out their preferences for P10's ongoing care (this remained implicit rather than explicit) and then sought opinions or commentary from P10 or her niece on that plan. While the team did not seek to involve the client or her relative in these ways (although it was evident that the niece had picked up on the team's belief about the inevitability of residential care), in other meetings a very active eliciting of clients' and families' concerns and the team's engaging with these happened infrequently. The second meeting, run by the disability team, identifies more-empowering practices.

P10's Family Meeting

This meeting was held partway through P10's rehabilitation following her fall and a partial hip replacement. P10 was in her eighties, very frail, with a hearing problem and with substantial short-term memory deficits. Apart from two key moments, she spoke infrequently and in a very wavering and almost inaudible voice. Most of her responses were restricted to "yes," but it was not always clear what the status of "yes" was and the team did not seek clarification. Those attending were P10's niece (who lived two hundred kilometers away), the charge nurse (who acted as chair), the occupational therapist, the social worker, the speech language therapist and her student, the physiotherapist, and P10's key worker (a nurse). The meeting lasted half an hour.

The charge nurse (admirably) opened the meeting with a statement of its objectives and process: the need for the meeting, what was to take place in the meeting, and her desire that P10 understand the process.

CN (*loudly, and leaning forward*) Um we are meeting to talk to about . what's been happening while you've been in Ward 7 P10.

P10 (*very softly*) Yes.

CN It's to give you feedback about all of the various assessments that you've been having while you've been here.

P10 (*softly*) Yes.

CN And it's to answer any questions or any concerns that your family or yourself may have about . anything . that's been happening while you're *here*, anything that comes out of what we tell you, and we're all also going to look at what's going to happen next.

P10 (*very softly*) Yes.

CN What we normally *do* is . we all go round and introduce ourselves and we tell you um what the kind of discipline we're from and, um, each person will give you their feedback from the assessment and then it's sort of open . slather as it were.

P10 mm hm

CN Is that *clear* ah the reason why we're here?

P10 Yes.

Although CN does outline the team's objectives for the meeting, this account is problematic. The word *assessment* crops up twice. The use of the word assumes that P10 understands both that she has been assessed and the purpose of assessments—that is, she understands the context for the meeting (planning for her future and the question of her safety). At the same time, a key sentence, "We're all going to look at what's going to happen next," is open to more than one reading. It could refer to some additional therapies that she may receive. It could mean that what is "going to happen next" will be decided during the course of the meeting; it also could mean that a decision about P10's future has already been made by the team, so that the "we all" is ambiguous. Further, this somewhat loose account is then rephrased even more loosely shortly after as "open . slather." While this may be a way of inviting P10 to participate in the discussion about her future, there is no explicit invitation to her to do so.

Moreover, P10 is not given a range of options that could be considered in relation to her ongoing care. In particular, the team does not clearly identify the issues associated with returning home, the nature and quantity of help that she may need if she is to remain at home and whether that can be provided in light of their restricted resources, or whether she needs to consider moving to a more sheltered environment, and what her options are in that context. Significantly, P10 is not specifically told that she will be asked her views about her future, this failure to ask being compounded by the absence of a previous discussion with her about her wishes. As it transpired, because of work pressures, the social worker, often an important source of advocacy for clients, had not met with P10 over the two or so weeks since her admission to the ward.

Following this statement of the meeting's objectives (to which neither P10 or her niece was asked to contribute), each member introduced herself and stated her discipline. Members then reported on the work they had done with P10. In the meetings I observed, a number of the therapists tended to direct their accounts of their work primarily to their colleagues rather than to the client. On this occasion, however, the therapists mostly did direct their comments to P10. However, while the chairperson did remind the OT (who typically spoke very quietly, in a voice that tended to trail off at the end of sentences) to speak louder, only the speech language therapist (SLT) held eye contact with P10 throughout her report to her (as distinct from looking around at team members, a practice that tends to move the focus away from the client and back to the professionals). During SLT's report to P10, in which SLT stressed what P10 *could* do as well as identifying her memory problem, P10 said "yes" at various points, as she did with the other therapists. She also offered some comments ("I think I need my ears done") and actively confirmed the SLT's evaluation.

SLT I looked briefly also at reading. and writing and you were writing . single words *just fine* for me this morning so there wasn't any problem there.

P10 Yes.

SLT And you could actually read . um sentences and get a lot of the meaning out of it. Sometimes you'd skip over words and that kind of would muddle up the meaning a bit but um, but ah, yeah short sentences and so again, it's not a specific reading or writing problem um that you're having.

P10 No I don't think there's a a—

SLT —no.

P10 A writing problem.

And she responded warmly when the SLT ended her report:

P10 I think you did very well.

SLT And so did you thank you very much. We got along just fine together. (*And both laughed.*)

This was the only moment during the meeting of positive engagement and of warmth and mutuality between P10 and members of the team. It was also the only point where there was clear evidence of an exchange relationship.

Following the report from the physiotherapist (concentrating on P10's difficulties in walking), some brief comments from the nurse about showering and dressing problems, and an explanation to the niece about the type of hip replacement P10 had had, the social worker, who had not met with P10, was asked to contribute. The discussion went as follows:

SW (*softly*) I haven't done anything yet. (*loudly to P10*) The physio's had a talk to me about . talking with you about your options, about you know what kind of help you're going to need so I'll still need to do that with you later this week.

P10 Yes.

NIECE Yes.

SW You've been living at home by yourself?

P10 Living at home by myself.

SW Mm, with no help?

P10 No help.

NIECE (*very softly*) No, no.

SW We'll need to talk about that me and you later in the week.

P10 Yes.

SW About how you would manage with those sorts of things . at home.

P10 Yes.

SW You've got some concerns?

P10 Pardon?

SW You've got some worries of your own?

P10 (*very softly*) oooh (*breathing hard*) . . .

NIECE Yes she is concerned about what's going to—

SW —yeah

NIECE To um

SW We can talk about your concerns later this week. Just me and you.

P10 Yes.

SW Okay.

My reading of this exchange is that it denies the stated purpose of the meeting ("we're all going to look at what happens next"). These issues are now only to spoken of in private with the social worker, P10 is effectively prohibited from expressing her concerns or her wishes, and the niece's attempts to act as an advocate for her aunt are not responded to.

The CN then speaks, emphasizing the staff perspective on P10's future and issues of risk management. It is not that these are not pertinent, complex issues that need to be raised, but there still have been no questions to P10 about her ideas about her future living arrangements. Further, the structure of CN's statement gives weight to the authority of the team, an authority that once stated may well complicate expressions of dissent.

CN Um, P10 from from a nursing point of view and from talking among . ourselves about the various things that have been going on we as a *staff* have some concerns about how you will manage by yourself at home and we just wanted you to know that so that you can be thinking about it before you talk to the social worker. We're quite worried about you being by yourself especially from a *safety* factor and because you do need quite a lot of reminding about things.

P10 Yes.

CN So we just wanted you to know about that so that when you talk with the social worker you you've already got that to think over.

P10 Yes.

CN Is there anything that you would like to ask any of us? . . . . . .

P10 (*softly*) No I/ I I don't think so.

CN (*to niece*) Is there anything that you would like to ask anybody?

At this point the niece commented on the unsuitable features of her aunt's house, suggested ways in which the team might be able to communicate more easily with her in relation to her deafness, and reminded the team of the stressful year her aunt had had (her husband, to whom she had been very close, had died). The charge nurse empathized with P10 over her "rough year" (to which P10 replied that the previous one had been worse) and then asked the niece if she had anything else she wanted to raise. The following exchanges then took place:

NIECE If you like um, it's just you know, some places would be *fine* um . . but um . . I was just sort of thinking for her, *her* comfort and for um, to know that that, for *her* to be . to be *really* confident about everything, you know it, when it comes time for her to leave here to . as an interim to, to go into a into a um, more *more homelike* surrounding and then take the step from there you know.

P10 (*loudly*) I I I *don't* er *agree* with that.

NIECE No I know.

P10 (*loudly*) *No* huh huh

SW These are things I can talk over with P10

NIECE Yes.

SW as the week goes on *anyway* What—

NIECE —I know that she's very—

SW —yeah.

NIECE (*to her aunt*) But um/ but but *everybody's* concern really is that um, for *your* (P10: mm) well being and care and that um, you know nothing else is going to go wrong. We wouldn't like you to go home and fall over again or something.

CN Well the social worker will talk to you later in the week P10 and if you have any worries about it in the meantime you can write them down and ask us any time through the week you don't have to wait for the meeting/ okay?

P10 Oh oh (*very softly*) all right.

What is so striking about this exchange is that it contains two moments in a twenty-minute or so meeting when P10 spoke loudly and in dissent from other participants. She assertively (even if briefly) rejected the framing of the discussion as being concerned with her comfort but at no point (again) was she asked to outline what she wanted or to discuss her understanding of her fitness to manage at home. Instead, her interjections were overruled, she was referred back to the social worker, and the meeting closed around the powerful and therefore difficult-to-resist question of others' concerns for her safety. The meeting finished almost immediately, with the niece being told not to hesitate to raise any concerns she might have and that the team would "carry on for another week and see if we can get you (P10) any better."

It is difficult to believe that P10 felt very empowered by this experience. Throughout the meeting she was almost entirely marginalized, a process to which undoubtedly her deafness and the onset of dementia contributed. There is no doubt that achieving a more empowering process for a client such as P10 is not simple. But neither is it completely unattainable, although a fully empowering process may be impossible. From the outset, most members positioned themselves as expert, offering detailed accounts of her functional abilities, defining the agenda for the meeting without identifying the objective of the assessments (to evaluate her safety) or spelling out their subtext (her admission to a rest home) until well into the interview. The CN stated initially that the team was interested in her concerns and in seeking her opinion. Yet on the two occasions when P10 sought to articulate those concerns and to resist her inscription as marginal, the social worker responded to her emphatic rejection of the team's and the niece's not very explicit proposed plan by saying she would discuss the question later. There was no process of exchange between the client and the team, although there was more between the niece and the team. At the end of the meeting, P10 was invited to write down in a communication book queries about her therapies so she could raise those with individual workers, but it was the niece who was invited to contact the team and continue the discussion of her aunt's future. It is possible that the niece left feeling empowered; her concerns about her aunt's future had been validated, as it was clear that the team also believed as she did, that P10 should go into a rest home. This highlights the importance of not assuming that family and client are always similarly positioned in relation to an issue, and it complicates assumptions that family members will necessarily advocate for the client's needs or wishes (McLean 1995).

P25's Family Meeting

This meeting, lasting about forty minutes, was organized by the disability team to discuss care issues of a young woman, P25, who had a degenerative illness, lived at home with her family, and attended a sheltered workshop several days a week. She had come onto the ward for reassessment largely because of the worsening aspects of her condition and a deterioration in the attitudes of the sheltered workshop staff toward her. As a consequence of these factors, it appeared that she might be asked to leave this workshop, an outcome that the team and family were keen to avoid. P25, her sister, her mother (M), the social worker, the nursing service coordinator (NSC), CNS (who took minutes), physiotherapist (PHYSIO), and occupational therapist (OT) attended the meeting.

The meeting began with each team member introducing him- or herself, and NSC, who was the chairperson for the meeting, outlined her role as key worker.

> My job is actually Nurse Service Coordinator in other words whether P25's *in or out* then/ it's I would be the point of contact if you've got problems/ I will be keeping in touch with P25 and so will the others with seeing what we need to do and looking ahead then you know

doing some of that planning and so on. (*softly*) Is that okay?; (*louder*) do you understand that? (yes) okay/ P25's just

CNS And I am just scribbling here because I am doing the minutes and you will get a copy of those, OK?

NSC then provided a short summary of the medical and physiological problems leading to P25's admission to the ward.

NSC Well P25 came in/ how long ago?

P25 26 April

NSC Yes/ its been a fair while/ it started really didn't it because I and your sister and Physio had a lot of concerns (mm) mainly about P25's bladder problems and also about her walking getting worse um and I couldn't/ we needed to look at it as an overall picture not just something that was happening so/ that's what we started too to do (*slight sigh*). So/ shall we/ what's happened since she's been here is that um/ we've done a lot of tests haven't we CNS? (CNS: yes). A *lot* of *really thorough* examinations from a neurologist and he ordered MRI scans and um (*softly*) *CT scan* (*louder*) and from the result of that we know that P25 has got one of these fibromas that (*raises tone of voice*) remember we talked about that in the car again P25? (*drops tone*)/ *hard to remember* I know/ but um you don't have to worry too much about it/ and that's probably what is causing her to be a lot worse with her walking/ and her bladder and so on/ we've *talked*/ everybody's talked about whether or not she should have surgery or not to remove that fibroma on her spinal cord and you have talked to RS about it, haven't you and um/ it is something that they wouldn't be very *keen* to do specifically but we have got an appointment with the specialist/ in July {gives precise date}/ now I am really happy to *go* to that with P25 and (*to M*) perhaps you would like to come too?

M Yeah I think I'd like to go.

NSC So that we need to be there to *see* what the surgeon says/ RS thinks that he will probably say leave it alone/ doesn't he but we (*softly*) just don't know until we get there and um because it is quite a big operation (*louder*) and so it needs very careful thought anyway wouldn't it P25? (P25: Mm) okay/ *so* what else do we/ shall we start with somebody else now since I've um/

NSC in this statement consistently refers to P25 and her family, to what they know ("*remember, we talked about that in the car*"; "*we've talked,* everybody's talked about whether or not she should have surgery (. . .) and you've talked, haven't you, to RS"). This was a practice she followed through the meeting, although she did not specifically seek the family's understanding of the reasons for the admission and its sequelae.

While NSC handed over to the physio at the end of her outlining of the issues resulting in P25's admission, she almost immediately reentered the discussion (in one sense as family advocate, to ensure that they were able to raise concerns) in order to get a seemingly small detail elaborated for P25's mother's benefit. This intervention led to a quite detailed interchange, some of which is reproduced below, between the physio and the mother about the reasons for using a particular type of frame, about P25's deteriorating walking ability, her level of safety, how she typically supported herself while walking inside (which the physio had not known about), and whether modifications to P25's shoes and the use of a splint would result in their longer life.

PHYSIO While P25's been in hospital we've working a lot on her walking/ um/ she came in walking with two elbow crutches and she's actually *not*/ bad on the crutches she's not entirely unsafe but um/ I've given her a walking frame that one over there and she walks a lot better on the walking frame/ she's more upright and she's *really* safe on it so/ I'm giving her the walking frame to take home and she keeps the crutches as well so she's got that/ option . um

NSC (*softly*) Can I just interrupt there because M had a/ query about—

M —have you got a smaller/ P25 said you had a smaller frame than that one. Have you or not?

PHYSIO You mean a different type of frame?

M Yes/ not so/ *wide*.

PHYSIO No.

M No they're all the

PHYSIO That's just

M same

PHYSIO And and that/ and that would be no different from what it is now (no) and see how that goes.

M Yes because a lot of the time she doesn't use those inside *either*.

PHYSIO Yeah she needs to.

M Just sort of hands along the wall.

The value of a knowledgeable key worker, able to raise issues unobtrusively, including those that the family may not have raised on their own accord, was demonstrated several more times during the interview. For example, NSC interrupted a series of exchanges largely between team members about P25's use of a wheelchair, which the team saw as a means of assisting her in maintaining her sporting interest, by asking,

NSC You find it a bit of a nuisance in the house don't you M?

M Well it is *really* (*sigh*)

NSC Yes.

M There's not/ not much room there and if we put it in the shed I'd be a bit worried.

NSC Yes/ would you/ it'll fold up.

M Well we've been broken into a few times.

NSC Have you?

M Into the shed I'm not really that keen on it. Oh well they'll take anything.

NSC Yes I think they will.

SISTER See it's handy when she stays/ it will mean that I can take her out/ (yes) if she comes and visits me on just a normal weekend I can't take her anywhere (no) (no) and my husband.

OT(1) Speed things up too/ yeah

SISTER Yeah well/ we walked to the shops one day and it took/ my husband said we were away an hour and a half.

NSC Yes.

SISTER You know it's not/ but if she comes to stay with me it's good I can get her out (NSC: oh yes) and go for a walk in the garden and shopping.

M It's a [.] at your place/ I mean if we go out it's just down the front door into the car and

SISTER Yeah I don't drive you see so it's my fault I'm (mm)

PHYSIO Well if we got a chair can we see how that goes? If we can borrow one of CNS' (mm) and just see how that goes (M: mm) and see if it does drive you crazy and you know/ ah

M Yeah because they're different sizes you can get small ones can't you?

In contrast to P10's and others' family meetings, the transcript of this meeting contains few lengthy statements by professionals. Instead, it demonstrates a high level of mutually informing professional and family interchanges about a range of issues pertaining to P25's needs and care. P25 was consulted throughout as to her understanding of issues and whether there are issues important to her that have not yet been raised. The meeting substantially concludes with CNS reading from the minutes about everyone's roles and tasks.

CNS Do you want me to read out what/ I've jotted down some outcomes um as to what's going to happen with her. Do you want to just comment about/ one person at the/ the Center just reminding P25 to go {to the toilet}?

SW I think Fiona {staff member at the Center} is/ Fiona isn't here. I mean it's important that um/ we contact have contact and actually set up some time with Fiona and P25 and that would be one of the issues that I'll talk about. It's not like everybody at the Center's going to be yelling (P25: mm) out to P25, "Go to the toilet" (yeah). We'll just/ try and um have a person who's going to remind you to be very quiet and discreet about it/ that would be one of the suggestions that we would be making (*very softly*) OK?

CNS Um/ I've just jotted these things down and that is P25 has an appointment to see Dr. Smith to assess the need for surgery and NSC and Sister will go with you, P25, for that/ and to go home on the walking frame which is much *safer* but that you can use the elbow crutches if you wish and um/ for safety/ reasons you should/ shouldn't be using/ *nothing*. You should be using either your walking frame or your elbow crutches/ and that the/ ankle [support] must be worn all the time for safety *as well* to stop your foot from dragging and it keeps your foot in the right position . . and we suggest you try and lie on your *tummy* for some time during the day/ particularly when you're resting and that travelling by public transport/ that is the buses should be avoided due to the difficulty of getting on and off/ SW is to meet with Fiona at work and to talk over issues regarding work and for her to be the person to remind you to toilet . . OT(1) has organized equipment for you to have at home and to ensure safety/ and she's applied for funding through Income Support. OT(1) will also keep in touch with you once at home and a wheelchair or a chair can be used/ {in the sport you play} and we will look at supplying one from the unit on a long term basis and that NSC will/ assist with the/ the supply of incontinence pads rather than/ Mother or Sister having to buy them.

NSC Does P25 like those big ones/ we've been using?

CNS P25, do you like the bigger pad?

P25 Yes.

NSC You do . . . . . . *any questions*/ anything you want to *ask?* . . . .

M I think we've pretty well covered/ *when* do you think she might be going home?

Developing Empowering Practices

At the beginning of this chapter, I discussed empowerment in terms of structural and more individually focused approaches. Achieving both modes requires professional and organizational attention to practices. As Chapman (1994), Smale and Tuson (1993), and Young (1994) demonstrate, both modes require a "dialogic," rather than an "expert," approach to discussions with clients and family members. Moreover, as the meeting with P10 suggests, working in an empowering way is likely to become more difficult the more vulnerable or frail the client becomes because professional concerns, such as those about safety, may well conflict with the client's wishes. What these meetings demonstrated was that teams seeking to empower clients require well-defined and clearly conceptualized practices, which take account of the fact that there will be some clients for whom holding such meetings is simply not empowering and for whom alternative processes need to be developed. In P10's case, the issue was not whether the team's evaluation of the dangers for her in living alone was correct (which they may well have been), but that in a major decision affecting her life, she was throughout the meeting rendered redundant and excluded. Although the team's intention may have been to empower, achieving other than this outcome was considerably complicated by the meeting's structure and professional practices, as one client who, for more than half an hour, had only been able to contribute minimally to the meeting, commented:

P22 Can we stop here? I haven't said anything yet.

COMMUNITY NURSE Sorry P22.

P22 Nobody's asked me for my view. I mean, I, I've commented here and
there and just been fobbed off. Um, I have some differences {from the
team} as to my capabilities.

Practicing empowerment in team meetings with families, then,
involves ongoing evaluations of process, practice, and development of
intervention strategies if the policy objective of the centrality of clients and
families in decision making is to be demonstrated. First, this means attention to team practices at the micro level and to the discourses that the team
is accessing. An "expert" discourse results, for example, in not focusing on
clients' and families' perspectives (and identifying any tensions between
them) or encouraging input rather than agreement to propositions. In
most of the meetings I recorded, the teams' detailed accounts of work
undertaken and its results foregrounded professional knowledge, professional input, and emphasized professional power and control.

Second, it requires that teams attend to how processes may well marginalize those whom the team intends to empower. For example, developing more-empowering processes, especially with frail or impaired clients,
could mean that:

1. Before the meeting, families and clients receive some information
about the objectives of such meetings and an outline of the process.
McClain and Bury (1998) include in their article the text of an information pamphlet distributed by the Department of Pediatrics at the University of New Mexico, Albuquerque, to parents and to staff in relation to family conferences.[5] The existence of such documentation highlights an organizational commitment to emphasizing the importance of families in the
team context and indicates how developing more-empowering practices is
a shared responsibility between organization and professional. This would
allow for the development of organizationally legitimated processes and
procedures.

2. Rather than a verbal presentation of the objectives of the meeting, a
written agenda over which there had been consultation and that specifically identified any differences in the clients', families', and team's objectives,
would be useful. This would require discussions with the client and family
before the meeting. Such an agenda may also demonstrate to the team that
a client may need an independent advocate in situations where families'
and clients' objectives differ.

3. The team evaluate whether meeting with a large group of professionals is appropriate for all clients and their families, a point that McClain and Bury (1998) also make.[6] Rather than routinely meeting as a team, part of a more-empowering procedure could be to decide on an appropriate format for the meeting, taking a client's abilities and the focus of a meeting into account. For example, McClain and Bury have suggested that presenting new information or sensitive news to a family in a large family conference is not helpful; nor are meetings helpful where there is strong professional disagreement over the appropriate courses of action. In light of P10's cognitive capacity, it may have been more empowering for her and her niece to have met with P10's key worker, who would have gained an evaluation of P10's (different) capacities from other members, and then discussed these with P10 and her niece in light of P10's elicited wishes.

4. The team attend to the technicality of its language in any reporting-back processes and to the structure of any report on work done. Highly detailed, complex reports, or loose, poorly organized feedback may well not be helpful to many clients. Provision of written material to which clients and families can subsequently refer may also be useful. It is also important to note that a primary focus on reporting back on what the therapists think has been achieved may exclude input from clients and families.

5. The team seeks to develop processes that focus on exchanges between client, family, and team to ensure that clients' and families' knowledge and concerns are foregrounded. An objective of a family meeting, therefore, would be to seek to create an environment in which dialogue is central, as happened more in the meeting with P25. This in itself challenges the traditional positioning of clients, families, and professionals. Undertaking this points to the difficulties in changing discourses. Professionals would be required actively to move beyond the "expert" role, which has proved difficult to shift, while also encouraging clients, some of whom may expect to take a more passive role, to take a more active role, as well as developing strategies that do not marginalize those who, by reason of frailty and disability, are able to participate only minimally.

The effect of these five points is to underscore how achieving more-empowering practices requires significant discursive changes in the processes by which professional and client bodies are produced. Discourses of empowerment inscribe a professional body that, while "knowing," is more modest in its claims to know, more able to acknowledge limitations in knowledge, and more receptive to knowledges articulated from other spaces/locations—a body, then, that is significantly more flexible, more attuned to the implications of different positionings in power than professional bodies have been in the past. The relationship between professional and client bodies thus shifts from a hierarchical to a more horizontal plane. A significant difficulty, however, with modernist empowerment discourses is that they are located within a binary framework. Their intention is to shift from discursively writing the client/family body as passive, subordinated to that of the professional and as neither knowledgeable nor able to articulate their knowledge, to discursively producing instead bodies that are authoritative, articulate, and powerful.

My argument is located within neither of these positions. I argue that empowering practice is based on recognizing that, collectively and even individually, clients may well occupy multiple positions within those polarized extremes, particularly in terms of their ability to articulate their knowledge. This therefore requires the production of flexible practices to accommodate and work with these differences. The production of changed/changing professional practices, though, is not simply a professional concern; it is also an organizational concern. The centrality of organizational discourses in effecting and maintaining effective practices in teams is taken up in the next chapter.

9

Performing Knowledge Work

The primary objective of this book has been to disrupt dominant representations of interprofessional teamwork and contribute to a new mapping of team practices more appropriate to the changing organizational settings, with their emphasis on professional accountability and effectiveness, in which teams work. The value of this text is that it locates the concept "teamwork" in postmodern theory and attends closely to the practice implications of that theorizing. The preceding chapters have foregrounded those elements of teamwork that have consistently been overlooked in conventional representations of that work, elements that are critical to the achievement of more effective team practices.

Rejecting a position that teams will in the end stand or fall by their own efforts (McKenzie 1994), I have written of the production of effective teamwork as intimately related to the clarification and elaboration of organizational discourses about teamwork. The production of effective teamwork also involves an understanding that clients and families, although not always physically present, constitute a part of the team, and it requires theorizing teamwork as knowledge-based work traversing different disciplinary and locational topographies. Moreover, I have stressed that knowledge-based work does not just address facts of difference. It focuses equally on the "effects of difference" (Haraway, quoted in Soja 1997:116). The work of this last chapter will be to explore some of the implications of this representation of teamwork as knowledge work.

Key objectives of knowledge-based interprofessional teamwork in health care settings are simultaneously to enhance the quality of clients' care (a word that in current discourses includes a reference to the concept of empowerment) and to contribute to organizational effectiveness. An effect of the use of interprofessional teams, rather than teams constituted by professionals from one discipline only, is that discursively the body of the client becomes a complex body, frequently fragmented by modern health care practices across multiple discursive (if not actual) sites (Atkinson 1995). The interprofessional team review or meeting, then, becomes the site where this fragmented discursive body may be reassembled through attention to the relationships between its dispersed fragments and the implications of those relationships worked with by the team through processes of knowledge collaboration and coordination of work. Working knowledgeably with clients in complex situations requires: first, a focused statement of the issues the team needs to address; second, the articulation (typically in a narrative format) of dispersed information about clients, including information about their situation held by them and their families; third, a recursive, spiraling process of knowledge generation produced by team members through discussion of information about clients/families and questioning of how the different representations of clients/families and their perceived needs generated from different positions (discipline-specific and lay) are to be worked with, and the implications of following particular (theoretical) lines of inquiry; fourth, the development of an evolving, contingent, and agreed-on team plan structured by the identification of immediate team, client, and family goals; fifth, the recording of the key elements of the discussion and confirmation of the accuracy and fullness of the minutes; and sixth, the subsequent effecting of this plan. A team discussion containing these elements will possess a recursive, fluid, yet also linear structure, by which the discussion is simultaneously shaped and progressed, its objective being a knowledge spiral that will contribute to tangible outputs (a well-informed client plan) as well as positive outcomes for clients.

As I have noted in chapter 6, Nonaka and Takeuchi (1995) described the initial process of the development of knowledge-based work as partly reliant on members' making explicit their tacit knowledge, that is, elaborating on the values informing the positions of different disciplines. If located within a humanistic rather than a postmodern framework of concepts and values, however, this position lends itself to the possibility of an unreflexive circularity. One implication is that members, confronted with "ideal" statements about the value positions of disciplines, would have the responsibility of choosing which value position should be adopted. Equally, a different result of the elaboration of value positions could be the identification of shared values between a number of disciplines, values reflecting concepts such as the autonomy of the individual and the potential for individual growth and development. It is not immediately apparent to me how either outcome would significantly advance knowledge-based teamwork as I have been defining it in this text.

The significant shift achieved by re-reconceptualizing teamwork through Foucault's theory of discourse lies in the foregrounding, not so much of members' articulation of tacit knowledge but of their consciousness of how operating from particular discursive locations (locations that are physical, as in their specific organizational/lay features, as well symbolic, as in their discipline-specific features) generate particular representations of clients, families, and team; and how such representations come to structure the ways in which clients and families are positioned by team members and shape the focus of ongoing teamwork. Representations of clients/families are thus generated in a complex, dynamic process involving teams' representational practices and their writing of clients/families; the representational practices within the team (the power/knowledge allocated to the different disciplines and to the representations of clients/families generated by each specific disciplinary site); and the manner of teams' engagement with clients'/families' representational practices about them (the team). The intersection of these modes of inscription results in the production of care plans and the effecting of ongoing work.

Teamwork is inextricably imbued with relations of power. Power circulates. It is everywhere. It is not the property of particular individuals but exists in discourse, so that the location of an individual within a more or less powerful discourse will define that person as more or less powerful. The issue for teams is not to seek to avoid power but, recognizing how crucially it structures their work, to engage with its discursive outcomes. The issue is not whether Mike (the doctor) is more powerful than Sam (the counselor) or whether Jane (the social worker) is more powerful than Mary (the nurse). The issue is how the relations of (disciplinary) power existing in a particular team affect how the team as a team elicits and engages with information from its different disciplinary sites and how, as a result of including or marginalizing particular types of knowledge, a specific team inscribes the bodies of its clients/families and itself, a process with material outcomes for all of the three groups involved. An effective knowledge-based team is therefore highly attentive to its management of relations of (disciplinary) power and to issues of inclusion and exclusion, visibility and

invisibility. It focuses on the margins as much as it focuses on what appears
to be the current team understanding of the center because what may
appear as insignificant, throwaway comments are often highly productive.
Its work is therefore intimately associated with questions such as those
posed by Haraway and cited in chapter 2. These questions inquire,

> How to see? Where to see from? What limits to vision? What to see for?
> Whom to see with? Who gets to have more than one point of view?
> Who gets blinded? Who wears blinders? Who interprets the visual field?
> What other sensory powers do we wish to cultivate besides vision?
>
> *(Haraway 1997a:289)*

A knowledge-based team (one open to addressing the inevitability of
power relations circulating within it) would, of course, be unlikely to ask
Haraway's specific questions. It could, though, as part of its everyday work,
ask questions such as "Who has not spoken who needs to?" "What disciplinary input/what information from the family/client are we missing
here?" "What are the differences in the accounts about this client/family
now circulating in the team?" "The contradictions between these accounts
are real, representing the different work of members. How do we make
sense of them?" "How would each account of this client/family structure
the work we undertake?" "How does this plan accord with family/client
goals or objectives?"

Because being aware of the discursive dimension of teamwork, including focusing on the effects of power relations, involves considerable conceptual shifts, I will ground the above comments in a concrete example. In
a discussion about a possible instance of spousal abuse of a physically disabled client, the doctor's firmly expressed annoyance toward the husband,
who pushed past her and demanded attention during a ward round, and
the annoyance expressed by an occupational therapist because of his continual modification of the wheelchair setting is more than the recounting
of an unpleasant interpersonal encounter and frustration about the necessity for redoing work. Such "interpersonal" encounters are, on all sides,
shot through with power relations and structured discursively, with the
effect that those who embody authority, expertise, and status override or
displace those who lack these qualities and are perceived as obstacles to the
achievement of discipline-based or team goals. A social worker's attempt to
challenge this powerful negative representation through advancing an
alternative representation (outlining areas of demonstrated concern by this

man for his wife) made no headway at all. The account she advanced remained, unattended and invisible, on the margins of the discussion.

All the team members involved in this discussion espoused humanistic, caring values. Analyzing this discussion by reference to value positions simply suppresses the power of discourse and its manifestations in micro-practices. Certainly, the interchange took place between individuals, but *how* that interchange took place was structured discursively.

The power of working from a position attentive to discourse is that it opens up a complex dimension of teamwork, the production of discursive bodies: as they are represented in team discussions, clients and professionals embody the intersections of organizational discourses and enact codified organizational and professional practices. Conceptualizing teamwork within a framework of discourse directs attention to knowledge work, the processes of knowledge generation and the implications of differently located knowledge. My emphasis in this analysis of teamwork is on how knowledge-based work includes not just information pooling but, critically, knowledge creation. The information that team members bring collectively to a discussion is not just passively held and recycled in its original form. Focusing on nodes of knowledge intersection, the team works with the initial informational input to reconstitute their knowledge in modes other than the parallel narratives in which it was first articulated. The process encourages and enables the team to refashion their collective and individual knowledge of the client.

There is one more point to be made explicit in relation to the concept "client/family as team members." I am not writing of their team membership in terms of a consistent physical presence at all team meetings. I am instead highlighting, if you will, their virtual presence. Clients/families are typically brought into the weekly team meetings through different disciplines' accounts of their concerns and the issues they require to be addressed. Members' capacity to articulate such accounts requires their gaining information from clients/families to determine these. Their ability to properly engage with these accounts means that members need to recognize that clients and their family may not agree on issues and may produce contradictory accounts of the same issues. Effective teamwork, however, requires trading in ambiguity and fluidity and the identification of alternative spaces that may be (temporarily) occupied and regarded not as oppositional but as augmentative.

It is not sufficient to write of knowledge-based teamwork simply as a process. The word *process* does not properly capture and highlight the performative dimension critical to effective teamwork, which requires more than haphazard, careless traverses over discipline-specific locations; instead, my intention is to note the rigorousness of that traverse, requiring of members a critical awareness, quickness to possibilities, flexibility, openness to multiplicities (fissures) and uncertainties. The map of the terrain "team discussion" sketched in chapter 6 provides some parameters to shape and guide such a discussion; it also allows for fluidity within those boundaries. The care plan that results is the outcome of a structured, creative process.

Organizational Issues in Creating Knowledge-Based Work

As I have argued extensively in chapter 3, because organizations create teams in order to advance organizational objectives, then it could be assumed that an organization operating within the current policy climate's emphasis on efficiency and effectiveness has a direct interest in the performance of the teams it has created. Further, the issue of the quality of team performances invokes current organizational discourses with their emphases on performance and knowledge work as necessary to the achievement of more effective work, if not to organizational survival. The production of effective, knowledge-based work in part requires the attraction and retention of skilled workers. It also requires organizations to clarify their expectations of how teamwork will be conducted and to support these public expectations through organizational micropractices: team design, policies (Galbraith, Lawler et al. 1993; Bowman and Kogut 1995), and attention to dimensions of practice.

There is, of course, an immediate problem with the above sentence. In my mapping of knowledge-based teamwork, I wrote of the need to avoid prescriptiveness, yet standards of practice (typically written in the imperative tense) are prescriptive. It would be quite possible for standards to result in inflexibility and rigid team procedures (Barker 1993). Substituting "guidelines" for "standards" may assist in maintaining an open process, but words may too easily slide into each other and acquire unintended effects. If organizations are to encourage the development of knowledge-based teamwork, then what they understand as "knowledge" and how they position themselves in relation to developing such work is highly significant. Nonaka and Takeuchi (1995) have noted that too often knowledge is defined as possessing formal and easily transmittable elements (as reflected in many standards of practice), where the emphasis is on content. An alternative mode of definition employed by learning organizations theorists distinguishes between the solving of identified, specific problems that draw on established premises and the establishment of new premises requiring different or new paradigms. Nonaka and Takeuchi suggest that the challenge for knowledge-based organizations is to create conditions allowing for fertile interaction and knowledge spirals. "The organization cannot create knowledge devoid of individuals. But if the knowledge cannot be shared with others or is not amplified at the group . . . level, then knowledge does not spiral itself organizationally" (Nonaka and Takeuchi 1995:225).

Nonaka and Takeuchi have suggested that the appropriate structure to facilitate knowledge work is a "hypertext" organization (225). Key features of such an organization include:

- the definition of the organizational knowledge domain and its vision, that is, the organization needs to address the type of knowledge that it creates;
- the development of a "knowledge crew" (229); and
- the building of a high-density field of interaction at the front line, as this is a key place where members are able to gain rich experience.

Highlighting the intersection between individual worker, the organization, and knowledge production, they write:

> It should be clear . . . that an individual and an organization are not at the opposing ends of a dichotomy. The individual is the "creator" of knowledge and the organization is the "amplifier" of knowledge. But the actual context in which much of the conversion of knowledge takes place is at the group or team levels. The group functions as a "synthesizer" of knowledge. . . . It provides a shared context in which individuals can interact with each other. *(240)[1]*

Such work, of course, may be organizationally risky. Training and practice development may not necessarily contribute to the perpetuation of particular stable and accepted organizational patterns and relationships. Because training requires a process of reassessing the familiar to expand cognitive maps, it is embedded in the engagement and management of paradox, uncertainty, and ambiguity (Nonaka and Takeuchi 1995). It

moves between the known and the unknown and, as Stacey (1996), drawing on Winnicott's and Klein's psychoanalytic theories, has noted, it challenges the organizational maintenance of accustomed patterns of behavior,
control procedures, and routines, a statement that draws attention to
micropractices as key nodes of change or perpetuation of the familiar. The
(discursively constructed) organization must be a key player in the production of effective knowledge-based teamwork. It must, then, be significantly
more than just "supportive" of teamwork.

Sketching the Organizational Role in Developing Knowledge Work

I have described how, in interviews with members, teamwork seemed to be
typically represented as "making a contribution" and, even more informal-
ly in the team meeting, as "discussing" or "talking about" clients. These
interviews also attested to the absence of an account of teamwork in job
descriptions, job interviews, and orientation programs, and the lack of
training in teamwork (within and beyond the organizations). I have
defined organizational practices in these areas as significant because,
although mundane, they nonetheless provide access to formal organizational accounts of teamwork and, even more significantly, to team and
organizational micropractices. How, then, might an organization concerned with the development of knowledge-based teamwork attend to
these three domains of teamwork?

The Job Description and Interview   The first formal contact that team
members are likely to have with the organizational and team representations of teamwork will probably be in the context of receiving a job
description in relation to a possible interview. A knowledge-based organization would attend to the weighting given teamwork and the description
offered of it in the job description. For example, the organizational conception of teamwork and objective(s) in establishing teams would be made
explicit, specific team tasks (such as running family meetings) would be
identified, performance indicators in relation to members' participation in
teamwork would be made explicit, and the organizational training available clearly noted. Knowledge-based organizations would include a written definition of knowledge-based teamwork as part of the accompanying
information package sent out to interviewees. This material could then
identify team-related issues on which they would be asked to comment in
an interview.

These issues would be extended in an interview situation. Rather than subordinating the focus on teamwork by primarily attending to discipline-specific issues and the interviewee's capacity to undertake such work (as happened at the research sites), the interview would be structured to ensure that both dimensions of work were adequately covered. In terms of teamwork, such an interview may well:

- Ask interviewees to outline what they understand teamwork to be about (based on their experience or training to date);
- Ask them, in relation to material made available before the interview, to comment on how knowledge-based teamwork is different from or complements their appreciation of teamwork and discuss the rationale informing the organizational account;
- Ask them to undertake a teamwork-related task. For example, having provided them with a transcript of a segment of a team meeting, ask them to identify how knowledge work was carried out or how the team discussion might have been more knowledge-focused;
- Review common team tasks (such as presenting a client, running family meetings, and taking minutes) and ascertain levels of experience and areas where additional training would be necessary, and discuss more fully the information relating to the organizational provision of training in teamwork; and
- Discuss how members' team performance would be assessed as part of their performance reviews.

Constructing Orientation Programs   A knowledge-focused organization that wanted to create "knowledge crews" (Nonaka and Takeuchi 1995: 229), would run formal orientation programs about such work for new employees. In addition to meeting individually with other team members to discuss their work and possible points of disciplinary intersection and overlap, the section of the orientation program addressing teamwork would expand (in writing and verbally) on the principles informing knowledge-based work. Such material could:

- Comment on the role of knowledge-based teamwork in increasing organizational effectiveness.
- Address issues of disciplinary power and power/knowledge claims. The organization could therefore comment on

The exclusory nature of all discipline-structured knowledge

The claims to power/knowledge within disciplines

The partial nature of disciplinary knowledge (hence the importance of understanding the team as a site of partial knowledges, the productive intersection of which create a fuller account of the issues confronting the team and provide the foci for its ongoing work)

The significance, in relation to the knowledge the team presents itself with, of members' accessing clients' and families understanding and knowledge, so defining them as team members, albeit members who are often physically absent from the team meetings. This would include noting that clients' and families' accounts are also representations and are imbued in power relations. Hence, the construct "client/family" cannot be read as homogeneous, and the possibility of different accounts of needs is a potential further point of difference for teams to attend to.

Indicate questions a team may ask in order to make explicit the different representations of clients/families circulating in the team

- Foreground the importance of working diffractedly with discipline-specific differences *and* difference effects, including (re)emphasizing how knowledge is affected by the location(s) in which it is constructed.

- Map the constituent elements of knowledge-based team discussions, noting the fluid, recursive, narrative, and more focused dimensions, all of which are necessary to build knowledge spirals.

- Identify common points of confusion, such as the distinction between "task" and "goal" and differences between goals of individual members and team goals.

- Outline the role of the leader and how team members are expected, in line with developing experience and practice, to assist in questioning the process of the discussion. This section might include questions traditionally asked in teams about team process, contrasting these with questions deriving from a knowledge-based paradigm.

- Emphasize organizational and team focus on *professional* critique and the expectation that members will be able to accept legitimate commentary about their professional work.

- Identify the frequency and process of teams' review of their work and other training provided by the organization in the context of its intention to build up its knowledge-based teamwork and to attract and retain skilled knowledge workers. The organizational commitment to reviews and training and resourcing in terms of members' time and through the provision of material required by the team to undertake its reviews would be indicative of its promotion of knowledge-based work.

- Outline key team procedures and their associated processes.

- Provide the group with some extracts of transcripts of team reviews and work with them to identify dimensions of knowledge-based work.

To summarize: The objective of the written material accompanying a job description and the orientation program would be to make organizational expectations about the structure of teams and their modes of interaction explicit. The orientation process would encourage discussion of the constituting features of teamwork and could include some role play focused on specific issues to assist new employees in beginning to make the necessary conceptual/practice shifts in their understanding of teamwork. It could be argued that recognizing the value and encouraging the development of work within this (postmodern) positioning of knowledge constitutes a significant indication of organizations' understanding of current changing intellectual spaces, the practice implications of such spaces, and its ability to engage with them.

Performing Knowledgeably   The team, as Nonaka and Takeuchi (1995) have remarked, is the site of "high-density interaction." It is within the interprofessional team that the mutually interactive processes of learning and performance of knowledge-based teamwork are played out. The organizational transition from an emphasis on function (reviewing clients) to an emphasis on effective knowledge-based work highlights teamwork as a conceptual activity, constituted and structured by discourse, its representational activities generating material outcomes.

The models of multi-, inter-, and transdisciplinary teamwork conventionally used to describe the features of teams engaged in increasingly complex knowledge intersections are, as I have suggested in chapter 2, somewhat unsatisfactory, in part because the transdisciplinary model (seen as the apotheosis of teamwork) posits the achievement by members of a shared language (for example, Antoniadis and Videlock 1991; W. Miller 1994). The "team" produced by such a representation is too smooth, too unconcerned with difference, for my liking, thereby collapsing key dimensions of the map of knowledge-based teamwork. In particular, it does not attend to the range of different representations of clients existing within the team as a result of differently located discipline-specific and lay knowledges. Nor does this representation comment on the importance of the team's attending to the implications of those differences.

Describing teamwork as intimately focused on difference emphasizes two aspects of team performance. One aspect is the production of information about clients. The other is how the team begins the shift from the production of information to the production of knowledge about the client. A key element is the team's commentary on and self-critique of its activity; in other words, the questions the team poses for and the statements it makes to itself as discussions proceed through their interactive spiraling in evolving reviews.

An effective, knowledge-based team discussion, then, would be punctuated by simple questions, such as those noted earlier. It would ask about what else the team needed to know; it would take stock of the direction in which the team was moving; it would note what disciplinary and client/family issues it was overlooking or eliding, and it might well, especially in complex discussions, actually map or track the answers it proposes on a board in order to visually highlight the (contradictory) positioning of different members of the team, drawing on differently located knowledge, about a family or client. It may write down key words of members' individual therapeutic goals in order to allow the team to conceptualize the immediate team goal. Equally, writing down intermediate goals against the longer-term goal could help alert the team to points of congruence and divergence.

Critiquing Performance/Reviewing the Team Production   Much of this text has emphasized the significance of how teams approach and work with their collective information and knowledge (information being the material enabling the creation of knowledge and knowledge that which enables the development of the new position, the achievement of a dynamic truth [Nonaka and Takeuchi 1995]). The model of teamwork I am advancing here places a considerable emphasis on ongoing training, with that training highly focused on how the team produces its work. This represents a significant shift in conventional training from paying attention to mem-

bers' psychological construction and degrees of trust and hostility, to paying attention instead to the structure of discussions, to dominant discursive representations and the questions the team asks itself about its work.
Knowledge-based team training therefore attends to teams' conceptual and
discursive practices.

Training can be thought of as operating across two planes. One plane
involves teams' attending to areas of work that have not gone smoothly in
the course of discussions of or with clients, such as a family meeting resulting in the polarization of that client, family, and team members, or the
problematics of dominant representations of clients circulating within the
team. Such discussions would be likely to occur during weekly meetings.

However, more intensive reviews of teams' general approach to their
work, focused on analyses offered by team members of selected sections of
a transcript of a meeting in order to develop critical and more diffracted
work and to avoid complacency, would also be likely to be necessary.
Teamwork relies largely on verbal interchange. Regardless of degrees of
experience, it is difficult without written evidence of their proceedings for
team members to identify easily where questions could have been asked
but were not, what problematic representations of clients were arrived at,
by what processes the team persistently overlooked clients/families' issues
and knowledge, what knowledge intersections were made and what ones
were missed, where disciplinary power struggles occurred, and so forth (all
issues determining how the team shaped its discussion and relating to the
representations of clients/families produced in discussions).

Further, the evidence in the selected transcripts, while nonetheless raising issues of weighting and interpretation, could also provide support for
individual members' critique of their team's work. Using transcripts would
shift any discussion onto an analysis of how such exchanges could have
been done differently, rather than falling into discussions of the accuracy
of recollections of what was said. The transcript material, then, would provide an excellent means for the team to review whether, collectively, the
team asked questions, what sorts of questions were asked, what were productive questions, and what questions were not being asked and what sorts
of responses questioning elicited. Reviews could also attend to developing
team procedures, including assessing whether these had become or were
becoming overprescriptive.

A review process of this kind becomes simultaneously a review of past
effectiveness *and* the training for structuring future work. While there
would be some preparation time in the choice and evaluation of the textual

segments to be discussed (the responsibility for this circulating among team members), the actual process of the review/training would not require an extensive amount of time. As with the team discussions, training sessions would be structured around how the team works in relation to a modifable map, with the expectation that members would have done some preparation ahead of time.

Bodies of Knowledge

The act of defining the client and family as members of the team falls, in broad terms, within current (modernist) discourses of empowerment. Its objective is to acknowledge significant information and knowledge existing beyond or outside of the team held by persons who are intimately affected by the outcomes of team discussions, and to ensure that that knowledge is not marginalized or suppressed. This process of rewriting the client and family as empowered shifts from the production of passive, uninformed bodies, in contrast to the expert professional bodies of the team, to the production of knowledgeable bodies, a term conjuring up assumptions of rationality, coherence, the absence of contradiction. It defines powerful bodies able to assert themselves and to articulate need or desire. Their differently located knowledge sits alongside that of the professional, thanks to the open and accessible processes of the team. But herein lies the rub. To "empower" someone immediately reinserts them in relations of dependency and subordination, the very positions that modernist discourses of empowerment were intended to undo. The liberatory moment turns illusory and, within teamwork, the whole issue is further complicated because these significant team members are necessarily absent for many team discussions, typically having to rely on professional others to insert their knowledge into team reviews.

Moreover, there is a danger of too closely linking knowledge articulation with qualities of coherency and rationality. Some clients and indeed some family members (for example, elderly frail people), although knowing, may not be able to articulate a position easily because of health reasons. Others, in an unfamiliar cultural context, may find such well-intended inclusive processes difficult to manage, or, as did P2, produce contradictory information about their situations, or regard the team as the "other," to be held responsible for what has happened to themselves or to their family member. Others again may not wish to be so closely involved and believe that responsibility for decision-making lies elsewhere. Teams may not find all families easy to work with and vice versa. In other words, "empowerment" or whatever more satisfactory word may come to replace it, is a difficult concept at the best of times. There is no simple way through.

Knowledge-based teamwork, in contrast, involves the writing of multiple clients' and families' bodies. Each team, in each local situation, will have to manage the inevitable tensions and contradictions associated with the allocation of a team role to clients and families and the realities of their different positioning, including the possibility of clients and families defining the team as oppositional. Teams would also have to expect to respond to clients' and families' different degrees of ability (because of health and cultural factors and their positioning of the team) to articulate their knowledge. If I take the micropractices of teams (how they attempt to include clients/families, the representations they develop of them, their engagement with the contradictions experienced by individuals about their situation, rather than their eliding/suppression of those contradictions) as a critical site of discursive production, then part of the effectiveness of teams' work relates to how they attend to such micropractices and the types of clients'/families' bodies discursively produced through them.

If the previous writing on teamwork is the outcome of its particular location within humanistic discourses of individual growth and development, so this text too cannot avoid participating in (different) inscriptive practices in its discursive production of professional bodies. The discursive body produced within the concept of knowledge-based teamwork as it has been elaborated in this text is an articulate, flexible, questioning, and conceptually quick body. It is attentive to differences in power as a consequence of location in a discipline and position within the team and the implications of such differential locations for the work of the team; alert to connections and possibilities; able to respond positively to difference and address the effects of difference, and work with the "and . . . and . . . and" (Deleuze and Guattari 1983:57) of contradictions rather than attempting to restructure such contradictions into a binary framework of "either/or." As with the bodies of clients, however, this body is not a smooth, uniform body. Here, too, it is necessary to write not of one professional body but of multiple bodies marked by different degrees of training and experience in knowledge-based teamwork.

It is important to emphasize that I am *not* writing of "ideal" bodies. Bodies with attributes such as those referred to above do not emerge from the ether. These professional bodies are discursive bodies, produced by specific discursive institutional practices within training institutions for health professionals and health care organizations. A total absence of training in teamwork, or a training deriving from psycho-dynamic, systems, consensus, or constructivist principles (Sands 1993) means that organizations are unlikely or unable to produce models or codifications of professional practice grounded in knowledge-based teamwork as it has been described here.

Conclusion: Teams and Organizations

A key area of concern for organizations is the effectiveness and the cost-effectiveness of specific work practices. Interprofessional teamwork has long been ambiguously sited in respect of both factors in health care organizations and other types of organizations. One consequence of locating this study within the concept of effectiveness and developing an analysis, informed by Foucaultian theories of discourse, of the problems associated with current dominant models of teamwork is to foreground the role of the organization in, and its responsibility for, maintaining or unraveling these ambiguities. The paradigmatic shift in conceptualizing teamwork presented in this text foregrounds effective teamwork as working with distinct kinds of professional and lay knowledge to enhance teams' accountability not only to specific organizations but also to clients and families. The organizational discourses circulating about teamwork and the micro-practices giving expression to those discourses are critical to the effectiveness of teamwork; staff in organizations whose discursive practices marginalize the production of knowledge-based teamwork cannot achieve these optimum levels of effectiveness. An overriding emphasis in organizations on professional accountability tends to occlude or suppress the necessary correlative, that is, organizational accountability to staff and the crucial role of the organization in the production of effective teamwork.

Appendix

Transcription Conventions

The following signs have been used in the transcripts of the audio-taped data quoted in the text:

word/ word	slash followed by space indicates very brief pause
. . .	period indicates pause; each period equals approximately one second
[.]	square brackets indicate inaudible section; each period indicates approximately one second
[word]	words inside square brackets represent guess as to what was said
words—	dashes at end of one speaker's statement and beginning of next speaker's statement (—words) indicate that one speaker interrupts another
{word}	words inside curly brackets indicate words added for clarification
word	italics indicate speaker's emphasis
word	boldface italics indicate speaker's very considerable emphasis
(. . .)	periods within parentheses indicate text omitted from manuscript

2. Shifting Boundaries

1. The choice of terminology to describe those people receiving assistance from human service organizations has become increasingly politicized by New Right discourses. Although the more common practice within economies structured around such discourses is to refer to "consumers," I have not used this term. *Consumer* implies an ability to choose (a key element in New Right ideology), hence referencing issues of knowledge, the ability to discriminate, the availability of a range of service providers, and the financial means to pay for the desired service. The teams involved in this research study were all located within publicly funded health services—the mode of service provision still most readily available to the majority of New Zealanders for whom, despite much rhetoric about choice in health care, privately funded schemes are not a viable option. Moreover, the word *consumer* suppresses differential power relationships between service users and the providers of services, relationships that require analysis, not occlusion.

2. This is not necessarily an easy task. In his discussion of Western representational practices and discourses defining the discipline of Orientalism, Edward Said (1978) wrote of the difficulties of inserting different representational practices into the field. He argued that Western scholarship, with its emphasis on citation of previous research as substantiating the authority of the current text, operates in two ways. It disguises its own modes of representation, and it results in the suppression of new knowledge in the field in favor of the older and more familiar paradigms. This means that the potentially destabilizing effect of new knowledge is subverted by a process in which the established view continues to retain its dominance. He described this process in terms of a metaphor of disruption, where "each individual contribution first causes changes within the field and then promotes a new stability, in a way that on a surface covered with twenty compasses the introduction of a twenty-first will cause all the others to quiver, then settle into an accommodating configuration" (Said 1978:273).

3. In commenting on the powerful and (unmentionable) aspects of the North American academe, Paul Rabinow wrote:

> One is led to consider the politics of interpretation in the academy today. Asking whether longer, dispersive, multi-authored texts would yield tenure might seem petty. But those are the dimensions of power relations to which Nietzsche exhorted us to be scrupulously attentive. There can be no doubt of the existence and influence of this type of power relation in the production of texts. We owe these less glamorous, if more immediately constraining, conditions, much more attention. The taboo against specifying them is much greater than the strictures of denouncing colonialism; an anthropology of anthropology would include them. Just as there was formerly a discursive knot preventing discussion of exactly those fieldwork practices that defined the authority of the anthropologist, which has now been untied, so, too, the micropractices of the academy might well do with some scrutiny.   *(Rabinow 1996:50)*

4. Webb and Hobdell (1980) have queried how the degree of team coordination and its resultant effectiveness are to be evaluated, raising questions about how much is better coordination worth; how it is to be recognized; and whether good coordination is a measure of effectiveness, resulting in improved quality of service; and if so, how is its impact assessed in relation to the client? Do attempts to achieve better coordination result in "an irrelevant and diversionary pursuit" (98) of interprofessional relations?

5. Uhl-Bien and Graen (1992:229) comment:

> Given that the . . . area which the individual represents is considered to be important for the effectiveness of the team (or else that area would not have been represented), the failure of a team member to contribute to the team means the lack of potentially vital information—information which may not be provided from any other source. . . .
>
> Individual team members become responsible for their own area of expertise and their collaboration with other team members to integrate their discipline area into the problem-solving processes of the . . . team. Moreover, since information is coming from a variety of sources, integration of the information provided by each discipline representative on the team into a cohesive final product requires team members to work together using teamwork processes. These teamwork processes are based on the potential of the team members to act as team players— to be committed to the goals of the team—and engage in those activities which will be most beneficial for a successful team outcome.

This does, though, rather beg the question of what are the beneficial team activities necessary to ensuring successful team outcomes.

6. This critique also applies to an extensive amount of the management literature, which abounds in texts offering exhortatory and highly generalized accounts of ways in

which teams changed for the better. See, for example, Larson and LaFasto (1989) and Rayner (1996) as recent texts that are typical of this genre.

7. Schwartzman (1986) is in fact critical of the general casting of research questions around the effectiveness issue. She suggests that researchers have too facilely adopted organizational assumptions about the purposes of meetings, and she proposes differently focused questions, the objective of which is to disturb simplistic researcher and organizational assumptions. These questions include:

- How do specific work groups define *work, effectiveness,* and *improvement?*
- Are individuals responsible for group activities?
- How do social forms such as meetings control and affect what happens in organizations?
- Do meetings exist because they facilitate making decisions or solving problems; or do decisions and problems exist because they generate meetings?
- Should interventions be directed to the content or form of group activity?
- How might "effective" activities actually be valuable for individuals, groups, or the entire organizational system?
- Is a focus on effectiveness the way to set the research problem? (Schwartzman 1986:266–267)

The problem with some of her questions, however, is that they posit an autonomous individual, unstructured by discourse, and they appear to bypass the fact that an organization creates teams for its purposes, although how that organization may resource teams is another question.

8. Gibbons et al. (1994:28) remark that the danger with transdisciplinarity is that it appears very attractive but much of what is regarded as transdisciplinary work "in reality amounts to a mere accumulation of knowledge supplied from one discipline." Further, "in the production of transdisciplinary knowledge, the intellectual agenda is not set within a particular discipline, nor is it fixed by merely juxtaposing professional interests of particular specialists in some loose fashion leaving to others the task of integration at a later stage. Integration is interdisciplinary; it cuts across disciplines—but is envisaged and provided from the outset in the context of usage. . . . Working in an application context creates pressures to draw upon a diverse array of knowledge resources and to configure them to the problem at hand."

9. Clark (1994) has discussed this issue at some length.

3. The Teams and Their Organizational Settings

1. The Mason Report (1996) was commissioned by the government to evaluate the effectiveness of mental health services in New Zealand. The report was highly critical of the structure and quality of service provision at that time. It linked improvements in services to better resourcing, more-integrated service provision, and the development of a more skilled workforce.

2. Here, as elsewhere in this text, I want to problematize the notion of "experience" and to disrupt any too rapid correlation between "experience" and ongoing refinement and development of practice. This does not necessarily happen. A worker who has been working in a particular domain for a number of years may have developed routine and/or unprofessional, rather than reflexive, practices.

3. While the majority of the team saw advocacy work as a critical part of their role, that perception was not shared by all. Some, such as a nurse, thought that advocacy work used energy that should be concentrated on addressing clients' immediate health needs.

4. The Core Health Services Committee was established in 1993 with the responsibility to define, following extensive public debate and consultations, the core health services to which all New Zealanders would be entitled. In the interim, services that had been available through the public health system would continue to be provided. At the end of two years, the committee described its task as impossible, redesigned its role, and changed its name to the National Health Committee. What appears to be happening is that the process of defining core services has continued in a significantly less open manner through contractual agreements.

5. One of the outcomes of the restructuring was that for a number of years hospitals were known as CHEs (Crown Health Enterprises). In 1997, however, they officially became "hospitals" again. Although at the time of the fieldwork, the sites where I carried out the research were still known as CHEs, I have used the more familiar (and current) term in this text.

6. The contracting process itself has appeared problematic. I am not aware of any research on the experience of different hospitals in conducting negotiations with their funding authority. However, research by the New Zealand Council of Christian Social Services (1996) into the contracting processes between the (now defunct) four regionally based funding authorities and rest homes and private hospitals indicated that negotiations with the funding authority to which the services involved in this research were responsible reported a lower level of satisfaction with the negotiating process, a higher level of difficulties, intractability, and refusal to negotiate contracts upward than did those contracting with other funders. The impression has been of a win/lose mentality on the part of this funder. (See Nishiguchi and Anderson [1995] for a discussion of different modes of contractual relationships between purchasers and service providers.)

7. Nocon and Qureshi (1996:37) have highlighted a number of problems with consumer satisfaction surveys:

Broad issues
- General questions may fail to distinguish between views about specific aspects of services
- Questions may not reflect issues of importance to users

Responses
- Respondents may be unwilling to criticize "free" services
- Respondents may fear that complaints will result in withdrawal of services

- Judgements about services may be influenced by views about individual staff
- Retrospective questions may fail to uncover details of past experiences
- Respondents may give answers to please the questioner

Relationship between expectations and satisfaction
- People may not have clear expectations
- Expectations will vary between individuals: basing provision on expectation leads to inequity;
- People make distinctions between an acceptable level of service and a subjective sense of what they deserve
- People distinguish between a preferred, ideal service and a lower expectation of what may be reasonably expected in reality
- Dissatisfaction may only [be] expressed if there is a gross discrepancy between expected standards and actual experience
- People's views vary in concreteness and specificity
- Expectations change as a result of receiving a service
- Satisfaction is not correlated with beneficial outcomes

Further, surveys are often based on providers', not clients', agendas, and surveys are often ritually carried out to justify existing service provision and to enable providers to claim that there is a consultative process.

8. *Pakeha* is now not an easily translatable word. The words *New Zealand European,* often used in the past as a definition of *pakeha,* are now under challenge, as the following quotes demonstrate. In an article on culture and landscape, Upton defines himself as a New Zealand European.

> I am happy to label myself as an English-speaking European, resident in the southwest Pacific. Not being surrounded by 300 million cuzzie-bros who wouldn't recognise a deserted beach or a barbeque if they stumbled upon one, I don't understand every nuance of European living. . . . But their culture is my culture. I am not Polynesian. And I am certainly not Asian. I am European.
> It doesn't, of course, mean a culture that resides exclusively in Europe. . . . its myths, symbols and intellectual crosscurrents are rooted in the experience of the peoples of Europe over, say, 2500 years. It is not a question of being able to talk knowledgeably about the nave of the Amiens Cathedral. . . . It is the unconscious embrace of ways of thinking, speaking, visualising and making music. And if, as a European New Zealander, you want to understand why you think as you do, your search will lead you back to European roots.

There is a considerable difference, though, between his account and Marilyn Waring's on being Pakeha, which Upton also cites. Her account points to a more pronounced sense of spatiality, a differently oriented gaze, an awareness of geographical specificities, and it refers to the linguistic intersections between Māori and English that constitute significantly changing speech patterns in Aotearoa/New Zealand. Waring, then, recalling a conversation, wrote of being Pakeha in this way:

> Beginning with my inability to describe my identity and where I come from without speaking te reo, the language of the indigenous to [sic] the tangata whenau of Aotearoa/New Zealand. I spoke of topographies and colours, of long and wide uncluttered spaces, of a texture of feathers and fauna not found anywhere else, of the remnant of dinosaurs called tuatara, of kakapo and kiwi, kauri and puriri. I again resorted to that non-European language. . . . And when I was moved to speak of the music and fashions of my generation's culture, I resorted to the lyrics of the two other local Waikato lads, Neil and Tim Finn, who began a song on an album released at the height of Split Enz fame in Europe, "I was born in Te Awamutu."   (Upton 1996:15)

See King (1991) for other accounts of "being Pakeha."

9. For example, see Ministry of Health 1997a and 1997b; Ministry of Health 1998; Mental Health Commission 1998; Mason Report 1996; National Health Committee 1998.

10. The effectiveness of governments' responses to continuing Māori marginalization within New Zealand society is under challenge from some Māori who consider that Māori autonomy and proper status as *tangata whenua,* or first comers, will be achieved only through major constitutional change leading to the creation of a separate Māori parliament with control over a proportional share of tax-generated finances (*Dominion* 2/2/99:6).

11. See Mitchell and Mitchell (1988) for a discussion in relation to the education system of the effects of token employment of Māori on Māori teachers.

12. Māori constitute 15 percent of the New Zealand population, and they have a much higher percentage of younger people than do Pakeha.

13. At two sites, the nurses did have some team training days of their own. To achieve this, however, they had to rely on their team colleagues to take over some of their tasks for the day.

4. Researching the Interprofessional

1. See Jacobs (1996) for a brief discussion of the problematics in postmodern theory of metaphors of travel.

2. I used the software package *HyperResearch* to undertake the first part of the analysis of the texts of team members. This involved a cut-and-paste process typically associated with the process of sorting text into first-order concepts. I have not, however, found software packages for qualitative analysis useful beyond this basic sorting function, in part, I think, because the sorts of conceptual and analytic work that they encourage is not the sort of work I am interested in doing, and, as with others, I feel somewhat critical about the way software packages have been persistently represented as necessary to the production of quality analysis and theory building (Coffey, Holbrook, and Atkinson 1996; Kelle 1997).

3. Fabian (1993:89) has written that "oralization, that is, recourse to audible speech, actual or imagined, is an essential part of our ability to read texts. Yet our 'ideology' of literacy seems to put a taboo on revealing what we actually do when we read, for fear that oralization might subvert the authority of the written text."

4. In the course of their interviews I asked some team members to tell me what happened in team meetings. The question was greeted with some amazement. Had I not seen for myself? And their responses indicated (as Garfinkel [1967] has demonstrated) just how difficult it is to describe a taken-for-granted, everyday activity, let alone produce a more conceptual account of that activity.

5. An effect of thinking about the meaning of *contribution* was that, although the project's focus was on the work of the team, not on the role of a particular discipline within the team, I realized at the end of the first round of fieldwork that, as a former social worker, I was expecting social workers to adopt a reasonably high profile in team meetings. Despite my critique of representations of social work literature positioning social workers as powerful, knowledgeable team saviors/leaders, my particular anxieties about the extent and quality of social workers' input demonstrated how much I was still located within this discourse.

6. I did not meet with the whole group after the first year of the project because of one member's relocation and another's absence from the country and changing work demands. Over the next two years I met twice (and helpfully) with two members individually.

7. For example, many of the community reviews conducted by the psychiatric team fell into the "brief" category, involving minimal informational exchange. It is not impossible to define a purpose for such an exchange, but in the context of very vulnerable clients and busy staff, the overall value of such meetings would seem questionable. A typical example of these meetings went as follows:

SP Okay. On to the community. P4. who's doing P4? SW and SSW? Okay, P5.

SW Um, he's/ doing *OK* um . . going straight back into that community employment agency hopefully next week. He's getting a bit desperate with the work/ situation.

SP Mm

SW But/ mentally he's presently stable.

SP OK, who's his doctor now?

SW That's um . . . (*very softly*) ooh . . . he's going to have/ oh is it/ no. It's not you.

PR2 Who is it?

SW PR2/ looking at the list.

PR2 No, it's not me.

SP What we did/ I I think what we're thinking of doing is given P5 was um looked after by CP3 in the *past* . CP3 will take him back on but that's just to be decided by the doctors so there's these *few weeks*.

SW I think PR(1) is covering.

SP *Covering*. OK, he, yeah.

SW PR(2) and I said/ well PR(2) said goodbye to him last week and I can't recall what we decided.

SP OK move on to P6.

SW He's doing okay. I'm going to see him next week.

SP Where's he living?

SW . . . Oh that's *old* {referring to a list of addresses}. He/ he's now in/ he's still in [.] flats

SP He is?

SW He's just moved flats/ into his own flat. That's really old information . . in a/ in a single flat his own/ his own flat . . at his own request (*very softly*) at his request.

SP Is George still running that?

SW No he had [. .]

SP Is he still doing the painting?

SW Yep.

CP(3) P7 he's doing/ *good.* He's got a special patient review on the 2nd of/ July . . . . . P8, SP he *is* . .the same P8 isn't it?

SP2 The same.

SP . . . . P13.

CO2 He is fine. CP(1) was going to drop down a prescription for him last week so/ he phoned and she *didn't* get round to it so I'll find somebody.

SP Mmm. P10. He's not here. CP(1)'s *left.* . . .

5. Mapping Effectiveness: Achieving a "More Subtle Vision"

1. For example, members of one team held different views on whether the meeting's primary objective was to discuss clients or to support nursing staff, the second objective interestingly positioning the nurses as subordinate in relation to their colleagues with whom they were organizationally defined as equal.

2. These discursive differences within the teams were of course circulating within the public domain. Members of one team defined their role with a person who had a head injury as doing what they could, given the considerable uncertainty about his future prognosis, to improve his quality of life. Achieving this was dependent in part on finding a less-secure but supervised environment where he could live. As it happened, the proposed placement would have been less expensive. Obtaining funding to resource this shift was unlikely to succeed, as the funding agency's criteria for funding placements were focused solely on the client's full rehabilitation prospects, and the team could not provide evidence of the certainty of this outcome. (Sections of the transcripts of the team reviews of this patient are presented in chapter 7).

3. It would appear that the medical argument about the appropriate shape for a team discussion is not peculiar to that discipline. Abramson (1989), writing in the social work literature, in a discussion of team leaders' role, refers to their responsibility for maintaining the team process and focus. *Focus* implies a narrowing-down, an exclusion of the irrelevant. It defines the appropriate shape for interprofessional discussions as more, rather than less, linear and implies easy discernment of and agreement about relevance. In an organizational context where members feel under pressure to complete meetings as quickly as possible and where the development of a case plan is defined largely as a series of actions to be carried

out by individual team members, then "being focused" may well exclude that more speculative dimension of team discussions, a dimension that I argue enables teams to engage with
the different discourses circulating within the team and with complex issues embedded in
developing care plans for some clients.

4. The function of "beyond," and therefore outside of, the team is to maintain a focus
on what knowledge gets excluded by the team because no member of that discipline is there
to actively represent it and ensure its inclusion in the team's deliberations (McClelland and
Sands 1993); equally, knowledge existing beyond the team includes knowledge held by
clients and their families, knowledge that may well be very differently located and structured from that held by professionals.

5. There were few questions in this team about the work that each member was undertaking with his or her clients. As the following exchanges illustrate, team members did not
appear to respond in any substantive detail to efforts to elicit a fuller account of their work,
outline what their work had achieved, or discuss the direction the team's work should be
taking:

UM .. I can't help thinking that um/ we've missed the boat well and truly with P10.

OT (*very softly*) mm hmm

PR .... In what way?

UM Well in that you know/ when is his six months up, must be *soon*

PR Well you know it's not/not as soon as I *thought* actually. According to the notes in the
section papers it's not till November

SP Mm mm

UM anyway

(*members mutter*)

SW Been here since April I think.

PR I/ I/ I thought that we had less time but I've looked in his section papers and they've got
his . his first year is running is running out at the end of *November*/it wasn't [.] till
May

UM .. but still don't have enough time to address the issues with him.

PR Just to um/ to feed *my* feedback from A & D is the same/ we are looking for any kind of
input really um *and* some suggestions for . possible . kinds of residential placement in
the first instance um, we're talking to R and I've discussed it with him [. .] him even
in the way of programs or any of the/ residential things because they're stuck . as to
accommodation.

UM The only thing that we've managed to achieve is the . probation and directing him to
live elsewhere besides his *mother* (mm) that's the only thing that we've actually
achieved in the time that he's been here/ which is a real concern. . . . . . .

PR2 Are we supposed to be having a meeting, probation soon [. .] this year?

UM Have you *started* work with him/ Pysch Intern?

PSYCH INTERN Um I, I met him yesterday I was certainly on the *phone*. We are going to
schedule regular sessions on the Thursday.

CNS Do you spend any time with him, SP?

SP Aah/ not a lot but um . . well it's reasonably regular but not long - 5 - 10 minutes.

CNS Mm, what do you talk about with him?

SP Oh (*very softly*) how's it going. That kind of/ level .

CNS Is anybody attempting to sort of/ look at the issues around why he came here or?

SW SP2's doing that.

SP1 SP2's doing that.

CNS She is?

SP1 Yeah/ yeah.

SW (*very softly*) She's doing that every week.

CP How long?

SP1 Two years.

SW Two years.

CNS1 Two years.

N It's almost impossible at the moment.

CNS1 Yeah I read *one report* about it and I just wondered what sort of ongoing issues she's continuing to work on.

SW Yeah (*overlapping*) she's doing [it].

CNS1 (*overlapping*) Oh I see.

N So it's very difficult/ and it's very difficult to put in place any kind/ of *behavioral* stuff around/ because of [his head] really.

CNS1 So it's a *non* issue then?

N Well no it's an issue. (*loud laughter*)

N A *huge* issue. (*speakers talk over each other*)

CNS1 It's an issue, a non issue.

N But it's very difficult to (*very softly*) get him (*louder*) . but SP2 is/ that's SP2's role.

The discussion about this patient ended at this point.

6. "We Talk About the Patients and Then We Have Coffee": Making and Shaping Team Discussions

1. In the research teams, all team members talked about being overworked and commented on their readiness for another relevant discipline to take on some of the work. The workers' protection of their discipline's boundaries, therefore, did not appear to be a markedly significant issue for these teams, although there was the occasional instance where this happened.

2. McKenzie (1994) has also focused on the knowledge dimension in teamwork, suggesting that effective teamwork requires pooling knowledge in order to generate a fuller picture. However, his identification of the relevant processes as "harmonizing" (reconciling differences), "gate keeping" (ensuring that shyer people get into the conversation), and "encouraging" (going along with ideas to see where they lead) tends to locate teamwork more in the management of the interpersonal domain and does not attend to issues of differential disciplinary power or of discourse. Nor does it offer a sufficiently detailed map against which the effectiveness of team discussions can be evaluated.

7. Teams as Author

1. However, this dichotomy between life-worlds and medical worlds is contested by Atkinson (1995).

2. The permeability of the line between "fact" and "fiction" is nicely emphasized in Korobkin's (1996) discussion of the way in which popular TV court dramas, movies, and novels have come to shape the conduct of "real" courtroom battles.

3. Deleuze and Guattari's theory of rhizomes and its relationship to knowledge-based teamwork is discussed in chapter 6.

4. His narrative about the meeting concludes on administrative and interorganization issues, an emphasis picked up by the next speaker. In any group setting, what is spoken last is more likely to be taken up, making it correspondingly more difficult for others to reflect back on earlier commentaries. Moreover, the issues about the transfer are of immediate concern to the team because if things work out, then the problem will no longer be theirs, i.e., there is a certain pragmatism about their approach. Other attempts to raise issues relating to the team's interaction with the guardians are met with a focus shift or a termination of the discussion, and although CP3 in the fifth review picks up the counselor's phrase about the guardians' significance as advocates, he does so in a somewhat belittling manner.

8. "Nobody's Asked Me for My View"

1. They write in critiquing the proliferation of different modes of "consumer" surveys:

> Representation had to be demonstrably extensive and wide ranging. Surveys were conducted on issues such as rationing, and public preferences for healthcare provision. These "public health" surveys did not stop at merely seeking the voice of the local population. They also established an individual reflexivity so that, in the process of being questioned, members of the public were taught to question themselves about their own (un)healthy lifestyles. Users could be losers too, as the focus shifted from a concern with meeting needs to a concern over managing risk. Those versions of the user's voice which are re-presented as needs appear only when professional strategies can be constructed to meet them. Re-presented as risk, they change the emphasis to one of caveat emptor, shifting the responsibility for health from the corporate representation of the people's needs to the individual's responsibility to preserve his or her own health. . . . Both the questions and answers to each survey, focus group and consultation exercise, remain the textual property of the professional groupings the state has entrusted to deal with the governance of health.

> This consumerist discourse has become insistent and pervasive. . . . No apparent mental or physical barrier is to be acknowledged in the pursuit of the authentic voice of the user. The moral authority vested in user representation cannot be directly challenged although it can be modified and often is. Once more we discover the interpretation of experts lying at the heart of the process. Whilst the patients may seem free to set the agenda, the manner in which that agenda becomes incorporated into the structures of power and provision remains firmly in the hands of the authorities. *(Gilleard and Higgs 1998:240–241)*

2. McLean (1995:1057) noted that Julian Rapapport underscored the ecological focus of empowerment, writing of empowerment as "a *proactive* meaningful engagement in one's world" where empowerment cannot be given but must be taken. While this focus on taking reinforces agency on the part of the disempowered, it excludes what I understand to be critical to the concept: the shift in power and changed position (however slight) within the social. Rather than writing within binary frameworks (power as given or taken), it is more helpful to conceptualize a more dynamic structure, where power is both taken and given in the light of changing discourses.

3. The consultation processes employed by the RHA, which funded the services in which the research teams were located, were widely regarded as inadequate by community organizations.

4. Government, however, has developed advocacy services, produced a list of patients' rights and responsibilities in relation to health services, and created the office of the Health and Disability Commissioner, to whom patients or clients may take concerns over treatment.

5. Headings in the document, *When Parents and Medical Staff Talk Together,* distributed ahead of time to families, are "Bring Someone," "You Know Your Child Best," "Write Down Questions," "Get Your Questions Answered," "Slow Them Down," "Don't Make Quick Decisions," "Need Another Meeting?," and "Thank Everyone." The Pediatrics Department has also written material for staff about issues they need to think about in conducting family meetings. Headings in the *Staff Guidelines for Talking with Families* are: "First, Prepare Yourself and the Family," "Second, Create the Setting," "Third, Manage the Conference," "Fourth, Follow Up Significant Conferences" (McClain and Bury 1998:153).

6. In presenting this research to different audiences, there have always been those who have argued that properly empowering teamwork would involve all clients' being present at all team discussions in which they were reviewed. This seems to me to present an oversimplistic understanding of teamwork and power relations. Many of the clients who were the "subjects" of the teams in this research were not physically or mentally in a state to contribute to (weekly) discussions about their well-being; nor, indeed, would it have been reasonable (or possible) for families of those clients to attend meetings so frequently. Participants in the research who had in the past been members of teams where clients were often present in discussions debated the empowering nature of such practices, suggesting that in these teams, the "real" team discussions occurred in more informal settings where clients were not present.

9. Performing Knowledge Work

1. At the risk of being repetitious, it is necessary to read "individual" here as the discursively constructed knowledge creator and to retain a focus on "interaction" as the interaction of discursively constructed knowledge.

References

Abramson, Julie. 1983. A non-client-centered approach to program development in a medical setting. In H. Weissman, I. Epstein, and A. Savage, eds., *Agency Based Social Work: Neglected Aspects of Clinical Practice*, pp. 178–186. Philadelphia: Temple University Press.

____. 1989. Making teams work. *Social Work with Groups* 12 (4): 45–63.

____. 1992. Health-related problems. In W. J. Reid, ed., *Task Strategies: An Empirical Approach to Social Work* 99: 225–249.

____. 1993. Orienting social work employees in interdisciplinary settings: Shaping professional and organizational perspectives. *Social Work* 3 (2): 152–157.

Abramson, Julie, and Terry Mizrahi. 1986. Strategies for enhancing collaboration between social workers and physicians. *Social Work in Health Care* 12 (1): 1–21.

Abramson, Julie, and Beth Rosenthal. 1995. Collaboration: Interdisciplinary and interorganizational applications. In D. Edwards and J. Gary Hopps, eds., *The Encyclopedia of Social Work,* 19th ed., pp. 1497–1489. Washington, D.C.: NASW Press.

Ancona, Deborah. 1990. Outward bound strategies for team survival in an organization. *Academy of Management Journal* 33 (2): 334–365.

Antoniadis, Anastasia, and Joyce Videlock. 1991. In search of teamwork: A transactional approach to team functioning. *Transdisciplinary Journal* 1 (2): 157–167.

Atkinson, Paul. 1994. Rhetoric as skill in a medical setting. In Michael Bloor and Patricia Taraborelli, eds., *Qualitative Studies in Health Medicine,* pp. 110–130. Aldershot: Avebury.

____. 1995. *Medical Talk and Medical Work: The Liturgy of the Clinic.* London: Sage.

Bailey, Donald. 1984. A triaxila model of the interdisciplinary team and group process. *Exceptional Children* 51 (1): 17–22.

Barker, James. 1993. Tightening the iron cage: concertive control in self-managing teams. *Administrative Science Quarterly* 38:408–437.

Barthes, Roland. 1986. From work to text. In Richard Howard, ed., *The Rustle of Language,* pp. 56–64. New York: Hill and Wang.

Biggs, Simon. 1989. Professional helpers and resistances to work with older people. *Ageing and Society* 9:43–60.

Boston, Jonathon, John Martin, June Pallott, and Pat Walsh, eds. 1991. *Reshaping the State: New Zealand's Bureaucratic Revolution.* Auckland and Oxford: Oxford University Press.

Bourdieu, Pierre. 1991. *Language and Symbolic Power.* Edited by John Thompson. Cambridge, Eng.: Polity Press.

Bowman, Edward, and Bruce Kogut, eds. 1995. *Redesigning the Firm.* Oxford and New York: Oxford University Press.

Braidotti, Rosi. 1997. Mothers, monsters, and machines. In Katie Conboy, Nadia Medina, and Sarah Stanbury, eds., *Writing on the Body: Female Embodiment and Feminist Theory,* pp. 59–79. New York: Columbia University Press.

Brem, Caroline. 1997. *Are We on the Same Team Here? Essential Communication Skills to Make Groups Work.* St. Leonards, N.S.W.: Allen and Unwin.

Briggs, Thomas. 1980. Obstacles to implementing the team approach in social services agencies. In Susan Longsdale, Adrian Webb, and Thomas L. Briggs, eds., *Teamwork in the Personal Social Services and Health Care: British and American Perspectives,* pp. 75–90. London: Croom Helm.

Burchell, Graham, Colin Gordon, and Peter Miller, eds. 1991. *The Foucault Effect: Studies in Governmentality.* London: Harvester Wheatsheaf.

Calvino, Italo. 1988. *Six Memos for the Next Millennium.* Cambridge: Harvard University Press.

Castel, Robert. 1991. From dangerousness to risk. In Graham Burchell, Colin Gordon, and Peter Miller, eds., *The Foucault Effect: Studies in Governmentality,* pp. 281–298. London: Harvester Wheatsheaf.

Castells, Manuel. 1996. The Rise of the Network Society. Oxford: Blackwell.

Chapman, Alan. 1994. Empowerment. In Alan Chapman and Mary Marshall, eds., *Dementia: New Skills for Social Workers,* pp. 110–124. London: Jessica Kinsley Press.

Clark, Phillip G. 1994. Social, professional, and educational values on the interdisciplinary team: Implications for gerontological and geriatric education. *Educational Gerontology* 20:53–51.

Clegg, Stewart. 1990. *Modern Organizations: Organization Studies in the Postmodern World.* London: Sage.

Clifford, James. 1983. On ethnographic authority. *Representations* 1 (2): 118–146.

Clifford, James, and George Marcus, eds. 1986. *Writing Culture: The Poetics and Politics of Ethnography.* Berkeley: University of California Press.

Coffey, Amanda, Beverley Holbrook, and Paul Atkinson. 1996. Qualitative data analysis: Technologies and representations. Sociological Research Online 1,1 http://www.socresonline.org.uk/socresonline/1/1/4.html

Cooper, Robert, and Gibson Burrell. 1988. Modernism, postmodernism, and organisational analysis: An introduction. *Organization Studies* 1:91–112.

Curnow, Alan. 1974. Landfall in unknown seas. *Collected Poems 1993–1973,* pp. 136–139. Wellington: A. H. and A. W. Reed.

de Certeau, Michel. 1984. *The Practice of Everyday Life.* Berkeley: University of California Press.

de Silva, Padmal, Penny Dodds, Jean Rainey, and Jan Clayton. 1992. Management and the multidisciplinary team. In Dinash Bhugra and Alistairs Burns, eds., *Management Training for Psychiatrists,* pp. 83–102. London: Gaskell.

Deeprose, Donna. 1995. *The Team Coach: Vital New Skills for Supervisors and Managers in a Team Environment.* New York: American Management Association.

Deleuze, Gilles, and Felix Guattari. 1983. Rhizome. In Gilles Deleuze and Felix Guattari, *On the Line,* pp. 1–68. New York: Semiotext(e).

Diamond, Irene, and Lee Quinby, eds. 1988. *Feminism and Foucault: Reflections on Resistance.* Boston: Northeastern University Press.

Dominion. Hikoi delegate sees clash over spending. February 2, 1999, p. 6.

Durie, Mason. 1998. *Whaiora: Maori Health Development.* 2d ed. Auckland: Oxford University Press.

Eco, Umberto. 1985. *Reflections on "The Name of the Rose."* London: Secker and Warburg.

Ely, Robin. 1995. The role of dominant identity and experience in organizational work on diversity. In Susan Jackman and Marion N. Ruderman, eds., *Diversity in Work Teams: Research Paradigms for a Changing Workplace,* pp. 161–186. Washington, D.C.: American Psychological Association.

Emy, Hugh. 1998. States, markets, and the global dimension: An overview of certain issues in political economy. In Paul Smyth and Bettina Cass, eds., *Contesting the Australian Way: States, Markets, and Civil Society,* pp. 17–37. Cambridge: Cambridge University Press.

Fabian, Johannes. 1993. Keep listening: Ethnography and reading. In Jonathan Boyarin, ed., *The Ethnography of Reading,* pp. 80–97. Berkeley: University of California Press.

Fook, Janis, ed. 1996. *The Reflective Researcher: Social Workers' Experience with Theories of Practice Research.* St. Leonards, N.S.W.: Allen and Unwin.

Foucault, Michel. 1977. *Discipline and Punish: The Birth of the Prison.* Guildford and London: Billing and Sons.

_____. 1980. *Knowledge/Power: Selected Interviews and Other Writings, 1972–1977.* Edited by Colin Gordon. Bury St. Edmonds: St. Edmondsbury Press.

_____. 1981. The order of discourse. In Richard Young, ed., *Untying the Text: A Post-Structuralist Reader,* pp. 48–78. London: Routledge.

_____. 1988a. *Michel Foucault: Politics, Philosophy, Culture: Interviews and Other Writings, 1977–1984.* Edited by Lawrence D. Kritzman. London and New York: Routledge.

_____. 1988b. *Technologies of the Self: A Seminar with Michel Foucault.* Edited by Luther H. Martin, Huck Gutman, and Patrick H. Hutton. Amherst: University of Massachusetts Press.

Fox, Nicholas. 1994. Anaesthetists, the discourse on patient fitness, and the organisation of surgery. *Sociology of Health and Illness* 16 (1): 1–18.

Fraser, Nancy. 1989. *Unruly Practices: Power, Discourse, and Gender in Contemporary Social Theory.* Minneapolis: University of Minneapolis Press.

Galbraith, Jay, and Edward Lawler and Associates, eds. 1993. *Organizing for the Future: The New Logic for Managing Complex Organizations.* San Francisco: Jossey-Bass.

Garfinkel, Harold. 1967. *Studies in Ethnomethodology.* Upper Saddle River, N.J.: Prentice Hall.

Gibbons, Michael, Camille Limoges, Helga Nowotny, Simon Schwartzman, Peter Scott, and Martin Trow. 1994. *The New Production of Knowledge: The Dynamics of Science and Research in Contemporary Societies.* London: Sage.

Gilgun, Jane. 1988. Decision-making in interdisciplinary treatment teams. *Child Abuse and Neglect* 12:231–239.

Gilleard, Chris, and Paul Higgs. 1998. Older people as users and consumers of health-care: A third age rhetoric for a fourth age reality? *Ageing and Society* 18 (2): 233–248.

Good, Byron. 1994. *Medicine, Rationality, and Experience: An Anthropological Perspective.* Cambridge: Cambridge University Press.

Gordon, Colin. 1991. Governmental rationality: An introduction. In Graham Burchell, Colin Gordon, and Peter Miller, eds., *The Foucault Effect: Studies in Governmentality,* pp. 1–51. London: Harvester Wheatsheaf.

Griffiths, Lesley. 1997. Accomplishing team: Team work and categorisation in two community mental health teams. *British Sociological Review* 45 (1): 59–78.

Gubrium, Jaber. 1980. Doing care plans in patient conferences. *Social Science and Medicine* 14A:659–667.

Guzzo, Richard. 1986. Group decision making and effectiveness in organizations. In Paul S. Goodman and Associates, eds., *Designing Effective Work Groups,* pp. 34–71. San Francisco: Jossey-Bass.

Hale, Sondra. 1992. Feminist method, process, and self-criticism: Interviewing Sudanese women. In Sherna Berger Gluck and Daphne Patai, eds., *Women's Words: The Feminist Practice of Oral History,* pp. 121–136. New York: Routledge.

Haraway, Donna. 1997a. The persistence of vision. In Katie Conboy, Nadia Medina, and Sarah Stanbury, eds., *Writing on the Body: Female Embodiment and Feminist Theory,* pp. 285–295. New York: Columbia University Press.

——. 1997b. *Modest_Witness@Second Millennium. FemaleMan©_Meets_OncoMouse™:* Feminism and Technoscience. New York and London: Routledge.

Holland, Martin, and Jonathon Boston, eds. 1990. *The Fourth Labour Government: Politics and Policy in New Zealand.* 2d ed. Auckland and Oxford: Oxford University Press.

Holstein, James. 1992. Producing people: Descriptive practice in human service work. *Current Research on Occupations and Professions* 6:23–39.

Hunter, Katherine Montgomery. 1991. *Doctor's Stories: The Narrative Structure of Medical Knowledge.* Princeton: Princeton University Press.

HyperResearch: A Content Analysis Tool for the Qualitative Researcher. Boston: Researchware.

Ittner, Christopher, and Bruce Kogut. 1995. How control systems can support organizational flexibility. In Edward Bowman and Bruce Kogut, eds., *Redesigning the Firm,* pp. 155–182. Oxford and New York: Oxford University Press.

Katzenbach, Jon, and Douglas K. Smith. 1993. *The Wisdom of Teams: Creating the High-Performance Organization.* Boston: Harvard Business School Press.

Kelle, U. 1997. Theory Building in Qualitative Research and Computer Programs for the Management of Textual Data. Sociological Research Online 2,2 http://www.socresonline.org.uk/socresonline/2/2/1.html

Kelsey, Jane. 1995. *The New Zealand Experiment: A World Model of Structural Adjustment?* Auckland: Auckland University Press and Bridget Williams Books.

King, Michael. 1991. *Being Pakeha: The Quest for Identity in New Zealand.* Auckland: Penguin.

Korobkin, Laura. 1996. Narrative battles in the courtroom. In Marjorie Garber, Rebeccah Walkowitz, and Paul B. Franklin, eds., *Fieldwork: Sites in Literary and Cultural Studies,* pp. 26–33. London and New York: Routledge.

Larson, Carl E., and Frank M. J. LaFasto. 1989. *Teamwork: What Must Go Right, What Can Go Wrong.* Newbury Park, Calif.: Sage.

Law, John. 1994. Organization, narrative, and strategy. In John Hassard and Martin Parker, eds., *Towards a New Theory of Organizations,* pp. 248–268. London and New York: Routledge.

Lewis, Jane, and Howard Glennerster. 1996. *Implementing the New Community Care.* Buckingham and Philadelphia: Open University Press.

Losoncy, Lewis. 1997. *Best Team Skills: 50 Key Skills for Unlimited Team Achievement.* Delray Beach, Fla.: St. Lucie Press.

Lyotard, J. F. 1984. *The Postmodern Condition: Report on Knowledge.* Minneapolis: University of Minnesota Press.

Malinowski, Bronislaw. 1967. *A Diary in the Strict Sense of the Term.* New York: Harcourt, Brace, and World.

Mankin, Don, Susan Cohen, and Tora Bikson. 1995. *Teams and Technology: Fulfilling the Promise of the New Organization.* Boston: Harvard Business School Press.

Mason, Kenneth. 1988. *The Psychiatric Report.* Report of the Committee of Inquiry into procedures used in certain psychiatric hospitals in relation to admission, discharge or release on leave of certain classes of patients. Wellington: Government Print.

Mason Report. 1996. *Inquiry Under Section 47 of the Health and Disability Act 1993 in Respect of Certain Mental Health Services.* Report of the Ministerial Inquiry to the Minister of Health, Hon. Jenny Shipley. Wellington: Parliament.

McClain, Catherine, and Jean Bury. 1998. The heart of the matter: Care conferences to promote parent-professional collaboration. *Pediatric Nursing* 24 (2): 151–159.

McClelland, Marleen, and Roberta Sands. 1993. The missing voice in interdisciplinary communication. *Qualitative Health Research* 3 (1): 74–90.

McCloskey, Donald. 1990. Storytelling in economics. In Christopher Nash, ed., *Narrative in Culture: The Uses of Storytelling in the Sciences, Philosophy, and Literature,* pp. 5–22. London: Routledge.

McKenzie, Leon. 1994. Cross-functional teams in health care organizations. *Health Care Supervisor* 12 (3): 1–10.

McLean, Athena. 1995. Empowerment and the psychiatric consumer/ex-patient movement in the United States: Contradictions, crisis, and change. *Social Science and Medicine* 40 (8): 1053–1071.

Means, Robin, and Rachel Lart. 1994. User empowerment, older people, and the UK reform of community care. In David Challis, Brian Davies, and Karen Traske, eds., *Community Care: New Agendas and Challenges from the UK and Overseas,* pp. 33–43. London: Arena, in association with the British Society of Gerontology.

Mellor, M. Joanna, and Renee Solomon. 1992. The interdisciplinary geriatric/gerontological team in the academic setting: Hot air or energizer? *Geriatric Social Work Education* 18 (3–4): 203–215.

Mental Health Commission. 1998. *Blueprint for Mental Health Services in New Zealand: How Things Need to Be.* Wellington: Mental Health Commission.

Midgely, Stephen, Tom Burns, and Carol Garland. 1996. What do general practitioners and community teams talk about? Descriptive analysis of liaison meetings in general practice. *British Journal of General Practice* 46 (February): 69–71.

Miller, Eric. 1993. *From Dependency to Autonomy: Studies in Organization and Change.* London: Free Association Books.

Miller, Hillis. 1995. Narrative. In Frank Lentricchia and Thomas McLaughlin, eds., *Critical Terms for Literary Study,* 2d ed., pp. 66–79. Chicago: University of Chicago Press.

Miller, William. 1994. Common space: Creating a collaborative research conversation. In Benjamin Crabtree, William Miller, Richard Addison, Valerie Gilchrist, and Anton Kuzel, eds., *Exploring Collaborative Research in Primary Care,* pp. 265–288. Los Angeles: Sage.

Ministry of Health. 1994. *Standards for Needs Assessment for People with Disabilities.* Wellington: Ministry of Health.

_____. 1995. *Policy Guidelines for Regional Health Authorities 1995/96.* Wellington: Ministry of Health.

_____. 1997a. *Mental Health Promotion for Younger and Older Adults.* Wellington: Ministry of Health.

_____. 1997b. *The Health and Wellbeing of Older People and Kaumatua: The Public Health Issues.* Wellington: Ministry of Health.

_____. 1998. *Whāia Te Whanaungatanga: Oranga Whānau: The Wellbeing of Whānau: The Public Health Issues.* Wellington: Ministry of Health.

Mitchell, Maui John, and Hilary Mitchell. 1988. *Māori Teachers Who Leave the Classroom.* Wellington: New Zealand Council of Educational Research.

Mizrahi, Terry, and Julie Abramson. 1994. Collaboration between social workers and physicians: An emerging typology. In E. Sherman and William J. Reid, eds., *Qualitative Methods in Social Work Research,* pp. 135–151. New York: Columbia University Press.

Mohrman, Susan Albers, and Allan Mohrman. 1993. Organizational change and learning. In Jay R. Galbraith and Edward E. Lawler III and Associates, eds., *Organizing for the*

Future: The New Logic for Managing Complex Organizations, pp. 87–108. San Francisco: Jossey-Bass.

Moore, Stephen, John Poertner, Elizabeth Goody, and Melissa Habacker. 1991. Performance guideline systems in social work practice: A team-focused approach. *Community Alternatives: International Journal of Family Care* 3 (2): 19–32.

Mumby, Dennis K. 1993. Introduction: Narrative and social control. In D. Mumby, ed., *Narrative and Social Control: Critical Perspectives,* pp. 1–14. Newbury Park, Calif.: Sage.

Myerhoff, Barbara, and Jay Ruby. 1982. Introduction. In Jay Ruby, ed., *A Crack in the Mirror: Reflexive Perspectives in Anthropology,* pp. 1–29. Philadelphia: University of Pennsylvania Press.

Nash, Christopher. 1990. Slaughtering the subject: Literature's assault on narrative. In Christopher Nash, ed., *Narrative in Culture: The Uses of Storytelling in the Sciences, Philosophy, and Literature,* pp. 199–218. London: Routledge.

National Health Committee. 1998. *The Social, Cultural, and Economic Determinants of Health in New Zealand: Action to Improve Health.* Wellington: National Advisory Council on Health and Disability.

New Zealand Council of Christian Social Services. 1996. Contracting with Regional Health Authorities for Residential Services for Older People. Overview. Wellington: New Zealand Council for Christian Social Services.

Nicholson, Linda. 1990. Introduction. In Linda Nicholson, ed., *Feminism/Postmodernism,* pp. 1–16. New York and London: Routledge, Chapman Hall.

Nishiguchi, Toshihiro, and Erin Anderson. 1995. Supplier and buyer networks. In Edward Bowman and Bruce Kogut, eds., *Redesigning the Firm,* pp. 65–84. New York and Oxford: Oxford University Press.

Nocon, Andrew, and Hazel Qureshi. 1996. *Outcomes of Community Care for Users and Carers: A Social Services Perspective.* Bristol, Pa., and Philadelphia: Open University Press.

Nonaka, Ikujiro, and Hirotaka Takeuchi. 1995. *The Knowledge-Creating Company: How Japanese Companies Create the Dynamics of Innovation.* New York: Oxford University Press.

Northcraft, Gregory B., Jeffrey T. Polzer, Margaret A. Neale, and Roderick M. Kramer. 1995. Diversity, social identity, and performance: Emergent social dynamics in cross-functional teams. In Susan E. Jackman and Marian N. Ruderman, eds., *Diversity in Work Teams: Research Paradigms for a Changing Workplace,* pp. 69–96. Washington, D.C.: American Psychological Association.

Oliver, Michael. 1990. *The Politics of Disablement.* New York: St. Martin's Press.

Onyett, Steve, Richard Standen, and Edward Peck. 1997. The challenge of managing community mental health teams. *Health and Social Care in the Community* 5 (1): 40–47.

Opie, Anne. 1995. *Beyond Good Intentions: Support Work with Older People.* Wellington: Institute of Policy Studies, Victoria University of Wellington.

_____. 1997. Thinking teams thinking clients: Issues of discourse and representation in the work of health care teams. *Sociology of Health and Illness* 19 (3): 259–280.

Orange, Claudia. 1987. *The Treaty of Waitangi.* Wellington: Allen and Unwin, in association with Port Nicholson Press.

Orchard, Lionel. 1998. Public sector reform and the Australian Way. In Paul Smyth and Bettina Cass, eds., *Contesting the Australian Way: States, Markets and Civil Society,* pp. 111–123. Cambridge, New York, and Melbourne: Cambridge University Press.

Orr, Jackie. 1990. Theory on the market: Panic incorporating. *Social Problems* 37 (4): 460–484.

Ovretveit, John. 1993. *Coordinating Community Care: Multidisciplinary Teams and Care Management.* Buckingham and Philadelphia: Open University Press.

Parker, Martin. 1992. Post-modern organizations or postmodern organization theory? *Organization Studies* 13 (1): 1–17.

Perkins, Jan, and Joyce Tryssenaar. 1994. Making interdisciplinary education effective for rehabilitation students. *Journal of Allied Health* 23 (3): 133–41.

Petersen, Alan, and Deborah Lupton. 1996. *The New Public Health: Health and Self in the Age of Risk.* Sydney: Allen and Unwin.

Pithouse, Andrew. 1987. *Social Work: The Organisation of an Invisible Trade.* London: Gower.

Pollit, Christopher. 1988. Bringing consumers into performance measurement: Concepts, consequences, and constraints. *Policy and Politics* 16 (2): 77–87.

Polyani, Michael. 1962. *The Tacit Dimension.* New York: Harper and Row.

Poulin, John, Carolyn Walter, and Jean Walker. 1994. Interdisciplinary team membership: A survey of gerontological social workers. *Journal of Gerontological Social Work* 22 (1/2): 93–107.

Priestly, Mark. 1995. Dropping "E"s: The missing link in quality assurance for disabled people. *Critical Social Policy* 44/45 (Autumn): 7–21.

Public Health Commission. 1994–1995. *He Matariki: A Strategic Plan for Māori Public Health: The PHC's Advice to the Minister of Health.* Wellington: Public Health Commission.

Rabinow, Paul. 1996. *Essays on the Anthropology of Reason.* Princetown: Princeton University Press.

Rangihau, John, Emarina Manuel, Donna Hall, Hari Brennan, Peter Boag, Tamati Reedy, and John Grant. 1986. *Puao-te-Ata-tu (The Daybreak).* Report of the Ministerial Advisory Committee on a Māori Perspective for the Department of Social Welfare. Wellington:

Ramsden, Irihapeti Merenia. 1988. *Kawa Whakaruruhau: Cultural Safety in Nursing in Aotearoa.* Wellington: Ministry of Education.

Rayner, Steven. 1996. *Team Traps: Survival Stories and Lessons from Team Disasters, Near-Misses, Mishaps, and Other Near-Death Experiences.* New York: John Wiley.

Roberts, Kay T., John C. Wright, Jane M. Thibault, A. V. Stewart, and Keith R. Knapp. 1994. Geriatric partnerships in health and care: The life span model. *Educational Gerontology* 20 (2): 115–128.

Ruwhiu, Leyland, Harata Baucke, Robyn Corrigan, Moana Herewini, Noramerle Davis, Pirihi Te Ohaki Ruwhiu. 1999. "'Whaka—whanau—nga—tanga': A touch of class— we represent." Published in the conference proceedings of the Joint Conference of the AASW, IFSW, APASWE, and AASWWE, Brisbane, 26–29 September, pp. 151–157.

Said, Edward. 1978. *Orientalism.* London: Penguin.

———. 1989. Representing the colonized: Anthropology's interlocuters. *Critical Inquiry* 15 (Winter): 205–225.

Salmond, George, Gavin Mooney, and Miriam Laugeson, eds. 1994. Health care reform in New Zealand. Special issue of *Health Policy* 29 (1–2): 1–182.

Salmond, Gill. 1997. Working in a multidisciplinary team: Need it be so difficult? *BMJ* 309, no. 6967, 1520.

Saltz, Constance. 1992. The interdisciplinary team in geriatric rehabilitation. *Geriatric Social Work Education* 18 (3–4): 133–143.

Sands, Roberta. 1993. Can you overlap here?: A question for an interdisciplinary team. *Discourse Processes* 16 (4): 545–564.

Saramago, José. 1996. *The History of the Siege of Lisbon.* New York: Harcourt Brace.

Schwartzman, Helen. 1986. Research on work group effectiveness. In Paul S. Goodman and Associates, eds., *Designing Effective Work Groups,* pp. 237–276. San Francisco: Jossey-Bass.

Senge, Peter. 1990. *The Fifth Discipline: The Art and Practice of the Learning Organization.* Australia: Random House.

Sheppard, Michael. 1992. Contact and collaboration with general practitioners: A comparison of social workers and psychiatric nurses. *British Journal of Social Work* 22 (4): 419–436.

Shipley, Jenny, and Simon Upton. 1992. *Support for Independence for People with Disabilities: A Government Statement on the Funding and Delivery of Health and Disability Services.* Wellington: Parliament Buildings.

Smale, Gerald, and Graham Tuson. 1993. *Empowerment, Assessment, Care Management, and the Skilled Worker.* National Institute for Social Work Practice and Development Exchange. London: HMSO.

Smith, Dorothy. 1990. *Texts, Facts, and Femininity: Exploring the Relations of Ruling.* London: Routledge.

Smyth, Paul, and Bettina Cass, eds. 1998. *Contesting the Australian Way: States, Markets and Civil Society.* Melbourne: Cambridge University Press.

Soja, Edward. 1996. *Thirdspace: Journey to Los Angeles and Other Real-and-Imagined Places.* Cambridge, Mass. and Oxford: Blackwell.

Solomon, Renee, and M. Joanna Mellor. 1992. Interdisciplinary geriatric education: The new kid on the block. *Geriatric Social Work Education* 18 (3–4): 175–185.

Stacey, Ralph O. 1996. *Complexity and Creativity in Organizations*. San Francisco: Berrett-Koehler Publishers.

Stevenson, Olive. 1980. Social service teams in the United Kingdom. In Susan Longsdale, Adrian Webb, and Thomas Briggs, eds., *Teamwork in the Personal Social Services and Health Care*, pp. 9–31. London: Croom Helm.

Taylor, Ian, ed. 1990. *The Social Effects of Free Market Policies: An International Text*. Melbourne: Harvester Wheatsheaf.

Tedlock, Dennis. 1983. *The Spoken Word and the Work of Interpretation*. Philadelphia: University of Pennsylvania Press.

Toseland, Ronald, Joan Palmer-Ganeles, and Dennis Chapman. 1986. Teamwork in psychiatric settings. *Social Work* 31:46–52.

Trinh Minh-Ha. 1992. *Framer Framed*. New York and London: Routledge and Chapman Hall.

Uhl-Bien, Mary, and George B. Graen. 1992. Self-management and team-making in cross-functional work teams: Discovering the keys to becoming an integrated team. *Journal of High Technology Management Research* 3 (2): 225–241.

Upton, Simon. 1991. *Your Health and the Public Health: A Statement of Government Health Policy*. Wellington: Parliament.

——. 1996. Making it all irreversibly ours. *New Zealand Books* 6 (5): 15.

Varney, Glenn. 1990. *Building Productive Teams: An Action Guide and Resource Book*. San Francisco and Oxford: Jossey-Bass.

Webb, Adrian, and Martin Hobdell. 1980. Co-ordination and teamwork in the health and personal social services. In Susan Longsdale, Adrian Webb, and Thomas Briggs, eds., *Teamwork in the Personal Social Services and Health Care*, pp. 97–110. London: Croom Helm.

White, Hayden. 1981. The value of narrativity in the representation of reality. In W. J. T. Mitchell, ed., *On Narrative*, pp. 1–23. Chicago: University of Chicago Press.

Whiteley, Alma. 1995. *Managing Change: A Core Values Approach*. Melbourne: McMillian Education Australia.

Whittington, Colin. 1983. Social work in the welfare network: Negotiating daily practice. *British Journal of Social Work* 13:265–286.

Whorley, Larry. 1996. Evaluating health care team performance: Assessment of joint problem-solving action. *Health Care Supervisor* 14 (4): 71–76.

Williams, David. 1989. Te Tirito o Waitangi—unique relationship between Crown and Tangata Whenua? In I. H. Kawharu. ed., *The Treaty of Waitangi: Māori and Pakeha Perspectives of the Treaty of Waitangi*. Oxford: Oxford University Press.

Young, Iris Marion. 1994. Punishment, treatment, empowerment: Three approaches to policy for pregnant adults. *Feminist Studies* 20 (1): 33–58.